National University of Ireland, Galway

Ollscoil na hÉireann, Gaillimh

Leabharlann James Hardiman

Níl sé ceadaithe an leabhar seo a choinneáil thar an dáta is déanaí atá luaite thíos.

This book must be returned not later than the last date stamped below.

Patrice Petro

AFTERSHOCKS OF THE NEW

Feminism

and

Film History

Rutgers University Press
New Brunswick, New Jersey, and London

Library of Congress Cataloging-in-Publication Data

Petro, Patrice, 1957–
    Aftershocks of the new : feminism and film history / Patrice Petro.
        p. cm.
    Rev. papers, presented on various occasions, most of which were previously published,
1986–1999.
    Includes bibliographical references and index.
    Contents: Introduction — The "place" of television in film studies — Feminism and film
history — German film theory and Anglo-American film studies — After shock, between
boredom and history — Historical ennui, feminist boredom — World weariness, Weimar
women, and visual culture — Nazi cinema at the intersection of the classical and the
popular — The Hottentot and the Blonde Venus — Film feminism and nostalgia for the
seventies.
    ISBN 0-8135-2995-6 (cloth : alk. paper) — ISBN 0-8135-2996-4 (pbk. : alk. paper)
    1. Feminism and motion pictures. 2. Women in motion pictures. 3. Motion pictures—
Germany—History. I. Title.
PN1995.9.W6 P485 2002
791.43'082—dc21   2001019803

British Cataloging-in-Publication information is available from the British Library.

Manufactured in the United States of America

FOR ANDY, NATASHA, AND SOPHIE

CONTENTS

ILLUSTRATIONS

ACKNOWLEDGMENTS

LL of the essays included here, whether previously published or new to this volume, were originally presented as papers that were subsequently revised according to the comments, criticisms, and suggestions I received from numerous colleagues, students, and friends in the United States, England, Germany, Canada, and Australia. Chapter 1 was first published as "Mass Culture and the Feminine: The 'Place' of Television in Film Studies" in *Cinema Journal* 25, no. 3 (spring 1986); chapter 2 was previously published in *Camera Obscura* 22 (1991); chapters 3 and 7 in *New German Critique* 54 (Winter 1991) and 74 (spring–summer 1998); chapter 4 in *Discourse* 16, no. 2 (winter 1993–94); and chapter 5 in *The Persistence of History: Cinema, History, and the Modern Event*, edited by Vivian Sobchack (New York: Routledge 1996). Finally, chapter 9 was first published, in altered form, in the *Canadian Journal of Film Studies* (fall 1999). All materials are reproduced with permission.

In these brief acknowledgments, I can only begin to thank some of the people who have encouraged and supported my work over the years. My gratitude is nonetheless deep, profound, and heartfelt. I would like first to thank Mark Anderson and Andreas Huyssen for inviting me to participate in the international symposium on "Siegfried Kracauer—The Critic in Exile," sponsored by the German Academic Exchange Service, the Max Kade Foundation, and the Deutsches Haus at Columbia University in 1990. I would also like to thank Jamie Daniel for years of advice, friendship, and lively debate about Kracauer and Adorno and other theorists associated with the Frankfurt School. I am grateful to the School of the Art Institute of Chicago for inviting me to think and write about Fritz Lang's *Destiny* in conjunction with the Art Institute's exhibition "Degenerate Art" in 1991. My ideas about this film were further refined in a presentation at the University of Chicago, which coincided with the Smart Museum's exhibition "The German Print Portfolio: Serials for a Private Sphere" in November of 1993.

I am particularly indebted to Maria Makela, who invited me to participate in a symposium she organized on Weimar culture at the Walker Art Center in Minneapolis in the fall of 1996. This symposium was held in conjunction with the opening of the exhibition "The Photomontages of Hannah Höch" that not only deepened my respect for Höch's work, but also introduced me to the work of her most perceptive contemporary critics, such as Jula Dech and, of course, Makela herself. I would like to thank Margaret Dériaz of the Goethe-Institut in London for inviting me to extend my ideas about newer German film historiography at a lively and engaging day-long symposium, sponsored by the Goethe-Institut and the National Film Theatre, "Weimar and Third Reich Cinema: A Different Take," in November 1997. Lectures by Erica Carter, Tony Kaes, Richard Dyer, and Ginette Vincendeau were especially memorable and helped to shape the arguments presented here. These ideas were further refined in a paper presented at the University of Iowa, following a generous invitation by my former doctoral advisor, Dudley Andrew, to speak to a group of students and former professors at the Institute for Cinema and Culture in November of 1997.

As always, I am especially grateful to Nataša Ďurovičová—my oldest friend, my fiercest critic, and one of the most profoundly original and intelligent voices in the field of film studies today. Nataša read and commented on most of the chapters included here, as did Charles Wolfe. I am forever in their debt, not only for always being there when I needed them, but also for the special kind of friendship they have afforded me over the years—a friendship that grew out of a shared love for cinema and that now extends well beyond cinema to include all aspects of our lives.

Although my work on boredom and visual culture was first developed at the Center for Twentieth Century Studies at the University of Wisconsin-Milwaukee in dialogue with a range of people, especially Patricia Mellencamp, Chris Lane, Lynn Worsham, Herb Blau, and Kathleen Woodward, these ideas were given new life and direction through conversation with Elizabeth Goodstein, who not only invited me to speak to the topic "World Weariness, Sexuality, and Boredom" at the University of Rochester in May 1998, but who also shared with me her own, incredibly perceptive and illuminating work on boredom and intellectual history. I am also deeply indebted to Jodi Brooks, who invited me to speak about boredom and visual culture at an international conference, "Cinema and the Senses," held at the University of New South Wales in Sydney, Australia, in November of 1998. This conference introduced me to the wonderfully rich and stimulating work of a range of Australian scholars and critics, notably Adrian Martin, Viki Dun, Helen Grace, Therese Davis, Paul Starr, Catheryn Vasseleu, Laleen Jayamanne, and Alan Cholodenko, and also restored my faith in the existence and vitality of a larger community of film scholarship that extends well beyond the borders of the United States.

In this regard, I would like to express my deep gratitude to Janine Marchessault and the Film Studies Association of Canada for inviting me to give the annual Martin Walsh Lecture at the 1999 FSAC Conference in Sherbrooke, Quebec. This conference was incredibly energizing and collegial and introduced me to scholars and critics (Graham Petrie, Peter Harcourt, Peter Morris, Tom Waugh, Dave Douglas, Zuzana Pick, Christine Ramsay, Angela Stukator, Michael Zyrd) whose commitment to film studies and warm reception made the world of difference at a difficult time. In this regard, I would like to especially thank Susan Lord, Brenda Longfellow, Catherine Russell, and, of course, Janine Marchessault.

Closer to home, there are several people who deserve special acknowledgment. Associate deans Richard Meadows and Charles Schuster have been extraordinary colleagues, as have Mark Bradley and Kristin Ruggiero. Working closely with them at the Center for International Education has made the completion of this book possible. I would also like to express my gratitude to James Sappenfield for his friendship, support, and encouragement (and copyediting skills) over the years. The essays included here are stronger and more elegantly argued as a result of his keen editorial eye. I would also like to acknowledge Eric Rentschler for his longstanding support of my work, and for the many hours of discussion and debate about several key issues raised in this book. Thanks go also to my former students, many of whom are now invaluable colleagues in the profession: Kathleen Green, Brent Keever, Jim Castonguay, Jon Beasley-Murray, Gary Weissman, Tony Grajeda, Connie Balides, Tara McPherson, Aine O'Brien, Brooke Thomas, and Ben Schneider. All of the ideas presented here are a result of discussion, debate, and argument with these individuals—both in and outside of the graduate classroom.

I am grateful to Leslie Mitchner for being such an enthusiastic and supportive editor as well as a valued and trusted friend. I am also indebted to Bobbe Needham for her meticulous job of copyediting. Sarah Hoadley, Sara Tully, Anne Banda, Rachel Schrag, and Amy Kuether at the Center for International Education at UWM deserve much credit for their help in preparing the manuscript for publication.

Finally, I would like to thank my sister, Mary Petro Doran, for her keen sense of humor and emotional support over so many years. But my deepest thanks go to my husband, Andrew Martin, for so many things, not least of all for his unceasing encouragement, unwavering support, and rare intelligence, which have left their imprint on every page of this book. More than anyone else, Andy has given my work—and my life—direction, perspective, sustenance, and inspiration. I dedicate this book to him, and to our daughters, Natasha and Sophie, for teaching me what I truly know about the aftershocks of everyday life, which remain, after all, both the condition of existence in the modern era and the source of hope for the future.

AFTERSHOCKS
OF THE NEW

INTRODUCTION

AFTERSHOCKS OF THE NEW

HIS volume brings together nine essays that address a constellation of issues regarding histories of film theory and theories of film history. It focuses throughout on *feminist* film theories and histories, viewed through the lens of German cinema, critical theory, and visual culture. Some of the chapters are published here for the first time. Others have appeared in journals or books or small circulation periodicals. Still others have been republished in various venues (in translation in international journals or as part of larger collections on feminism, film history, or German theory). The obvious and immediate questions for this introduction are, Why bring these essays together here, in this book, and why now?

The beginning of the new century has brought with it a host of assumptions about the newness of our technologies, globalized economies, and transnational media practices. As a consequence, there has been a great deal of interest in exploring the prehistory of our own modernity, in an effort to understand where we are now, and how we got to where we are today. Of course, our own time, both pre- and postmillennial, is typically described as a time marked by refined mechanisms of power, accelerated growth and accelerated obsolescence, and experiences of fragmentation, dispersal, sensation, and shock. In this volume, I concur with this general view, arguing that fragmentation, dispersal, speed, and shock are indeed hallmarks of our contemporary age. But I also contend that these mechanisms and experiences must be understood historically, through reciprocal relation to a host of other, simultaneous developments, such as boredom and waiting, not to mention slowness, banality, and repetition—and this as much in our culture as in our intellectual lives.[1]

The essays collected here, although written at different times, under different circumstances, and for distinct audiences, are joined by their common concern to explore the pre- and post-history of our own modernity, specifically in the field of film studies. They are linked by their focus on modernism, German cinema, and feminist film theory, and by their effort to show, not how feminism or film or modernism itself ushered in the "shocks of the new" but, rather, how they continue to shape and define the *aftershocks* of our own modernity. I will have more to say in this introduction about feminism and film studies, after the shock of their newness and novelty, and in the context of an emergence of new constellations of institutional forces, activities, and arrangements. I would like to begin, however, by saying more about the impulse for this collection, which appears at a moment when we are witnessing a proliferation of books and monographs and collections about feminism, recent film theory, and the institutional status of film studies more generally.

It seems fair to say that there is currently a widespread interest among film scholars in taking stock of and making interventions into our current understanding of the history of film theory, particularly since the 1970s, when film studies was first institutionalized as a specific discipline or field.[2] My own efforts here are obviously part of this trend, although they are also intended as a considered response to it. Indeed, although the essays gathered here were written over a period of more than a decade, they come together in a volume at a time when cinema itself has been subsumed within new configurations (in the process of globalization and media convergence, for instance) and when film studies itself is being dispersed (into newly formed departments of "media studies" or "cultural studies" or "visual studies").

Rather than lament such developments, I attempt in this collection to ask what new possibilities might be imagined—for film studies, feminist women, and cross-disciplinary scholarship—in the wake of the aftershocks of the new: the aftershocks of feminism, most centrally, but the aftershocks of cinema as well. It is of course ironic that film studies emerged as a discipline at the very moment that the cinema itself had ceased to be the major cultural force in the realm of media. But, then, the cinema has been challenged and transformed by new technologies throughout the twentieth century (by photography, gramophone, radio, television, and computer) and has been, at least since the time of Lumiere, considered "an invention without a future." In this regard, and in thinking about the introduction to this volume, I was drawn to Siegfried Kracauer's introduction to his last, posthumously published book *History: The Last Things before the Last* (1969). There, Kracauer remarks on the connection between his interest in transient phenomenon and historical contingency and his commitment to the study of photographic media, particularly photography and film. "At long last," he writes, "all my main efforts, so incoherent on the surface, fall into line—they all have served, and continue to serve—a single purpose: the rehabilitation of objectives and modes of being which still lack a name and hence are overlooked and misjudged."[3]

Along with Walter Benjamin, whose historical analysis of modern subjectivity continues to inspire spirited commentary and debate, Kracauer was drawn to the transient and fleeting qualities of modern life, offering a phenomenological interpretation of the everyday world of modernity. He adopted an attitude of extreme commitment that was matched by an unwillingness to surrender to any critical or theoretical absolutes. As Gertrud Koch explains in a recent monograph, Kracauer always raised doubts, always retained a critical attitude toward systematic historical or philosophical constructions. He was always "of the opinion that the overall outline of the course things take over time remains hidden from our view—all we see are the traces it has left"[4]—hence, his commitment to photography and cinema as distinct modes of knowledge in the modern age. Like Benjamin, Kracauer was guided not by an interest in history in the service of the present, but rather by a passion for lost causes, for failed opportunities and unrealized promises in the past that might be revealed and redeemed in the future.

This critical, indeed utopian, attitude, especially in its commitment to locate the newness of the new within its reciprocal banality and repetition, remains, for me, both inspirational and timely. As I argue throughout this collection, the newness and familiarity of film theory must be understood in relation to the practices and theories of cinema that emerged in the teens and twenties, the proverbial site of the "shock of the new" in popular culture, the arts, and social practices. In drawing on German film theory, and especially on Kracauer's theories of history, I aim not simply to make connections between twenties and seventies film theory or to repeat the ideas or attitudes or approaches of another time. Instead, I am motivated to redeem multiple approaches to film studies, and to feminism and film theory especially, against the relentless pursuit of novelty—a novelty that fails to remember its past and hence fails to bring about anything new in history.

The essays collected here are organized in the order in which they were written, but there is another logic to their organization that became clear to me only retrospectively. The first three chapters—"The 'Place' of Television in Film Studies," "Feminism and Film History," and "German Film Theory and Anglo-American Film Studies"—were all written in the late eighties and early nineties, largely in response to a variety of issues circulating around French poststructuralism, semiotics, psychoanalysis, or what is now simply called "seventies film theory." At stake in each chapter is the status of film studies as an emerging academic discipline in the United States. As their titles suggest, the questions they raise remain at once familiar and topical. What is the place of television and other media in the field of film studies? What is the place of feminist film theory in our conceptions of film history, and how does this theory function, more fundamentally, in defining periods, genres, historical evidence, and objects of study? Finally, what is the place of German film theory in film studies, given the inaccurate translations and the more general inability of German film theory to circulate in or seriously influence a discipline built on French and British intellectual foundations?

In one sense, perhaps, it would seem that these questions have already been adequately and properly answered. Television studies now have a firm place in film studies, or at least an established identity in the U.S. academy and in its national organization, the Society for Cinema Studies (SCS). Feminist theory likewise has established its academic credentials in monographs and essays and book-length studies of directors, historical periods, national cinemas, and stars. Finally, German film theory has an incontestable place in the history of film, with new translations of central texts by German theorists being published almost every year, and new assessments of this work informing contemporary debates about the nature and history of perception, representation, and modern subjectivity.[5]

But to leave it at this would be to miss the ongoing importance of debating, expanding, defending, and redefining the place of German film theory, the status of feminism, and the relevance of technologies of representation in film studies. If television studies, for instance, no longer seems an issue for some in film studies, certainly the prospect of internet studies raises issues—and problems and misunderstandings— similar to those raised in early debates about the place of television in the field. The status of German film theory likewise remains of pressing concern, because it is largely German studies scholars who have extended the insights of early German film theory texts, outside of the purview of film studies, which has remained relatively unaffected by much new work. Finally, the status of feminist film theory in a postfeminist era remains perhaps the most urgent and pressing issue of all. As I suggest in chapter 9, feminist film theory, now largely relegated to some variant of "seventies film theory," is either bypassed as hopelessly outdated or dropped entirely from current discussions of film studies and its prospects for the future.

The problem here, of course, is both historical and conceptual. Catch-phrases like "seventies film theory" or "gaze theory" or even "feminist film theory" tend to suggest a unity that fails to capture the energy or variety or constructive tensions at work within and among these constellations of terms. In the seventies and eighties, of course, no one referred to psychoanalytically inflected semiotic film theory as "seventies film theory," most likely because film theorists writing in the 1970s and 1980s did not see themselves or their ideas as confined to a single decade—or to a single approach or view. But in the repackaging of film studies for a new generation, the diversity of intellectual debate—with its competing tendencies, aspirations and activities—has been the first victim of easy and simplistic understanding of the past. Indeed, the very rubric "seventies film theory" flattens out the complexity of a vibrant and contested series of intellectual debates, reducing them to a chronological view of a fairly self-contained "period" or spirit of a (postsixties) time.

In a 1998 essay, Laura Mulvey goes some way to refute this current view by attempting to situate her own work within a specific historical and national context.[6] She explains how, in the sixties and seventies, the combination of anti-Englishness (on a cultural front) and a rejection of indigenous Left traditions (on a political front) allowed U.S. popular culture and French poststructuralism to meet productively in Britain. She makes this observation in order to reflect on the intellectual traditions of Anglo-American film studies, and especially feminist film theory's interest in Hollywood and commitment to psychoanalysis and French poststructuralism. She points out how difficult it was, for many feminist film theorists in the seventies, to "think innovatively and traditionally at the same time."[7] By "traditionally," she means to signal the inability to think historically or economically or internationally:

In the early/mid 1970s, not only was history not a particular intellectual priority but many of the French ideas that were influential at the time were formulated in opposition to traditional Marxism's preoccupation with history and its determinisms. As a result, feminist analysis of Hollywood cinema had lost any relation to wider economic considerations,

any sense of changing historical contexts and its intense, complex relations to the rest of the film-going world.[8]

These remarks have a particular resonance for us today, coming as they
do from someone whose name has become virtually synonymous in our
own time with "seventies film theory," an identification that has effectively reduced Mulvey's own history—as a thinker, writer, and critic—to
a single essay written in 1975.[9] But certainly Mulvey speaks, in this 1998
essay, from a more complex position as a British feminist who, along with
other feminists in the seventies and eighties, was fundamentally concerned with the psychoanalytic mechanisms that shaped the patriarchal
unconscious of representation. Nonetheless, it would be a mistake to then
assume that there was not a range of feminist thinkers, in the seventies or
eighties or nineties (often including Mulvey herself, whose own thinking
changed and evolved over time), working in tandem who disagreed with
the kind of psychoanalytic feminism for which Mulvey is now, individually
and emblematically, associated.

The first three chapters in this book are best read in the context of this
broader—more complex and varied—tradition of feminist thinking about
film in the last three decades. My own approach to feminist film theory
has always been attentive to historical questions and suspicious of psychoanalytic generalizations. But it has also engaged with psychoanalysis and
with attempts to initiate a more historical approach to questions of subjectivity and perception—an approach inspired by early German film
theory and developed through dialogue and debate with feminist thinkers.[10] Each of the first three chapters therefore aims to challenge and
complicate and engage with semiotic and psychoanalytic film theory.
"The 'Place' of Television in Film Studies," written in response to a Society for Cinema Studies plenary, takes its cue from early German film debates by situating questions of television's "place" in film studies within a
larger discourse about the status of cinema in the early part of the century.
And it does so in order to restore a more complex vision of the function
of mass culture in relation to other social institutions and phenomena of
modernity than much poststructuralist or psychoanalytic theory at the
time allowed.

The second chapter, "Feminism and Film History," written for *Camera
Obscura,* a journal previously dedicated to psychoanalytic and French
poststructuralist thought, endeavors to underscore the importance of historical study for feminist film theory. Extending themes raised in chap-

ter 1, it argues the necessity of theorizing the more intangible historicity of concepts and categories by which we attempt to understand film history, and it locates feminist film theory as central to any conceptualization of film's historical field.

The third chapter, "German Film Theory and Anglo-American Film Studies," delivered first as a talk at a symposium at Columbia University and later published in *New German Critique* under a different title, attempts to show how German film theory has been virtually unreadable in Anglo-American film studies.[11] In an earlier time, the problem could be traced to faulty and misleading English translations. By the late 1980s and 1990s, the more substantial difficulty involved the lack of any understanding of German film theory's historical antecedents, given the French orientation of so much film studies, whether phenomenological, poststructuralist, or auteurist. Although this essay was originally delivered and published in a German studies context, it was written and conceived with a film studies audience in mind, hence the decision to include it here. Indeed, despite the fact that German studies scholars have rehabilitated many writings by early German film theorists (especially Kracauer's Weimar essays), they have done so largely without concern for the significance of this work for the conceptualization of issues in film studies (such as representation, perception, or historical subjectivity). Film scholars, for their part, tend to relegate German film theory to the sidelines of film studies and persist in assuming that Kracauer's writings pale in comparison to the celebrated (if often equally misunderstood) essays of Walter Benjamin.

The first three chapters thus set forth the central terms for the chapters that follow by exploring a history of film studies and its engagement with other media and other scholarly traditions, notably feminist and German film theory. The second three chapters take up where these first chapters leave off, mapping a theory of film history rather than tracing a history of film theory, as in the case of the opening chapters. Chapters 4, 5, and 6 might be said to constitute something of a "boredom trilogy." Indeed, they share a concern with theorizing another side to modernity—precisely *after* the shock of the new—when the new ceases to be shocking, and when the extraordinary, the unusual, and the sensational become inextricably linked to the boring, the prosaic, and the everyday. Feminist film theory is central to these chapters, as is the tradition of German film theory. Kracauer's Weimar essays, for instance, are described in some detail in chapters 1 and 3. His ideas about the contradictory place of women in emerging economies of work and leisure are then productively brought to bear on what I call, in the chapters on boredom, the *aftershocks of the new*. These aftershocks encompass both photographic media and feminist practice, since each exists "in between" boredom and history—in other words, between the psychic and the social, after the "fact," so to speak, between that which happens and that which fails to occur. Indeed, whereas the "shock of the new" is conventionally linked to modernism and to new technologies of representation and transportation, there were also the shock effects engendered by the newly visible presence of women in the world of work and as producers and consumers of mass culture. Alongside what were frequently perceived as the (often shockingly) sensational behaviors of modern women, however, were the *aftershocks of the no longer novel*, registered in the work of feminist artists and female performers, which I explore in greater detail in chapters 5 and 6.

Chapter 4, "After Shock, between Boredom and History," sets the theoretical agenda for the chapters that follow, tracing a history of boredom as theory and practice of modernity. Chapter 5, "Historical Ennui, Feminist Boredom," builds upon this theoretical and historical framework, but with a specific focus on modernist theory and modernist practices at the point where they intersect with discourses about the new woman and emerging practices among feminist women in literature and film as well as the other arts. Finally, chapter 6, "World-Weariness, Weimar Women, and Visual Culture," takes these theoretical ideas about modernism, modernity, and boredom theory and locates them within a founding moment of Weimar visual culture, exploring now conventional views of the time as they merged with images of sexual violence and otherness—androgyny, homosexuality, femininity, and race—and the shock value associated with them.

Although it may seem at first counter-intuitive, even perverse, on my part to describe Weimar culture as a culture of boredom, this is in fact what I attempt to do through close analysis of Hannah Höch's photomontages and the popular reception of Marlene Dietrich as world-weary Weimar icon. From Höch's desensationalized images of exhausted maternity to Dietrich's performances of a sexually sophisticated and knowing self-consciousness, the play with sexuality and gender identity in this period effectively dispensed both with the ideology of love and with the notion of an already achieved liberation for women. Thus did Weimar culture suggest that sexuality and gender were as much a source of boredom as shock or sensation, and this particularly for Weimar's female artists, who were in a unique position to document just how much, and how little, had changed for women at this time.

The final three chapters extend boredom theories and practices to address film history and feminist theory within an international context, suggesting how international economies, transnational audiences, and global
media practices predate our current discoveries of the complex and far-
reaching circulation of peoples, popular practices, and cultural norms.
Chapters 7 and 8 explore the international nature of national cinemas,
focusing on Berlin and Hollywood in the twenties and thirties, with attention to issues of classical Hollywood cinema, popular European film, and
the peculiar continuities, discontinuities, interchanges, and borrowings
that shaped these national traditions. Chapter 7, "Nazi Cinema at the Intersection of the Classical and the Popular," looks at recent research on
Weimar and Nazi cinema—and the inevitable comparisons with Hollywood traditions—in order to challenge familiar oppositions between art
and propaganda, popular and national cultures, in our theories of film
history. It concludes—in ways that are both remarkable and unsurpris-
ing—that Nazi cinema best exemplifies our theories of classical narrative
cinema and remains perhaps the most emblematic and successful popular
European cinema of all time.

Chapter 8, "The Hottentot and the Blonde Venus," continues this analysis, turning from questions regarding the impact of Hollywood in Berlin
to focus on the reciprocal (and simultaneous) impact of Berlin in Hollywood. Josef von Sternberg's *Blonde Venus* (1932) is the key text here, as are
the intersections between the New Woman (in both New York and Berlin), the New Negro (itself a product of the Harlem Renaissance), and the
star personas and performance styles of Dietrich and Josephine Baker. Significantly, *Blonde Venus* has been central to the development of feminist
film theory in Britain and the United States and remains at the center of
debate even today. But whereas feminist film scholars assume that the film
has nothing to do with Weimar culture, German studies scholars consider
it to be a Hollywood film and thus fail to see its relevance to their recent
work on gender, ethnicity, and race. My aim is thus to bring Anglo-
American feminist film theory and German cultural studies into dialogue,
given their shared concerns and focus on the same historical period. Such
crossing of disciplinary and national borders, I argue, enables us to see
larger transnational systems of entertainment and their fictionalized constructions of national and racial identities, in this case, for instance, the
way in which the German Dietrich copied the African American Baker,
who performed an ultramodern primitivism, itself a product of an imaginary African American culture in postwar Europe.

The final chapter, "Film Feminism and Nostalgia for the Seventies," offers both a summary of the issues raised throughout this volume and a polemic about the need to recall the past in order to creatively imagine new possibilities for feminism and film studies in the future. Whereas chapter 1 takes as its starting point a contentious SCS plenary session in the mideighties about the place of television in film studies, chapter 9 is inspired by a more nostalgic SCS plenary in 1999, in which the past, present, and future of feminist film studies were at stake. What is remarkable, when thinking about debates in film studies over the past decades, is not simply the shift in mood from anxiety about television to nostalgia about feminist film theory. Rather, it is the persistent attempt to come to terms with the meaning and legacy of seventies film theory and thus, in a fundamentally related sense, with the legacy of feminism and film studies, themselves developed in dialogue with radical theories and practices of the teens and twenties.[12]

The final chapter of this volume takes on these issues directly by focusing in large part on B. Ruby Rich's 1998 book *Chick Flicks: Theories and Memories of the Feminist Film Movement*. Rich's book provides a wealth of insight into questions about writing, memory, activism, and the generational bonds and divisions among feminist women. Written in an autobiographical mode, it revisits the highly politicized film theory debates of the 1970s in an effort to reflect on the place of feminism, both inside and outside the academy, from the seventies to the present. As one reviewer has remarked, however, the book's very title ("one that only the marketers of the 1990s would inflict on a reading public supposedly leery of unhip feminism")[13] suggests that more than a behind-the-scenes look at the recent history of film feminism is at stake. Indeed, Rich is a vocal and relentless critic of semiotic, poststructuralist, and especially psychoanalytic feminist film theory, whose academic ascendancy in the 1980s she holds singularly responsible for closing off the richness and vitality of earlier feminist debates. In Rich's estimation, the 1970s were a time of enthusiasm and inclusion and political activism, in which a broad and international coalition of feminist women struggled to invent new forms, new forums, and new theories. By the 1980s, however, she argues, the feminist *movement* evolved into a narrowly conceived academic *discipline*, with its own conferences, its own journals, and its own "professionalized, parochial, self-absorbed, deracinated writing." For Rich, it is no wonder that feminist work has come to a certain impasse in the nineties. As she puts it, "What sprang up in the seventies and was institutionalized in the eighties has been stagnating in the nineties, its vigor bypassed by queer

culture, on the one hand, multiculturalism on the other, and cultural studies in general." [14]

These are strong words, to be sure, and as a partisan critic with pas-
sionate views about the development of feminism within the university,
Rich has much of value to say from the standpoint of a position on the
academy's margins. But her characterization of film feminism in the nineties as somehow exhausted or depleted fails ultimately to convince, given
how she conceives of its history through the lens of her own political and
personal relationships, rooted almost entirely in the 1970s and articulated
in a chronological, oppositional, and one-dimensional way. Curiously,
feminist film theory in the eighties and nineties becomes, for Rich, an
entirely unified academic activity (not unlike the characterization of "seventies film theory" advanced by its detractors). She therefore fails to account for the more complex matrix of sensibilities, voices, and impulses
among feminist film theorists, during this time and beyond, who have
written and theorized and debated about gender and sexuality and race
with greater attention to difference—and to history—than was previously the case. Feminist film theory, in other words, continues to exist
beyond any self-contained or unified historical "period" and endeavors to
refine and expand, in subtle and often unsensational ways, the parameters
established by Rich and so many others nearly three decades ago. This has
been a time for feminism that I have characterized as coming *after the
shock of the new*—the new of modernism and the modern, to be sure, but
also after the new of so-called seventies film theory as well.

Of course, Rich is not entirely wrong, and certainly she is not alone in
sensing a certain feeling or attitude of ennui among feminists today.
Sometime in the 1990s, for a variety of obvious and complicated reasons,
feminist theory was charged with aridity and abstraction, and attacks
were leveled against feminist women, especially, although not exclusively,
within the academy. The popular image of a moralistic and humorless
feminism was reinforced by media-induced accounts of generational divisions among women, pitting younger, supposedly more sexually radical
feminists against older, allegedly sexually conservative ones. Popular representations were accompanied by critical justifications for a new, sexually
adventurous, and sensationally youthful postfeminism (whose cultural
icon was Madonna). Such seemingly novel attempts to shore up women's
sexual and cultural power are testament to the desire to reinvent feminism
for another generation. Unfortunately, such reinventions often lacked the
irony or self-consciousness of an earlier proto-feminist moment, such as

I analyze in this collection through the examples of Brassaï's Parisian photographs or the performance styles of Dietrich and Baker.

Both feminist theory and popular culture have registered the estrangements and banalities of twentieth-century life and demonstrated how they are bound up with representations of women's experiences (and disillusionments) with the promises and failures of modernity. Hence, the efforts by women artists and feminist theorists to defamiliarize the familiar understanding of modernity—not by seeing things anew, but by seeing them as no longer novel, thereby perceiving and sustaining the promise and possibility of social change. This is why I argue that boredom offers such a useful conceptual language with which to address issues in feminist theory today. Indeed, the ennui that haunts the feminist project in our own time (and that has haunted feminism in the past) may ultimately prove an enabling condition rather than a cause for despair. Indeed, boredom and repetition have been central to feminist aesthetics as well as to mass culture and to women's experiences of everyday life throughout the twentieth century. Thus, while some may now find feminism (rather than the limitations placed on women) tiresome and repetitive, it is important to remember that dead moments and dead ends in the past can be the source of new ideas and new creations in the present.

Aftershocks of the New: Feminism and Film History is dedicated to redeeming these seemingly dead moments so that, once revealed anew, they may provide innovative ways of thinking about where we have been and how we might imagine new possibilities for the future. In addressing the place of television (and other media) in film studies, the status of feminist film theory in our conceptions of film history, and the place of German critical theory in cinema studies more generally, this collection endeavors to raise questions that remain thought provoking and timely. And in exploring the complicated relations among shock and boredom, and innovation and repetition, in our histories and theories of visual culture, it aims to lower the volume (although not the stakes) of debates over our own place within a modernity at once intractable and in transition. Finally, this collection hopes to contribute to the larger task of restoring richness, complexity, and vitality to our understanding of feminism and film history in the recent past as well as today. And it does so precisely by being attentive to the *aftershocks* of our own modernity, and to the ways in which they continue to reverberate in our culture, our writing, and our everyday lives.

THE "PLACE" OF TELEVISION IN FILM STUDIES

The fear of the vulgar is the obverse of the fear of excellence, and both are aspects of the fear of difference.

— LESLIE FIEDLER

HE final session of the 1984 Society for Cinema Studies Conference held in Madison, Wisconsin, was titled "The Place of Television in Film Studies." The question of television's "place" in film studies was nevertheless soon displaced by an intense debate about what were proper objects for scholarly attention, a debate that encouraged some conference participants to voice their fears about the precarious status of film within the academy and to express their anxieties over television's potential threat to that status.

To begin with, some conference participants feared that once television was incorporated into film studies, a return to various positivist methodologies would soon follow, thereby undermining the more sophisticated approaches to spectatorship and textuality carried over from continental philosophy and literary theory to film studies proper. Furthermore, the emphasis on content analysis, audience survey, and controlled experiment in mainstream television study, in short, the "number crunching" empiricism of communication research, was seen by some to threaten the already beleaguered position of film study within the university by moving it further away from the humanities and in the direction of the social sciences.

In addition to this was a second, less articulated, fear that the study of the vulgar, popularized medium of television would undercut the artistic and educational goals of film study within the university. In support of this fear, and serving as further evidence to indict television as medium, were quoted the apparently different modes of reception assumed to follow from "viewing a film" and "watching television." As many theorists have pointed out, when viewing a film, the spectator centers attention on the screen, becoming absorbed in the narrative and with the characters. The viewing of television, however, seems to be marked by discontinuous attention, by the spectator's participation in several activities at once among which televiewing may not even rank as third in importance.[1] Drawing upon these assumed differences between perception and spectatorship in film and television viewing, the debate over television's place in film studies came to rest upon the (unexamined) assumption that while film encourages attention to the work itself, television merely contributes to the tendency toward distracted and indiscriminate reception.

It would be hasty to dismiss the fears outlined here as entirely illusory or to generalize about all film scholars' tunnel vision with respect to their discipline (thus overlooking the extremely productive work on television carried out by film scholars both in Britain and the United States).[2] It nevertheless seems to me that the anxiety expressed over the prospect and consequences of positivist methodologies inundating film studies is rather misplaced. For a start, not only have such methodologies long existed in film studies (as represented by the work of I. C. Jarvie, for instance), but they have in no significant way obstructed the development or refinement of film theoretical concerns. It is for this reason that the second fear, expressed in terms of television "debasing" the cultural and education goals of film studies, seems to me highly suggestive in its assumption of what, precisely, constitutes knowledge, education, and value. As Hélène Cixous has remarked, every theory of culture, "every theory of society, the whole conglomeration of symbolic systems—everything, that is, that's spoken, everything that's organized as discourse, art, religion, family, language, everything that seizes us, everything that acts on it—it is all ordered around hierarchical oppositions that can only be sustained by means of a difference posed by cultural discourses as 'natural,' the difference between activity and passivity."[3]

The difference between art and mass culture—understood by means of a "natural" opposition between activity and passivity—has long been assumed in our theories of culture. And it is remarkable how theoretical discussions of art and mass culture are almost always accompanied by gendered metaphors that link "masculine" values of production, activity, and attention with art, and "feminine" values of consumption, passivity, and distraction with mass culture. To be sure, this dichotomy is not exclusive to those seeking to valorize high art. As Tania Modleski has argued, even theorists of mass culture continually make "mass culture into the 'other' of whatever, at any given moment, they happen to be championing—and, moreover, to denigrate that other primarily because it allegedly provides pleasure to the consumer."[4] Given the tenacity of hierarchical gender oppositions both in our culture and our theoretical discourses, it is not surprising that debates over the "place" of television in film studies should echo the oppositions between activity and passivity when assigning value to different representational practices. What is surprising is that some film scholars assign a place to television outside the domain of legitimate culture, outside the arena of academic respectability, particularly since as this was (and in some cases, continues to be) precisely the "place" assigned to cinema by educators, intellectuals, and artists.

In the following discussion, I would like to suggest possible reasons for the attribution of feminized values (with their implicitly pejorative connotations) to television by analyzing developments within film criticism as well as within critical theories of television. I must emphasize, however, that I am not concerned to argue that either television or film is in fact feminized. While at least one film scholar has valorized television as psychically and essentially feminine, thereby providing television with an ontology to match the masculine ontology of film provided by Jean-Louis Baudry and Christian Metz, I believe that this kind of approach not only collapses the historical and theoretical issues raised by television as a social technology, but also replicates the very terms that ally femininity with passivity, consumption, and distraction.[5] In my view, it is precisely these terms that must be called into question if television theorists are to avoid reproducing the problems already encountered by theorists of film. Indeed, what I would like to argue is that before we can begin to theorize the historical and perceptual difference between film and television viewing, we need first to scrutinize our critical vocabularies that assign hierarchical and gender-specific value to difference. My aim in this essay will thus be less to advance a new theory of television than to demonstrate how critics of mass culture, from civic reformers to postmodern theorists, employ gender-specific oppositions in order to evaluate the differences between art and mass culture. In this way, I hope to suggest why debate over the "place" of television in film studies may have been necessary to begin with.

CINEMA AND MASS CULTURE

Since its beginnings, the cinema has been interrogated in almost every Western society for its function and meaning in culture. Rather than presume to give an extensive account of the various discourses on cinema as a manifestation of mass culture, I will merely suggest a pervasive preoccupation with gender oppositions in mass culture criticism. In fact, before turning to television directly, it is useful to look at how debates over television have not only borrowed from, but also virtually replicated, earlier debates over film.

Quite consciously, I have chosen to draw my examples from Anglo-American and German mass cultural criticism and to divide various approaches into three major areas: (1) moral and educational discourses—concerned to discuss cinema's effects upon children (those presumably unable to distinguish reality from fantasy) and marked by analogous inability to distinguish representation from presentation, given their assumption that film maintains an immediate and direct relation to the real; (2) artistic and intellectual discourses—generally concerned to distinguish artistic from popular practices and to defend the status of art by setting it in opposition to mass culture's triviality and vulgarity; and (3) political and cultural discourses—usually involving critics on the political Left and distinguished by an attempt to discern the social and ideological effects of mass-produced forms on audiences themselves produced by an increasingly industrialized culture. At this point I must emphasize that these categories are not mutually exclusive, since moral evaluations of the cinema are never confined to the discourses of reformers, just as analyses of the effects of industrial culture are not limited to critics on the Left.

I must also make explicit my reasons for privileging examples from Anglo-American and German mass cultural criticism. Most obviously, institutional and historical factors have made possible the interchange between Anglo-American and German intellectuals (e.g., the impact of the German university on U.S. intellectual life in the late nineteenth century and the influence of the Institute for Social Research on U.S. sociology and communications research in the 1940s and 1950s). Furthermore, it seems to me that early German film theory may have much to offer contemporary film and television scholars.[6] Without a doubt, problems of translation (both literal and cultural) have often stood in the way of sophisticated assessments of early German theory: the narrow and predominantly formal understanding of that theory as either realist (Kracauer), modernist (Theodor Adorno), or postmodernist (Walter Benjamin) may indeed be attributed to this. And although early German film theory does not escape the patriarchal bias found in its Anglo-American counterpart, I do believe that it holds perhaps the most promise for any historical analysis of perception and identification in film and television media. For instance, Benjamin's discussion of aura and its demise provides an important historical and ideological explanation (rather than a formal or epistemological one) for the current denigration of television by scholars who have only recently succeeded in restoring aura to the study of film art.

The writings of U.S. educators and reformers in the early twentieth century are especially revealing in their construction of the differences between education and mass culture through their reference to the "demands" of national traditions and the "seductions" of popular entertainment forms. As early as 1926, Donald Young, a sociologist at the University of Pennsylvania, argued that the cinema was helping to promote a "reckless appreciation of true values," and this precisely because it was designed to be cheap, available, and easy to understand. Following the observations advanced by Young, and popularizing the research of prominent sociologists and psychologists, Henry James Foreman, author of *Our Movie-Made Children* (1933), explicitly distinguished between the "rigors" of national education and the "promiscuity" of the cinema. Foreman acknowledged that the cinema might one day provide instruction more valuable "than the present text-book variety." For the time being, however, he believed the cinema to be "vast, haphazard, promiscuous . . . [and] ill-chosen" in its output, and thus "extremely likely to create a haphazard, promiscuous, and undesirable national consciousness." [7]

The concern of U.S. academics and reformers with regulating the cinema for the good of national consciousness found similar expression in the writings of German educators and reformers. As Miriam Hansen forcefully demonstrates in her essay "Early Silent cinema: Whose Public Sphere?" educators and literary commentators in Germany in the early twentieth century aimed to establish the educational mission of the cinema by curbing what they saw as the explicitly sexual excesses inherent in its appeal. Cautioning against the irrational tendencies of mass tastes, German cinema reformers specifically warned against what they perceived as the increasing—and much deplored—sexualization of cinema audiences.

The high percentage of women in film audiences, combined with an apparently sensual and intoxicating atmosphere of the cinema auditorium, was perceived, in fact, as such an alarming phenomenon that, as Hansen explains, the fear of mass culture was translated into a fear of femininity more generally, "of female presence on both a pragmatic and metaphoric level."[8] Quoting from Alfred Döblin, Hansen makes this point especially clear:

> Inside the pitch-black, low-ceilinged space a rectangular screen glares over a monster of an audience, a white eye fixating the mass with a monotonous gaze. Couples making out in the background are carried away and withdraw their undisciplined fingers. Children wheezing with consumption quietly shake with the chills of evening fever; bad-smelling workers with bulging eyes, women in musty clothes, heavily made-up prostitutes leaning forward, forgetting to adjust their scarves. Here you can see "panem et circenses" fulfilled; spectacle as essential as bread; the bullfight as popular need.[9]

As this quote from Döblin suggests, the polemic against the cinema's "monstrous," "devouring" pleasures was not limited to civic-minded reformers: A number of established artists and intellectuals also decried the cinema's function as vulgar alternative to the cultural heritage of genuine art. Franz Pfemfert, editor of the expressionist journal *Aktion,* for example, called the cinema "barbaric," arguing that while "the torchbearers of culture hasten to new heights, the people . . . listen to the babbling of the cinema and place a new record on the phonograph."[10] Significantly, many German artists and intellectuals directed their attack against the cinema by way of an attack on the U.S. film, that form of cinematic representation not only emblematic of mass industrial culture, but also most threatening to the maintenance of a uniquely German cultural heritage. As one German publisher wrote in 1926: "The number of people who see films and don't read books has reached into the millions. . . . They all surrender to American tastes, they conform, they become uniform. The American film is the New World militarism. It is more dangerous than the Prussian world militarism. It doesn't devour single individuals, it devours whole peoples."[11] Not only is a dividing line drawn here between book culture and film culture, between a traditional mode of written expression and an emerging mode of visual expression, but it is also remarkable how the metaphorical threat slides from the masculine, the militaristic, and the national to the feminine, the insidious, and the all-enveloping. (The comparison between residual and emerging modes of representation, and the values attached to each, will, of course, find similar articulation when television is discussed as a threat to the dominance of film.)

Metaphors that refer to the cinema's insatiable appetite, to its appeal to the most promiscuous and undiscerning of tastes, can also be discerned in the writings of leftist cultural critics. As Heide Schlüpmann points out in her brilliant essay *"Kinosucht"* (literally, "Cinema Addiction"), the writings of Kracauer, Benjamin, and Adorno are instructive both in their attack on bourgeois notions of artistic value and in their simultaneous contempt for feminized reception.[12] For example, in contrast to Kracauer's later work, *From Caligari to Hitler* (1947), where mass culture is associated with a specifically male mob psychology, Kracauer's early writings often focus upon female spectators and the potentially liberating effects of mass culture. (This is not to say, however, that femininity and liberation are ever equated, a point to which I will return shortly.) As Kracauer writes in his 1927 essay, "The Mass Ornament":

What is entertainment for the masses is judged by intellectuals as distraction of the masses. Contrary to such a position, I would argue that the aesthetic pleasure gained from the ornamental mass movements is legitimate. . . . When great amounts of reality-content are no longer visible in our world, art must make do with what is left. . . . No matter how low one rates the value of the mass ornament, its level of reality is still above that of artistic productions that cultivate obsolete noble sentiments in withered forms—even when they have no further significance.[13]

As Kracauer makes clear, the perceptual "distraction" structured by the mass media carries with it a double meaning. On the one hand, distraction in the cinema is progressive, since it translates forms of industrial organization into a sensory, perceptual, and highly self-conscious discourse: "in the pure externality of the cinema, the public meets itself, and the discontinuous sequence of splendid sense impressions reveals to them their own daily reality. Would it be concealed to them, it couldn't be attacked or changed." On the other hand, distraction in the cinema contains reactionary tendencies, since it encourages passivity and mindless consumption on the part of the spectator that work to block the imagination and distract from the necessity to change the present order: "reason is impeded . . . when the masses into which it should penetrate yield to emotions pro-

vided by the godless, mythological cult." The emotionality and irration-
ality of the cinematic spectacle, those apparently reactionary effects of
distraction, are in turn linked by Kracauer to an overidentified and specifically female mode of spectatorship. As he argues in his series of sketches
"The Little Shop Girls Go to the Movies" (1927): "Many people sacrifice
themselves nobly because they are too lazy to rebel; many tears are shed
and they only flow because to cry is sometimes easier than to think. . . .
Clandestinely, the little shop girls wipe their eyes and powder their noses
before the lights come up." [14]

In this passage, Kracauer implies that a truly progressive cinema must
encourage an intellectual distance if the spectator is to guard against the
lure of a passive, emotional, or feminized reception. Kracauer's emphasis
upon an active or intellectual stance toward cinematic distraction, moreover, clearly informs the discussion of mass culture one finds in the writings of Benjamin and Brecht. [15] While all three theorists sought to redeem
mass culture, and this in spite of the apparent irrationalism of its appeal,
their all too easy linkage of irrationalism with the feminine poses a serious
problem for any reevaluation of their writings.

It should nonetheless be remembered that early German film theorists
directed their attention to the social function of representation, and thus
their analyses of mass culture remain far more dialectical, far more historical, than those one finds in much contemporary film theory. For
example, in their well-known essay, "Cinema/Ideology/Criticism," Jean-
Louis Comolli and Paul Narboni restate the distinction between art and
mass culture that one finds in the writings of early German film theorists,
only now this distinction is displaced onto a formal opposition between
radical practice and classical Hollywood cinema, where Hollywood cinema becomes virtually synonymous with ideology, with mass culture as
the expression of a thoroughly degraded consciousness. In marked contrast to early German film theorists, Comolli and Narboni also maintain
that the perceptions afforded by mainstream cinema simply reproduce a
closed system, a mystified, illusory, and one-dimensional perceptual experience: "The notion of a public and its tastes was created by the ideology to justify and perpetuate itself. And this public can only express itself
via the thought-patterns of ideology. The whole thing is a closed-circuit,
endlessly repeating the same illusion. . . . Nothing in these films jars
against the ideology, or the audience's mystification by it. They are very
reassuring for audiences for there is no difference between the ideology
they meet every day and the ideology on the screen." [16]

To be sure, Comolli and Narboni recognize that some classical films do escape the dominant ideology in which they are inscribed. Nevertheless, because they conceive of classical cinema as a monolith and a closed system, without any attention to the dynamics of reception, they must resort to text-bound notions in order to theorize that which is transgressed: that which ruptures, displaces, or disperses the "false and easy pleasures" of the Hollywood cinema is seen as a strictly formal gesture. However formalistic Comolli's and Narboni's theory of perception in the cinema may now seem, their understanding of transgressive practice continues to hold sway in even the most sophisticated of film theories. Stephen Heath, for example, defines the classical system as that which regulates, binds, and unifies the viewing subject. And fundamental to this binding, this all-consuming—again, devouring—process, is the system of suture, defined by Heath, somewhat unguardedly, as a "stitching or typing as in the surgical joining of the lips of a wound."[17] Heath theorizes an aesthetics able to transgress or "rupture" this dominant visual economy through recourse to a modernist practice that radically exposes the contradictions or gaps in the classical system. To quote Heath, once denied the pleasures of unity, coherence, and binding in, "the individual as spectator loses his epicentral role and disappears . . . 'he is no longer a simple consumer, he must also produce' . . . the spectator, that is, is to be divided, displaced, pulled into the radical exteriority of his / her process as subject which poses the construction of subjectivity in the objective contradictions of the class struggle."[18] Heath's emphasis upon work and production, and his invocation of the mutilated self in the service of the class struggle, serve as explicit contrast to the unified, consuming product of bourgeois ideology. The gendered metaphors here are clear: masculinity, production, and the divided self are again valorized in opposition to femininity, consumption, and the unified body.

Theorists of postmodernism have questioned the modernist and explicitly formalist impulse of Heath's argument and are skeptical of claims for the transgressive or negative potential of mass cultural forms.[19] And yet even postmodern theorists tend to reproduce rigidly text-bound distinctions between spectatorial perceptions of unity (or realism) and dispersion (or postmodernism). In an essay that concludes a volume dedicated to Frankfurt School debates, for example, Fredric Jameson argues that since modernism has "become the dominant style of commodity production," it has now lost its political, contestatory, and perceptual value. "In these circumstances," Jameson writes, "there is some question whether the ultimate renewal of modernism, the final dialectical subversion of the now automatized conventions of an aesthetics of cultural revolution, might now simply be . . . realism itself! For when modernism and its accompanying techniques of 'estrangement' have become the dominant style whereby the consumer is reconciled with capitalism, the fragmentation itself needs to be 'estranged' and corrected by a more totalizing way of viewing phenomenon." In a later essay, "Postmodernism and Consumer Society," Jameson checks the utopia of this realist solution and argues against all forms of mass culture that he sees as debasing the critical or emancipatory potential of art. "The erosion of the older distinction between high-art and so-called mass or popular culture," Jameson now writes, "is perhaps the most distressing development of all from an academic standpoint, which has traditionally had a vested interest in preserving a realm of high or elite culture against the surrounding environment of philistinism, of schlock and kitsch, of TV series and *Reader's Digest* culture, and in transmitting difficult and complex skills of reading, listening, and seeing to its initiates." [20]

Given the history of mass culture criticism, Jameson's remarks hardly seem original, reproducing as they do the familiar distinctions between art's complex and difficult skills and mass culture's cheap and easy pleasures that consume, incorporate, and trivialize everything. At this point, we might want to question the rigid distinctions between art and mass culture that organize our critical discourses. More precisely, we may even want to ask whether mass culture is really as monolithic and all-consuming as it has frequently been constructed to be, or whether, in fact, it is mass cultural *criticism* that has a vested interest in consuming and trivializing the different experiences of mass cultural reception. Before answering this question directly, I would now like to turn to television and to the discourses generated by this mass cultural form, perhaps considered to be the most vulgar and most implicated in the "environment of philistinism" that Jameson describes.

TELEVISION AND MASS CULTURE

"Television," writes Jerry Mander, "has so enveloped and entered us, it is hard for most of us to remember that it was scarcely a generation ago that there was no such thing as television." [21] Mander's use of the metaphor of penetration to describe and condemn television as medium evokes an audience for television that is passive, vulnerable, and inherently feminized. And not only is Mander's discourse representative of a

great deal of television criticism, but it also reaffirms the real and metaphoric fear of femininity previously articulated by critics of cinema—
a fear that simultaneously directs itself against women as viewers and
against the perceptual distraction assumed to follow from mass cultural
reception.

The earliest studies of television, for example, were conducted by sociologists and psychologists concerned with uncovering the effects of
television violence on children, those viewers most easily seduced by ag-
gressive behavior presented on the screen.[22] Similar to early studies of the
cinema, early studies of television aimed to intervene in the shaping of
consumer tastes so as to regulate television programs and to educate
television viewers by presenting "themes and characterizations which
are morally and socially more worthwhile."[23] What "morally and socially" worthwhile might have meant to early television reformers may be
gleaned from the response of one television producer to the pressures for
television regulation. Worthington Miner, executive producer of National
Telefilm Associates, wrote in 1961 that any censorship of televisual reality
will merely effect the return of a repressed, and presumably more detri-
mental, violence than that which currently organizes social relations:

> When all searching into politics, religion, and sex is removed—when
> every "damn" and "hell" is gone—when every Italian is no longer a
> "wop" and every Negro is no longer a "nigger"—when every gangster
> is renamed Adams or Bartlett, and every dentist an incipient Schweit-
> zer, when indeed, every advertiser and account executive smiles—what
> is left? For this the censor must answer. What is left? Synthetic hogwash
> and violence! Shot through the guts, the head, or the back—the blood-
> ier the better—Nielsen and Trendex demand it! Let woman blast her
> man in the face with a shotgun—but please, no cleavage. Tears? Oh,
> yes—lots of tears—for the poor misunderstood woman, or man, who
> just happened on the side to be selling heroin—or themselves. And in
> the daytime—Woman! The backbone of the home, the family, the busi-
> ness, the works. Oh, yes, within the censor's acceptance, the woman is
> forever a giant of integrity, loyalty, force—while generally misunder-
> stood and abused. Man—a poor, fumbling, well-meaning idiot—or a
> martyr. This is what the censor declares every American adolescent
> should know about his father.[24]

The racism and sexism of Miner's remarks are outrageous in their very
explicitness. And yet the conservatism implicit in Miner's belief that tele-

vision programs and social relations are best left the way they are can also be detected in the writings of less hysterical television commentators. Paul Robinson, professor of history and author of an essay entitled "TV Can't Educate," reverts to the familiar distinctions between education and entertainment in order to argue that attempts to regulate or promote educational values through TV are fundamentally misguided because television is "structurally unsuited to learning." In learning, Robinson maintains, "one must be able to freeze the absorption of fact or proposition at any moment to make mental comparisons." And because television is always "a matter of seconds, minutes, and hours . . . it can never teach." Significantly, Robinson does not confine his critical remarks to the educational pretensions of TV, or to television alone. "There is a new form of slumming among intellectuals," Robinson writes, "watching 'bad' (i.e. commercial) TV and even writing books about it." This trend, Robinson argues, should not be taken seriously, for if television and film are equipped to "entertain, divert, above all to amuse," they cannot provide the time or absorption required for true knowledge. The opposition between the absorption of learning and the distraction of television thus leads Robinson to conclude that there is, in fact, "only one way to learn: by reading."[25] (Following this line of argument, one wonders why universities require professors to meet with students at all.)

Robinson's argument clearly aims to preserve the traditional boundaries that define educational value in the academy and, in this, his position is hardly less conservative than Miner's. Furthermore, it is important to stress that the terms and oppositions that organize Robinson's discourse also pervade writings on television by critics on the political Left. For example, in his essay "Of Happiness and Of Despair, We Have No Measure," Ernest van den Haag, a critic indebted to the pessimistic strain of Frankfurt School theory, also denies any educational function to television because education is itself implicated in the logic of commodity production. Van den Haag goes one step further than Robinson, however, by claiming that television (and mass culture more generally) cannot offer genuine pleasure either, for pleasure, too, has been commodifed and drained of its true significance: "Condemned to pleasure, people often find themselves out on parole, craving to be distracted from distraction by distraction." In van den Haag's view, the commodification of labor under capitalism "depletes people psychologically and makes them weary and restless." And, as people desperately search for genuine experience and involvement, the mass media offer them only vulgar, duplicitous, and vacuous pleasures. The bonds that once existed between producers and consumers, van den Haag continues, have been severed with the advent of the impersonal market system, which increases the sense of "violation [that] springs from the same thwarting of individuality that makes prostitution (or promiscuity) psychologically offensive." [26]

Not surprisingly, van den Haag's characterization of the "promiscuous" marketplace lends itself to a description of the relationship between producers and consumers of mass culture more generally: "The cost of cheap and easy availability, of mass production, is wide appeal; and the cost of wide appeal is de-individualization of the relationship between those who cater and those who are catered to; and of the relationship between both to the object of transaction. By using each other indiscriminately . . . the prostitute and her client sacrifice to seemingly more urgent demands the self which, in order to grow, needs continuity, discrimination and completeness in relationships." The "cheap and easy" pleasures that lead van den Haag to personify mass culture as a prostitute also serve him to identify the values of genuine art. Like love, he argues, "art can only be experienced as a cumulative relationship." That is to say, in contrast to the promiscuity and noninvolvement of mass cultural reception, the reception of art encourages a continuous and individualized devotion to the work itself. "New, doubtful, and difficult" in its appreciation, art therefore negates mass culture's "loud, broad, and easy charms." While van den Haag does acknowledge that mass culture may provide pleasure to some, he maintains that this pleasure is only a "substitute" for the true pleasures of art, which restore man's need for unity, "penetrate deeper experience and lead to a fuller confrontation of man's predicament." [27]

Man's predicament and man's need for unity are recurrent themes in much mass culture criticism. And given the pervasive expression of these themes, it is hardly surprising that the televisual form most condemned in mass culture criticism is the soap opera, that form which makes its appeal explicitly to women. In his essay "Soap Time: Thoughts on a Commodity Art Form," Dennis Porter argues that soap time is "for and of pleasure, the time of consumption, of a collectivized and commercially induced American Dream." In Porter's view, the consumption of soap operas is thoroughly mystified and illusory, for soap operas completely efface the traces of their production and thus deny the distance that would "subvert [their] commercial function." Porter continues: "Not only is [the soap opera] itself made to be sold for a profit on the open market, it is also designed as a purveyor of commodities, an indiscriminate huckster for

freeze-dried coffee, pet food, and Carefree panty shields. As a consequence, it mystifies everything it touches." Although Porter does not state
it directly, it is clear from his argument that the soap opera primarily mystifies its audience—an audience implicitly coded as female. (Indeed, the
presumed customers for panty shields and, perhaps, for coffee and pet
food, are women; hence, women are those consumers who are, according
to Porter, most easily duped by the phony spell of the commodity.) Porter
does express his moral disgust with the function of soap operas in perpetu-
ating the domestication of U.S. women. And yet, he nevertheless con-
demns women's pleasure in watching soap operas, and he goes so far as to
suggest that "the speech of the soap opera . . . is voiceless." In so doing,
Porter assumes his experience of watching soap operas to be the same for
women, thus silencing the voice that may speak to women in even the
most banalized and commodified of forms.[28]

A similar inability to acknowledge the function of television for different audiences marks Noël Burch's discussion of television in his essay
"Narrative/Diegesis—Thresholds, Limits." Like Porter, Burch is also concerned to emphasize how television's commodification of pleasure makes
it the newest and most "potent weapon in the media arsenal of capitalism." And yet, unlike Porter, Burch adopts a postmodern stance that does
not allow for the hope of distancing to guard against television's hypnotic,
consuming, and narcotizing effects. In striking contrast to his earlier,
modernist stance, Burch argues that television's return to the dispersed
structures of identification that marked the primitive cinema is "anything
but innocent." "For years, we have assumed that the alienation effect was
necessarily enlightening, liberating, that anything which undercut the empathetic power of the diegetic process was progressive." Now, "having
observed the way in which Americans relate to a television," however,
Burch is forced to conclude, like Jameson, that "distanciation . . . has been
coopted." The incorporation of a variety of genres in U.S. network television, while apparently innovative or modernist in its mixture of styles,
is thus for Burch "designed to place everything on the same plan of
triviality . . . in which the repression in El Salvador is no more nor less
involving than 'The Price is Right.'" The television spectator is not
encouraged to think, to know, to take action, but instead to become
entranced by a "fascinated non-involvement that is several removes in
passivity away from the 'spell of motion pictures.'" Explicitly set in opposition to the cinema, television for Burch becomes the bad object from
which to promote radical practice. And given television's alleged modern-

ism, now Burch, too, argues for a return to realism, to a strong diegetic effect characteristic of classical forms, which will restore spectatorial unity and "elicit some kind of emotional, intellectual, and perhaps even ideological commitment."[29] With Burch, as with Jameson, mass culture criticism comes full circle: from an attack on unity or realism, to a privileging of negativity or modernism, to a call for involvement through realist forms.

In this circular movement, however, the "place" accorded to the feminine remains constant, forever made to bear the composite marks of passivity, mystification, and vulgarity. To quote from Cixous, it seems as though everything "must return to the masculine," to the realm of the "proper," which sustains itself only by locating a place for the feminine outside the realm of respectability, outside the sphere of activity and knowledge.[30]

And yet, while the eternal return of the masculine may pervade our theories of mass culture, it would be both a mistake and a serious omission on my part to suggest that all contemporary writings on mass culture are caught within the terms of a repetitive, masculinized discourse. A brief look at recent film and television scholarship will serve to emphasize that a certain shift is underway in contemporary writings on mass culture, a shift that contests the traditional view of mass culture as essentially passive, or, when used as a term of opprobrium, feminized in its modes of consumption and address.

For a start, what contemporary theorists have diagnosed as our postmodern condition—a condition marked by an apparent erosion of older distinctions between high and low culture—has been implicitly questioned by theorists who demonstrate that mass culture, from the nineteenth-century novel to the TV serial, has always quoted from high art or legitimate forms. Rather than situate either film or television as the privileged metaphor for the (often deplored) proliferation, overproduction, or diffusion of signs, some recent theorists of mass culture have attempted to analyze the function of intertextuality historically and in relation to competing representational forms. Jane Feuer's work on the Hollywood musical, for example, traces the quotation and erasure of high art intertexts as central to the development of the musical as a genre. The elision of boundaries between popular and elite forms, Feuer emphasizes, is by no means an invention of the last several decades or the mark of our postmodern, despairing condition. Instead, Feuer argues, the Hollywood musical's process of intertextual appropriation (or "quotation") from both legitimate and popular forms (i.e., theater, popular recordings, television) marks that genre as a hybrid from its very inception. Furthermore, as Feuer emphasizes, the self-consciously hybrid character of the Hollywood musical is itself a form of self-promotion, an attempt at product differentiation in an intensely competitive entertainment market. And, as Feuer concludes, a narrowly formal evaluation of the Hollywood musical's textual effects will not suffice to explain its complex social function. As she puts it, "unless we put the Hollywood musical in its proper place in the history of entertainment, we may mistake it for a modernist film, or, worse, we may never see what its revelations are trying to conceal."[31]

Feuer's work on the Hollywood musical, along with other theorists' work on popular forms, also casts doubt upon the pervasive view of mass culture as either formally or ideologically homogeneous. Scholarship on the woman's film and the maternal melodrama, for example, has insisted upon a differentiated view of the so-called classical Hollywood cinema so as to understand its historically variable structures of address and modes of reception.[32]

What is true of feminist film scholarship is also true of feminist writing about television. Tania Modleski's work on daytime soaps, for example, examines the assumption that they are feminized forms by analyzing the construction of women as social readers and the construction of soap operas as social texts.[33] Proceeding from the assumption that soap operas are organized differently from popular forms aimed at a masculine visual pleasure, Modleski maintains that the discontinuous, often fragmented rhythm of soaps is organized around the rhythm of women's work. Although she quotes approvingly from Benjamin, who claims that reception in a state of distraction marks the experience of mass cultural consumption, she does not then glibly endorse a reading of daytime soaps as simply progressive but stresses instead their function in habituating women to "interruption, distraction, and spasmodic toil."[34] At the same time, however, Modleski's negative appraisal of the effects of daytime soaps does not lead her to argue that they are irredeemably reactionary. On the contrary, she maintains that soap operas serve as the site for the expression of repressed desires that, if openly articulated, "would challenge the psychological and social order of things."[35] The contradictory social function of daytime soaps brings Modleski, finally, to question the patriarchal bias in theories of spectatorship and identification. Indeed, Modleski argues that while the female viewer of soaps may lack the distance supposedly required for mastery over the image, she does not pathologically overidentify with soap opera characters "but rather relates to them as intimates, as extensions of her world."[36] And, as Modleski concludes, we must not condemn this empathetic mode of identification if we are ever to understand how mass culture "speaks to women's pleasure at the same time it puts it in the service of patriarchy, keeps it working for the good of the family."[37]

Following from Modleski's remarks, we may now want to pursue a different reading of mass culture, one that begins from the assumption that mass culture is intrinsically neither progressive nor reactionary, but highly contradictory and historically variable in its forms, its meanings, and its effects. It is here that early German film theory, when combined with a feminist perspective, may provide a more precisely social and historical explanation for the construction of subjectivity and identification in film and television viewing as at once dispersed and distracted while at the same time intensely preoccupied and absorbed. In other words, rather than revert to uncomplicated or merely formal oppositions in our analyses of textual and subject effects, we must attend to the complex interplay between psychic, social, and cultural processes in the construction of visual pleasure and identification. From this perspective, if female spectators find it difficult to assume a fetishistic distance from the image (as feminist theorists and theorists like Kracauer have claimed), then it would no longer follow that they therefore lack the ability to attain pleasure or a critical understanding of the image. Indeed, rather than subscribe to an epistemology that privileges the masculine, to the notion that an emotional identification is always regressive, we would do better to understand that different spectators may recognize themselves differently, and that this recognition, itself an effect of cultural and institutional processes, may entail a complex response of concentration, distraction, and emotional identification. While in some instances an empathetic mode of identification may very well put women's pleasures in the service of patriarchy, in others it may in fact encourage an understanding that leads to strong emotional response, which, in turn, may lead to recognition and to action.

Theorists of film and television must begin to acknowledge the complex and competing modes of perception and identification in mass cultural practices and avoid theorizing in an immanently textual or formal manner. As we have seen, not only is such an approach fundamentally ahistorical, but it also lends itself to a pernicious patriarchal bias that elides the social function of representation by continually returning to an epistemology that privileges the masculine and, by extension, legitimate cultural forms. This is not to suggest, however, that we embrace mass culture uncritically or assume it to be inherently liberating, progressive, or some-how problem free. Neither do I mean to deny the real perceptual and historical differences between film and television viewing or to dismiss the important institutional changes resulting from differences between, for example, collective and privatized reception. I would only insist that these differences are theorized historically and not through recourse to essences that reduce the question of difference to a mere application of gendered metaphors and manmade oppositions.

Two

FEMINISM AND FILM HISTORY

It's now too easy to assume that if a text is labeled "feminist" theory, then it can't properly "count" or "figure" as anything else ("woman's sphere," again).

— MEAGHAN MORRIS

T A time of inflated rhetoric about the importance of history for textual analysis and criticism, it is perhaps not surprising that film studies has recently experienced a turn to history and historical inquiry. Well before the new historicism in literary studies, however, film scholars had engaged in extended debates about the problems and inadequacies of traditionally conceived histories and attempted to bridge the critical separation of texts from contexts, and history from theory.[1] For all of their self-consciousness and theoretical sophistication, these early debates about film history nevertheless remained curiously silent about feminist challenges to conventional ways of thinking about the past. And some of the most recent work in film history (or, at least, the work that most explicitly and unreservedly names itself as such) has only exacerbated this trend, either by excluding feminism from consideration altogether, or by relegating feminist work to the specialized realm of gender criticism and speculative theory.[2]

The repeated call for greater rigor in film studies, an argument typically cast in terms of a need for archival research and hard empirical study, has had the additional effect of implying that feminists working in film theory have had relatively little to say about questions of film history.[3] As a result, it would appear from the writings of some film scholars that a certain division of labor has come to characterize film studies as a discipline in which "historians" pursue the realm of the empirical, the quantifiable, the concretely known (the realm of history proper), and "feminists" explore the more intangible realm of theoretical speculation (the realm of interpretation).

There are, of course, obvious and immediate problems with situating such an impassable (and impossible) divide between historians and feminists, history and theory, empirical research and theoretical analysis. Such a divide not only simplifies the current state of film historical debate. More important, by ignoring feminist film theory's longstanding concern to differentiate and particularize notions of subjectivity, it also functions to consign to oblivion much feminist work on film history.

To be sure, feminist film criticism and theory are often unrecognizable as "history" understood in a conventional way (history as the study of unique individuals; history as the development of aesthetic forms; history as the evolution of industrial and legal structures, what one feminist has called "history as usual").[4] Not surprisingly, the methods and approach of traditional histories have proven problematic for feminists, not least of all because so many documents preserved from the past offer limited traces of women's presence, while presenting massive evidence of their marginality and repression. But what is fundamentally at issue here is not a lack of adequate documentation. Indeed, as many feminists have shown, the project of reconstituting film history from a feminist perspective is not merely a matter of making the invisible visible. It also involves submitting regimes of visibility to a general critique of objectivity and subjectivity in the writing of film history, and rethinking critical methods and theoretical procedures in contemporary film theory (e.g., the status of textual analysis, the relationship between authorship and biography, the role of extratextual determinations on the cinema and its audiences).

A larger and more important distinction in film historiography is therefore obscured by debates over the relative merits of empiricism and theoretical speculation: namely, the difference between a history of film as institutionally and formally *produced* (the history of film as a privileged object) and a history of film as it is *received* in culture (the history of the spectator-subject). As Fredric Jameson has remarked, there are always two historicities, and thus two paths of historical inquiry: "the path of the object, and the path of the subject, the historical origins of the things themselves and that more intangible historicity of the concepts and categories by which we attempt to understand those things."[5]

The difference between these two historicities in film studies is perhaps best described as the difference between a *formal* history of filmic conventions and institutions and a *cultural* history of film reception and spectatorship. Whereas formal film histories are characterized by an attempt to discern developments within institutional constraints and generic conventions, for example, cultural film histories aim to locate films within the history of larger cultural forces, such as consumerism, censorship, or reform. Given these alternatives, it is no coincidence that feminists have chosen to pursue issues in cultural history, thereby following the path of the subject and the more intangible historicity of subjectivity. In contrast to formalist film historians, who seek to recover what is increasingly becoming a lost object, feminists have been primarily concerned to unearth the history of the (found) female subject.

Having posed the issue in this way, I would not want to imply that the distinction between formal and cultural histories exhausts the kinds of historical writing in film studies today, or, indeed, that there is no overlap between formalist and culturalist approaches. Furthermore, as I will suggest later on, the very opposition between subject and object remains inherently problematic and especially limiting for feminist film histories, failing as it does to account for the paradoxical status of woman in film history as both subject and object of representation, as both consumer of images and as the quintessential image of the consumer. Finally, as the history of feminist film theory so clearly demonstrates, the very attempt to "find" a female subject has led to a paralyzing situation in some feminist film histories, which tend either to affirm a socially constructed feminine identity, or to reject any attempt at self-naming at all.

This said, there is something to be gained by recognizing the historical dimension of feminist film criticism and theory, and by discerning the more general feminist concern with mapping the path of the (female) subject in history. Although feminist work in film studies has rarely been thought to "count" or "figure" as history, I would like to suggest how it reveals a consistent concern with questions of history and representation, as well as a shift from grand, teleological narratives of the representation of women in film to more limited histories of authorship, spectatorship, and consumerism. In the analysis that follows—an analysis that admittedly remains suggestive rather than exhaustive—I hope to show how historical questions loom large in feminist writings on film, where the stakes of historical knowledge turn less on debating the merits of empiricism and interpretation, and more on rethinking the vexed relationships between identity and difference in culture.

FEMINISM AND REFLECTION THEORY

Women have served all these centuries as looking glasses possessing the magic and delicious power of reflecting the figure of man at twice its natural size.

—VIRGINIA WOOLF

The earliest accounts of film history written from a feminist perspective—Marjorie Rosen's *Popcorn Venus: Women, Movies, and the American Dream* (1973) and Molly Haskell's *From Reverence to Rape: The Treatment of Women in the Movies* (1974)—are now dismissed as popularized and theoretically unsophisticated histories, noted for their sweeping and teleological historical claims.[6] Detailing the decade-by-decade repression of women in the Hollywood cinema, both books are also criticized for their historical reductionism, for their assumption of an identity between text and context, audience and screen, in short, for their reliance on what is commonly referred to as "reflection theory."[7]

"Movies are one of the clearest and most accessible of looking glasses into the past, being both cultural artifacts and mirrors," writes Molly Haskell in the introduction to *From Reverence to Rape*.[8] Similarly, in the preface to *Popcorn Venus*, Marjorie Rosen asks whether "art reflects life," only to provide the following unequivocal answer: "In movies, yes. Because more than any other art form, films have been a mirror held up to society's porous face. They therefore reflect the changing societal image of women—which, until recently, has not been taken seriously enough."[9] The metaphor of the mirror that is invoked here, while serving to establish a relationship between film and culture, the textual and the social body, nevertheless fails to consider the far more difficult issue of the relationship between text and ideology. Thus, according to Jameson's formulation: "Is the text a free-floating object in its own right, or does it reflect some context or ground, and in that case does it simply replicate the latter ideologically, or does it possess some autonomous force in which it could also be seen as negating that context?"[10]

Rosen's account of women and film history remains unconcerned with the question of the relationship between text and ideology, invested as it is in the terms of traditional sociological analysis. Haskell's account, by contrast, often suggests a far more nuanced view of how films can function as historical evidence, addressing the ways in which the cinema both reflects social conditions and distorts women's experiences of those conditions. In one of the most frequently cited passages from her book, Haskell writes:

Women have grounds for protest, and film is a rich field for the mining of female stereotypes. At the same time, there is a danger in going too far the other way, of grafting a modern sensibility onto the past so that all film history becomes grist in the mills of outraged feminism. . . . We can, for example, deplore the fact that in every movie where a woman excelled as a professional she had to be brought to heel at the end, but only as long as we acknowledge the corollary: that at least women *worked* in the films of the thirties and forties, and, moreover, that early film heroines were not only proportionally more active than the women who saw them, but more active than the heroines of today's films. Here we are today, with an unparalleled freedom of expression and a record number of women performing, achieving, choosing to fulfill themselves, and we are insulted with the worst—the most abused, neglected, and dehumanized—screen heroines in film history.[11]

In this passage, Haskell challenges the conventional view of "progress" and "development" in the Hollywood cinema and insists that critics respect the otherness of the past and account for its fundamental difference from the present. Questioning the basic tenets of reflection theory, she also maintains that the mirror held up to women in film does not simply "reflect" their social reality but rather reveals how the cinema has functioned historically to obscure women's accomplishments and further invest the male point of view with what she calls the "big lie" of Western civilization—the idea of women's inferiority.

Interestingly enough, Haskell avoids the pitfalls of reflection theory by setting up an atemporal and normative ideal of heterosexual romance against which the trajectory of film history is judged. Significantly, the metaphor of the mirror is often invoked pejoratively in Haskell's text, usually in reference to contemporary cinema and in relation to questions of sexual difference. In recent seventies films, for example, Haskell detects a breakdown in the representation of heterosexual romance, claiming that the male-female protagonists, "like so many modern couples, come together in their weaknesses rather than their strength; they are mirror reflections of each other's neuroses" (27). The male buddy film, moreover, is analyzed in strikingly similar terms, although it comes in for additional criticism for its exclusion of women and its narcissistic indifference to heterosexuality:

Sexual desire is not the point, nor "homoeroticism" the term for these relationships or for men fighting together shoulder to shoulder at the front . . . ; rather, the point is love—love in which men understand and support each other, speak the same language, and risk their lives to gain each other's respect. But this is also a delusion; the difficulties of the adventure disguise the fact that this is the easiest of loves: a love that is adolescent, presexual, tacit, the love of one's *semblable,* one's mirror reflection. (24)

Despite her remarks to the contrary, Haskell's critique of the buddy film is at least in part a critique of homoeroticism that she extends to contemporary cinema as well. "We have succumbed to a kind of emotional laziness and passivity," Haskell writes, "a state in which only violence can rouse us, and we are inclined to choose as our partners those who are reflections of, rather than challenges to, the soul. The homophile impulse, like most decadent tropisms, like incest, is, or can be, a surrender, a sinking back into one's own nature" (28).

Although critical of the institution of marriage and what she refers to as "a disease called middle-class family life," Haskell upholds the "male-female chemistry" as a standard by which to evaluate film history, and she indulges in an uncritical celebration of heterosexual romance (as represented by "films in which the two points of view are separate but equal," such as those starring Lauren Bacall and Humphrey Bogart or Katharine Hepburn and Spencer Tracy [25]). While commonly criticized for its sweeping and teleological claims, *From Reverence to Rape* can also be criticized for imposing an identity on film history—for reducing the history of women and film to the (failed) history of heterosexual romance in contemporary U.S. cinema and culture.

In any case, Haskell's narrative version of film history was quickly abandoned in favor of more theoretically sophisticated, and more historically limited, approaches to women and film. Questions of authorship, in particular, allowed feminist theorists to challenge established ways of writing about film history, and to rethink, at the level of production, the complicated relationships between gender identity and sexual difference in film.

FEMINISM AND FILM AUTHORSHIP

Women and film can only become meaningful in terms of a theory, in an attempt to create a structure in which films such as Arzner's can be examined in retrospect.

— CLAIRE JOHNSTON

It has often been remarked that the poststructuralist critique of authorship functioned to exclude the very questions of identity and subjectivity central to an emerging feminist literary criticism. As Nancy Miller explains, "The removal of the Author has not so much made room for a revision of the concept of authorship as it has, through a variety of rhetorical moves, repressed and inhibited discussion of any writing identity in favor of the (new) monolith of anonymous textuality." [12]

In the context of film studies, however, the advent of poststructuralism had the opposite effect on feminist criticism; at least initially, it enabled the discussion of women directors in the cinema and revitalized debates about authorship that had dominated film studies since the early 1960s. Appearing in 1975, only a year after the publication of *From Reverence to Rape*, Claire Johnston's and Pam Cook's essays on Dorothy Arzner effectively redefined the terms of traditional *auteur* criticism by submitting the concept of film authorship to poststructuralist revision and to a thoroughgoing feminist critique. (Arzner was a director, editor, and writer whose career spanned the heyday of the Hollywood studio system.)

Importantly, Johnston and Cook understood their project to be a *polemical* intervention into contemporary debates about the function of feminist criticism and an emerging feminist film practice. Challenging established ways of writing film history for excluding the contributions of women (e.g., the auteurism championed by Andrew Sarris and the sociological histories of Kevin Brownlow and Lewis Jacobs), they also challenged feminist "discoveries" of female directors in the Hollywood cinema and criticized attempts to reclaim films directed by women for an unbroken tradition of "feminist art." A feminist film history, Johnston argued, is not simply a matter of "reintroducing" women into an untransformed history, as yet another series of "facts" to be assimilated into a preexisting chronology:

> "History" is not some abstract "thing" which bestows significance on past events in retrospect. Only an attempt to situate Arzner's work in a theoretical way would allow us to comprehend her real contribution to film history. . . . This is not, however, to ignore the political importance of asserting the real role women have played in the history of the cinema. . . . [But] the role of women in film history . . . inevitably raises questions about the nature of film history as such, and it is for this reason that this pamphlet has approached Dorothy Arzner's work from the point of view of feminist politics and feminist theory, as prerequisite research before any attempt at insertion into film history can be undertaken. [13]

For Johnston, as for Cook, the place of the female director in the Holly-wood cinema can only be assessed in relation to a *history* that made it impossible for feminist statements to emerge from the studio system, and in terms of a *theory* that understands film authorship to be a function of discourse rather than individual intent. In Arzner's case, this amounts to analyzing the ways in which her films displace identification with charac-ters and generate a series of competing discourses that "denaturalize" pa-triarchal ideology and "disturb" the fixed position of the spectator. "In Arzner's work," Johnston explains, "the discourse of the woman, or rather her attempt to locate it and make it heard, is what gives the system of the text its structural coherence. . . . These women do not sweep aside the existing order and found a new, female order of language. Rather, they assert their own discourse in the face of the male one by breaking it up, subverting it, and, in a sense, rewriting it" (4).

Arzner's 1940 film *Dance, Girl, Dance* provides both critics with a wealth of examples to support this idea of the "subversive text." The final scene, in which Judy O'Brien (Maureen O'Hara) discovers Steve Adams's identity as director of a dance academy, and hence the real reason for his pursuit of her (i.e., her abilities as a dancer), is cited by Johnston as a compelling instance of denaturalization:

> *Dance, Girl, Dance* shows Judy exchanging the humiliation of the spec-tacle for the defeat of the final embrace with Steve Adams, the pa-triarchal presence which has haunted her through the film. . . . As she turns to camera, her face obscured by a large, floppy hat, Judy, half crying, half laughing, exclaims "when I think how simple things could have been, I just have to laugh." This irony marks her defeat and final engulfment, but at the same time it is the final mark of subversion of the discourse of the male." (7)

Of this same scene, Cook writes:

> In this final ironic reversal Judy "gets what she wants" at the expense of any pretensions to "independence" she had. Again, by displacing our expectations of identification with Judy's positive qualities into a recog-nition of the weakness of her position within male-dominated culture, the film's ending opens up the contradictions inherent in that position (our position) thus encouraging us as spectators to recognize the all-important problematic of the difficulties of the working through of fe-male desire under patriarchy.[14]

Four years after the appearance of their work on Dorothy Arzner, Johnston's and Cook's approach to the analysis of the subversive text was subjected to detailed criticism by Janet Bergstrom and Jacquelyn Suter.[15] Bergstrom, in particular, questioned Johnston's attempt to specify—on the basis of a largely thematic analysis—reactions or reflexive thoughts on the part of the spectator. For all of Johnston's interpretive claims, Bergstrom argued, she fails to provide a textual analysis that adequately demonstrates "the working through of the woman's desire" or the positioning of the woman's discourse in terms of a larger system: "The irony which Johnston sees operating in these Arzner endings is stated as if it is part of a factual account of the narrative. It is assumed that these endings will be understood as ironic by everyone, and that this irony will work, for all spectators, in the woman's favor."[16] In addition to Johnston's problematic use of textual evidence, Bergstrom further contends, her analysis of the "rupturing activity" of the classical film relies on a rather dubious view of the workings of Hollywood cinema:

> Although Johnston refers to Stephen Heath's analysis of *Touch of Evil* . . .
> his article serves to demonstrate what, at the very least, presents a ma
> jor paradox for what she is arguing—that is, the seemingly unlimited
> capacity for classical narrative film to create gaps, fissures, ruptures,
> generated most of all by its difficulty in containing sexual difference,
> only to recover them ultimately and to efface the memory, or at least
> the paths, of this heterogeneity. It is just this rupturing activity that is
> said to be characteristic of the classical text, and which, moreover, is
> thought to be the condition of a large part of its pleasure. (85)

In underscoring the problems that follow from highly interpretive analyses such as Johnston's, Bergstrom provides a compelling critique of attempts to generalize audience response on the basis of a single analysis and, in the process, raises important reservations about assigning subversive or feminist readings to classical texts. Bergstrom's description of the Hollywood cinema, which draws largely upon the work of Raymond Bellour, Stephen Heath, and Thierry Kuntzel, nevertheless presents its own problems for the study of female authorship in the classical film— problems that become strikingly apparent in Jacquelyn Suter's analysis of Arzner's *Christopher Strong*. Simply put, if the classical film functions, consistently and inevitably, to contain the excesses and contradictions it so clearly generates, is the study of female authorship in the Hollywood cinema a questionable endeavor, merely another version of what Constance Penley calls "the easily accepted (because narcissistically desired)"?[17]

Suter's discussion of Arzner's film attempts to provide a provisional answer. In her view, a film like *Christopher Strong* generates certain formal transgressions that might be associated with a feminine discourse, and yet these "isolated interruptions do not necessarily deconstruct the narrative discourse in any significant way." According to Suter, the classic text is bound up with a narrative logic that necessarily precludes the forceful articulation of authorship that one finds, for example, in Chantal Akerman's films. In *Jeanne Dielman,* Suter contends, "instead of isolated interventions into a classic text, we have a systematic reordering of certain crucial elements upon which the classic text depends, and a recognition of other elements which the classic text chooses invariably to ignore."[18] For Suter, the Hollywood film thus remains a self-contained and, by implication, a closed system—at least insofar as female authorship is concerned.

While Johnston and Cook, and Bergstrom and Suter, generally agree about what constitutes authorship in the cinema—that is, they all define it as a discursive practice—they nevertheless disagree as to what constitutes a subversive reading and hence about critical methodology. Importantly, however, none of these theorists (with the exception of Johnston) addresses the difficulty or the necessity of thinking about authorship in extratextual terms, and therefore they fail to consider the problem of authorship as it intersects with issues of history, biography, and textuality.

Paradoxically, then, what began as an attempt to *revise* the concept of film authorship by rethinking the place of the female director in the history of the Hollywood cinema ended up in debates about the concept of the subversive text, and in arguments (to borrow from Nancy Miller) for a "(new) monolith of anonymous textuality" that inhibited further discussion of female authorship in the development of the classical film. To be sure, feminists continued to consider the possibility of locating female enunciation in the Hollywood cinema, and studies of female authorship in the independent and avant-garde cinema proceeded as if the relationship between biography and textual analysis were simpler, or at least less problematic, than in Arzner's case. In any event, both the role of the woman director in Hollywood and the troubling theoretical question of biography were virtually set aside as theorists turned from the production context to explore questions of film history through a consideration of spectatorship and discourses on consumption.

FEMINISM, SPECTATORSHIP, AND CONSUMERISM

If the apparatus stages an eternal, universal and primordial wish to create a simulacrum of the psyche, then Baudry's argument is blind to the economic, social or political determinations of cinema as well as its basic difference from other art forms.

— CONSTANCE PENLEY

What is elided in the conceptualization of the spectator is not only historical but sexual specificity.

— MARY ANN DOANE

Studies of consumerism and female spectatorship emerged in response to the most significant film theories of the 1970s: Jean-Louis Baudry's and Christian Metz's theory of the cinematic apparatus, and Laura Mulvey's theory of narrative cinema and visual pleasure.[19] Both apparatus theory and the theory of the spectator developed by Mulvey signaled an important conceptual shift in film studies: the shift from a formal analysis of the film text (the structural organization of the fiction) to a consideration of the metapsychology of film viewing (the place of the spectator with respect to the fiction).

Although setting the terms for a sophisticated analysis of perception and identification in film, apparatus theory, and the conceptualization of the spectator that underpinned it, quickly became the focus of extensive criticism and debate. Feminist theorists, in particular, challenged claims for the eternal, universal effects of the cinematic apparatus, as opposed to its historically specific and sexually differentiated constructions.

As Jacqueline Rose has pointed out, Metz's psychoanalytic reading of visual perception and, specifically, his use of the concept of disavowal to describe the ways in which cinema achieves its impression of reality failed to address the problem or the difficulty of sexual difference.[20] In a similar way, Baudry's assumption of a transhistorical, indeed primordial, desire for cinematic pleasure neglected to consider pleasures and subjectivities that were historically produced as well as sexually inflected. Baudry's model, as Penley has explained, is "not only ahistorical but also strongly teleological."

The shackled prisoners fascinated by the shadows on the wall of Plato's cave are the first "cinema" spectators; the only historical changes in the apparatus since then have been little more than technological modifications. . . . Baudry's teleological argument [further] asserts that the cinema aims at pleasure alone, and that it unfailingly achieves it, an

assertion, moreover, that is merely stated and not supported. . . . The
question of pleasure has been a crucially troubling one for feminist
theory and filmmaking and the theory of the apparatus appears to answer the question before it is even raised.[21]

The question of sexually inflected pleasures was, of course, central to
Mulvey's now classic theory of visual pleasure in the Hollywood film.
However, in assuming masculine subjectivity as a sole point of reference,
Mulvey's analysis of structures of looking in the cinema tended to reproduce the problems and blind spots of apparatus theory. In an effort to
reintroduce both historical and sexual specificity into theories of cinematic perception, feminists therefore increasingly turned to questions of
consumerism and female spectatorship, exploring the ways in which a
particular history (the history of consumer capitalism) transformed not
just the organization of narrative and visual pleasure, but also the forms
of subjectivity associated with a female spectator-subject.

Mary Ann Doane's book *The Desire to Desire: The Woman's Film of the
1940s* (1987) stands as the most important contribution to the reconsidera-
tion of spectatorship and apparatus theory from a feminist perspective.
Challenging the assumption that the cinematic apparatus is sexually indifferent—that it stages a "universal and hence ahistorical condition of the
human psyche"—Doane sets out to trace the contours of female subjectivity in the woman's film, charting the difficulties and failures of Hollywood's attempt to construct a position for the female spectator. The
woman's film, Doane explains, "does not provide us with an access to a
pure and authentic female subjectivity, much as we might like it to do so.
It provides us instead with an image repertoire of poses—classical feminine poses and assumptions about the female appropriation of the gaze.
Hollywood women's films of the 1940s document a crisis in subjectivity
around the figure of woman—although it is not always clear whose subjectivity is at stake.[22]

As this quote implies, Doane's challenge to apparatus theory remains
within the terms of its own analysis. Her study of the woman's film for
example, does not address the habits and responses of actual moviegoers
but rather provides an investigation of "classical feminine poses" or discourses of feminine subjectivity during the period. This is not to say, however, that Doane is unconcerned with questions of history or the context
of reception. Indeed, although she is careful to distinguish between social
and psychical descriptions of the subject, she nevertheless attempts to ex-

amine the historical process whereby the address to women as consumers became indistinguishable from the objectification of woman as image.

Drawing on the work of Charles Eckert and Jeanne Allen, Doane sketches the relationship between the cinema and commodity fetishism, and shows how the commodity form inflected filmic representation and spectatorship.[23] With reference to Walter Benjamin's argument about large-scale historical changes in human perception, Doane further suggests how the commodity form collapses traditional distinctions between subject and object and restructures spatial and temporal registers of looking and perception.[24] "It is not accidental," she writes, "that the logic of consumerism and mechanical reproduction corresponds to a logic of perception attributed to the female spectator whose nonfetishistic gaze maintains a dangerous intimacy with the image."[25] Proximity rather than distance, a disabling closeness to the image—these are the tropes that link femininity and consumerism and the female spectator. As Doane explains:

> In her desire to bring the things of the screen closer, to approximate the bodily image of the star, and to possess the space in which she dwells, the female spectator experiences the intensity of the image as lure and exemplifies the perception proper to the consumer. The cinematic image for the woman is both shop window and mirror, the one simply a means of access to the other. The mirror/window takes on then the aspect of a trap whereby her subjectivity becomes synonymous with her objectification. (32–33)

Doane's efforts to historicize apparatus theory represent a remarkable achievement, and yet her assessment of female spectatorship during the 1940s raises important questions about historical periodization and critical method. One could argue, for example, that Doane describes a form of spectatorship that embraces the history of the cinema in its entirety, rather than a particular subjectivity at a precise historical moment. To be sure, the history of consumer capitalism provides a more limited temporal frame for an analysis of cinema and subjectivity than does Baudry's appeal to Plato's allegory of the cave. Nevertheless, in situating her discussion of the female spectator within such an expanded historical perspective, Doane might be faulted by historians for subordinating historical analysis to theoretical interpretation—for producing a theory of the woman's film instead of a history.

Importantly, however, Doane's attempt to *theorize* the context of film reception in the 1940s allows her to explore questions of historical spectatorship through textual analysis. In contrast to other recent studies of cinema and consumerism, *The Desire to Desire* seeks to integrate film analysis with a larger, and more extensive, discussion of film culture during a historical period—hence, the appeal to consumerism as a critical concept, and the close analysis of films like *Caught*, which inscribe female desire according to the logic of the commodity.[26] This is not to say, however, that Doane aims simply to respond to the formalist question, Can film history survive without the analysis of individual films? Indeed, by considering consumerism as it inflects modes of looking and representation, she also confronts a far more crucial issue, namely, Can a feminist film history be confined to a history of film? From this perspective, studies of consumerism and the female spectator, rather than necessarily implying the triumph of theory over history or the disappearance of film as a privileged object, might more usefully be understood as redefining the object of a specifically feminist film history. As Doane herself has written: "Feminism cannot be a formalism. The object is cinema only insofar as cinema is understood not as formal object or as a repository of meanings but as a particular—and quite specific—mode of representing and inscribing subjectivities which are sexually inflected."[27]

All of this is not to suggest some sort of teleology in the development of feminist film theory, in which consumerism replaces authorship, which replaced social history, as the most viable concept for organizing film history. Studies of the female spectator-consumer, moreover, pose a number of difficulties and problems, most obviously with respect to the history of U.S. consumer culture itself. One might ask, for example, what distinguishes discourses on consumption in the 1940s (a privileged area for feminist research) from discourses on consumerism in the early part of the century? Does the history of consumer capitalism form an unbroken continuum, or does it rather reveal a series of radical shifts and dislocations? And what of the relationships among cinema, sexual difference, and consumerism in second- and third-world nations? Given the inordinate amount of attention to the Hollywood cinema in feminist film theory, it is now important to begin to account for the history of other national cinemas from a feminist perspective.[28] But can the model of the spectator-consumer developed by feminist theory be easily exported to explain developments in other cinemas or national traditions?

While studies of consumerism raise important questions and suggest areas for further research, I believe it is also crucial for feminists to return to earlier debates on film history and address issues that were too hastily dismissed or prematurely foreclosed. The relationship between biography and textuality, for instance, remains a crucial issue for feminist film history, although more attention has been paid to the biographical dimension of filmic textuality than to the textual dimension of biography. Certainly, a study like Haskell's highlights the place of the female star in the Hollywood cinema, and biographic information remains central to her attempt to detail the contradictions between cinematic representation and the everyday lives of female stars. In view of recent theoretical work on cinema and the star system, however, Haskell's social history could be usefully extended and updated. How, for example, might the concepts of biography and textuality be theorized to enable the study of differences outside of a heterosexual problematic? As Judith Mayne points out in her book on feminism and women's cinema, "it was well-known in Hollywood, and it is well-known amongst feminist critics, that Arzner was a lesbian, but rarely if ever does this enter into discussions of Arzner's work." [29] How, then, might studies of female authorship open up discussion about tensions and negotiations of the production context and hence generate accounts of sexual *differences* in the history of the Hollywood film?

Finally, as the history of feminist film theory so clearly demonstrates, the analysis of individual films goes only so far in explaining the complexities of audience expectation and spectator response. But if film theory cannot exist without film analysis, and if feminism cannot be a formalism, then what precisely is the role of textual analysis in feminist film history? The issue here, as I suggested earlier, is not one of retrieving film analysis from the perceived excesses of theory, or of reducing feminist film history to a formalist study of film. It is instead a matter of rethinking what claims can be made on the basis of film analysis, and of reconceptualizing what constitutes textual evidence in relation to questions of sexual difference. For what is finally at stake for feminism is not so much the problem of claiming too much for textual analysis, but that of claiming too little, thereby leaving the writing of film history to those who would exclude sexual difference from the study of the cinema entirely.

GERMAN FILM THEORY AND ANGLO-AMERICAN FILM STUDIES

T HAS often been remarked that, until fairly recently, Siegfried Kracauer's reputation in film theory rested upon the two books he wrote in English: *From Caligari to Hitler* (1947) and *Theory of Film* (1960).[1] These two books, which established Kracauer as a major, if fundamentally flawed, thinker on film, have frequently been compared to the essays and more aphoristic writings of the French film theorist André Bazin, who shared Kracauer's concern for an aesthetics of realism in the cinema. In standard surveys of film theory, however, the comparison between Kracauer and Bazin is made only to underscore the tendentious and one-dimensional quality of Kracauer's thought. Dudley Andrew, for example, characterizes the difference between Kracauer and Bazin in the following way: "Kracauer is the kind of man who decided after forty years of viewing film that he ought to work out and write down his ideas about the medium; so he went straight to the library and locked himself in. There, reading widely, thinking endlessly, and always working alone, always cut off from the buzz of film talk and film production, he slowly and painstakingly gave birth to his theory." Andrew continues: "Unlike Kracauer, who spent years alone in the library generating *Theory of Film*, Bazin seems always to have been with people who were making films or discussing them. . . . It has been suggested that the best of his criticism has been lost because it occurred in the form of oral presentations and debates. . . . In any case, Bazin displayed little concern for the future of his ideas. He seemed satisfied that his thoughts could be of service in particular situations.[2] In Andrew's account, Bazin is upheld as the quintessentially French intellectual, collegial in his approach to scholarship and aware of the contingent nature of thought. Kracauer, by contrast, emerges as the stereotypical German pedant, shut off from the world of practical criticism and obsessed with the future of his own ideas. Indeed, what Andrew values most in Bazin is directly related to what he finds most lacking in Kracauer. The local and specific nature of Bazin's theorizing about film—its provisional and essayistic quality—is precisely what prevents it, according to Andrew, from becoming the formidable and formidably closed system represented by Kracauer's ponderously Teutonic thought.

This obvious caricature of both Kracauer and Bazin is not merely the expression of an opinion, nor simply the reflection of a Francophile sentiment. For it is that, but it is also much more, pointing to the intellectual and historical origins of contemporary film theory. No attentive reader of Anglo-American film theory over the past three decades would fail to miss its distinctly French orientation. From auteurism to poststructuralism, French traditions of thought have had the most significant influence on the development of film studies as an academic discipline, both in the United States and in Britain. To be sure, German theory has been enlisted along the way to expand the domain of a critical film theory. But it is Freud as read through Jacques Lacan, or Marx through Louis Althusser, that has set the terms for the reception of German film theory. Even initial attempts to restore a phenomenological dimension to film study appealed to existential phenomenology rather than to critical theory, Maurice Merleau-Ponty and Jean-Paul Sartre rather than Kracauer or Benjamin, in order to challenge the analytic and overly scientific approach of early film structuralism and semiotics.[3]

What this points to, among other things, is the relative ease with which ideas have circulated between French and Anglo-American traditions, and the fundamentally impaired or more limited movement of German theories in the United States and Britain—at least insofar as the recent history of film theory is concerned. The rise of Nazism, which forced some of the most sophisticated theorists of cinema and mass culture into exile, certainly accounts for the loss of texts and traditions that contributed to a vital film culture in Germany during the 1920s. More significant than this, however, was the temporal lag between the translation of important German texts into English and the clearing of an institutional space in the 1970s for serious academic film study.

With no understanding of German theoretical traditions, and with no

knowledge of the German language, some of the most prominent film
scholars in the seventies had considerable difficulty in seeing any connection between Kracauer's final work on history and Benjamin's *Illuminations*, or, for that matter, any relationship between Kracauer's study of the
Weimar cinema and Max Horkheimer and Adorno's *Dialectic of Enlightenment*. In a thumbnail sketch of Kracauer's career, for example, Andrew
mentions only four of his major studies—*From Caligari to Hitler, Theory of
Film, History: The Last Things before the Last*, and *Offenbach and the Paris of
His Time*—books originally written in English, or, in the case of the Offenbach study, books readily available in English translation. Had Andrew
considered Kracauer's writings for the *Frankfurter Zeitung*, he might have
suggested how they share the improvisational character of Bazin's essays
and how they connect to a wider history of German thinking about film.

Unaware of this early work, and failing to appreciate the circumstances
under which *Theory of Film* was written, Andrew therefore fails to assess
adequately the reasons for Kracauer's and Bazin's different working methods. Kracauer, Andrew tells us, "decided after forty years of viewing film"
to write down his ideas about the medium, and "so he went straight to
the library and locked himself in." Bazin, by contrast, is valorized for the
social nature of his criticism, for having always "been with people who
were making films or discussing them." With Kracauer forced into exile
in the early 1930s, his mode of scholarship can hardly be compared with
Bazin's, since Bazin was never forced to leave his native France. And while
risking, in the very writing of *Theory of Film*, the possibility of appearing
out of date and overly ambitious, Kracauer also risked what Edward Said
has described in relation to Erich Auerbach as the very real "possibility of
not writing and thus falling victim to the concrete dangers of exile: the loss
of texts, traditions, and continuities that make up the very web of a
culture." [4]

Said's discussion of the effects of exile on Auerbach's writing of *Mimesis*
bears further comparison with Kracauer's *Theory of Film*, not least of all
given the two men's shared affiliation with a formidable tradition of
European literature and letters. Said points out that in the epilogue to
Mimesis, Auerbach casually mentions his experience of exile in Istanbul,
thereby invoking not merely a place outside of Europe, but also "the ultimate alienation from and opposition to Europe." As Said explains, "For
centuries Turkey and Islam hung over Europe like a gigantic composite
monster, seeming to threaten Europe with destruction. To have been an
exile in Istanbul at the time of fascism in Europe was a deeply resonating
and intense form of exile from Europe." [5]

Said concludes by suggesting that Auerbach's experience of exile ultimately served an enabling purpose, allowing him to convert his sense of pain and alienation into a work of literary criticism whose insights derive not simply from the culture it describes but also, and more crucially, from a necessary and agonizing distance from it. The same might be said of Kracauer's analysis of the Weimar cinema in *From Caligari to Hitler,* and yet the parallels between Kracauer and Auerbach go further than this. For instance, Auerbach's own admission of the need to transcend national boundaries ("our philological home is the earth," he writes, "it can no longer be the nation")[6] certainly illuminates the final section of *Theory of Film,* where Kracauer, drawing directly on *Mimesis,* argues for an aesthetics of cinema derived from the texture of everyday life. Films whose composition "varies according to place, people, and time," Kracauer writes, "help us not only to appreciate our given material environment but to extend it in all directions. They virtually make the world our home."[7]

Even more striking than Auerbach's and Kracauer's shared commitment to a realist aesthetic, however, are the similar effects of their different destinations as refugees from Nazi Europe. If Istanbul was a particularly intense form of exile for a literary critic like Auerbach, so, too, was the United States a deeply resonant experience for a film theorist like Kracauer. Since at least the 1920s, Hollywood cinema represented not merely an alternative to European filmmaking but also the very ethos of consumer capitalism that threatened to overtake and subsume other national traditions. Although Kracauer never shared Adorno's antipathy to Hollywood or, indeed, to U.S. culture, he was certainly aware of the dangers of consumerist logic, even if, on the surface, this seems more obvious in his early writings than it does in *Theory of Film.*

In any case, it would be impossible to see Kracauer today as the author solely of *From Caligari to Hitler* or *Theory of Film,* or to assume that these books contain all of what he had to say about the cinema. The translation of some of Kracauer's most important early writings in the pages of *New German Critique* has gone a long way to ensure a reevaluation of his reputation in film studies and has in fact inaugurated a veritable Kracauer renaissance in contemporary film theory. What has emerged from recent discussion is a view of not one theory but two successive and autonomous theories of the cinema in the corpus of his writings; in other words, one finds a view of "two Kracauers" in contemporary film theory: the early Kracauer of *Das Ornament der Masse* and the later Kracauer of *From Caligari to Hitler* and *Theory of Film.*

The early Kracauer, for instance, is characterized as the practical film critic of the *Frankfurter Zeitung*, the anticapitalist practitioner of a "material dialectics" (if not a dialectical materialism), the phenomenological observer of the local, the ephemeral, the everyday. The later Kracauer, by contrast, is seen to be the massive system builder and conceptual thinker of *Caligari* and *Theory of Film*, the anticommunist émigré intellectual, the sociological critic turned melancholy realist. While retaining Dudley Andrew's pejorative assessment of Kracauer's American work, this new view also assumes that the inconsistencies in Kracauer's writings constitute overwhelming evidence of a schism or epistemological shift in his thinking about film—a shift that separates the early, improvisational essays of the 1920s from the later, academically imposing studies of the postwar period.

To be sure, some commentators have suggested that Kracauer's writings exhibit a continuity of concerns, despite apparent inconsistencies in his method or chosen format, be it the exploratory essay or the book-length study. Karsten Witte, for example, maintains that the link between early and later work "lies in [Kracauer's] intention to decipher social tendencies revealed in ephemeral cultural phenomenon." For others, however, Kracauer's work evidences a significant theoretical division, with the later work marking a lapse into a fundamentally flawed or one-dimensional reasoning. Heide Schlüpmann, for example, writes that "in *From Caligari to Hitler* and *Theory of Film*, Kracauer's tendency to generalize, to subsume particulars within conceptual constructs, presents an obstacle to the expression of his ideas." The strength of the early essays, she further contends, "lies in their phenomenological procedure, their taking up of individual manifestations of daily life and dwelling upon them reflectively." Thomas Elsaesser similarly stresses the differences between Kracauer's work written in Germany and in America, claiming that between his 1927 essay "The Mass Ornament" and the 1947 book *From Caligari to Hitler,* Kracauer abandoned the dialectical core of his early criticism in favor of a sociological reductionism and an unredeemed humanism. In Elsaesser's estimation, the early Kracauer's emphasis on the impossibility of separating high art and mass culture distinguishes him as a proto-poststructuralist, whereas the later work places him squarely within the traditions of U.S. sociology and cold war anticommunism. Although the divide between early and later work is therefore variously interpreted, there is little dispute over the fact of a division—a division separating Marxist critique from a theory of realist aesthetics, and Weimar Germany from postwar America.[8]

Given the terms of Kracauer's reception in film studies, there is some question of whether we must speak of *Kracauer's* epistemological shift, or, rather, of an epistemological shift in *Kracauer criticism*. Of course, in the context of film studies, to speak of an epistemological shift at all is necessarily to invoke David Bordwell's essay on "Eisenstein's Epistemological Shift," which attempts to show how Sergei Eisenstein's writings turned from a materialist aesthetic informed by Pavlovian physiology and dialectical materialism to a romantic aesthetic grounded in psychology, organicism, and empiricism.[9] In a surprising reversal of classical film theory's traditional separation of formalist and realist aesthetics, Eisenstein and Kracauer have come to be discussed in remarkably similar ways. In Bordwell's view, Eisenstein's later writings evidence a shift toward political conformity as well as a move from a practical engagement with film to a stance of isolated self-absorption. According to recent commentators like Elsaesser, Kracauer's writings similarly reveal a turn away from dialectical thinking to political conservatism, as well as a shift from practical film criticism to academic film theory. What is at stake, then, in claims for epistemological shifts in the development of film theory are assumptions about intellectual responses to Stalinism and to communism in the cold war era. As one critic has put it (without, however, making any reference to Kracauer): "It is strange to see how the philistinism of the Stalinist regime in the 1930s finds its belated double in the United States of the Cold War two decades later."[10]

Of course, the concept of "epistemological shift" has a wider theoretical lineage, one that can be traced to Louis Althusser's structuralist rereading of Marx, with its claim for a divide separating the young, humanist Marx of the 1844 Manuscripts from the mature, scientific Marx of *Das Kapital*.[11] While clearly an intellectual response to Stalinism and its cult of personality, Althusser's concept of epistemological shift also finds parallels in assessments of other Marxist thinkers, notably Georg Lukács, whose work is typically interpreted as split between an early idealism and romantic anticapitalism, and a later orthodox Marxism and realist aesthetics.[12] The notion of epistemological shift, however, has even deeper historical resonances in film studies and can be traced to postwar film criticism (before the rise of auteurism), which stressed the negative impact of U.S. culture on various European directors' careers.[13] Within this tradition, the British Hitchcock was compared to the American Hitchcock, the German Fritz Lang to the American Fritz Lang, and, almost invariably, the American work was found wanting. Recent discussions of Kracauer's epistemological shift would therefore seem to partake of both the Marxist critique and the pre-auteurist legacy in film studies, as his writings are said to split upon both a critical response to Stalinism and an uncritical embrace of U.S. culture.

Kracauer himself would not object in principle to the concept of epistemological shift, since his final study of history provides a compelling analysis of historical time as profoundly fractured and disjunctive.[14] He would, however, insist on seeing his German and U.S. writing as part of a common project, and this, in fact, is one of the main arguments of the *History* book, which attempts to situate his life's work within a continuum of concerns. Some have suggested that Kracauer manipulated his image for posterity in this final study.[15] Yet it is clear that he was attempting to respond to the critique leveled against him by his longtime friend and former colleague, Theodor Adorno, who argued in a 1964 radio talk that Kracauer's work became increasingly affirmative in the United States, that it embraced the possibility of happiness in the world and failed to sustain a critique of the status quo.[16]

The image of Kracauer conveyed by Adorno suggests a familiar story of the émigré intellectual in the United States: The refugee fleeing from fascist Europe ultimately settles in America, where, feeling himself exiled, displaced, and alienated, he writes a scathing critique of his former culture. He then goes on uncritically to accept the English language and is eventually seduced by U.S. culture (not to mention its cinema), finding in it a haven from forced exile and voluntary emigration, thereby mirroring the "end of ideology" criticism fashionable in the United States in the 1950s. To be sure, Adorno ultimately conceded that the source of Kracauer's conservatism must be sought in the very tensions and pressures of emigration. And yet, by reading Kracauer's career as a mirror reflection of wider historical developments in cold war politics, he failed to consider the range of institutional changes that necessarily separated Kracauer's early and later work.

First, Kracauer confronted very different audiences and institutional arrangements in the United States than he had known in Weimar Germany. Needless to say, in the United States of the 1940s and 1950s, there was little place in film journalism for a man of Kracauer's training and expertise, though he was able to find a congenial environment for intellectual work on the margins of academic life. The shift in his writings from practical criticism to academic film theory must therefore take into account the very different sense of place and belonging, as well as the very distinct forms of association and community, entailed in the movement from Europe to the United States at the time.

Second, it is important to note the changing status of film as a cultural object in the period spanning Kracauer's migration. In the 1920s, Kracauer wrote about the cinema as a marginal sphere of life and about film viewing as an experience that marked the cultural disintegration of absolute values and objective truths. By the 1940s, the cinema could no longer be construed as a marginal phenomenon, for it had clearly emerged as one of the central institutions in modern cultural life. Without an established institutional place for film studies in the 1960s, however, *Caligari* and *Theory of Film* failed to find a wide or appreciative audience. And when academic film study was formally institutionalized in the 1960s and 1970s, these books became even further marginalized and unreadable, antithetical as they were to the reigning critical orthodoxies of auteurism, structuralism, and antirealist film theory.

Today, of course, all of this has changed, as some of Kracauer's early writings have been translated into English and interpreted from the perspective of contemporary film theory, which has itself moved away from psychoanalysis and semiotics in search of a more historical approach to the most pressing issues in the field. No longer is there any doubt of Kracauer's connections to critical theory, and it has become nearly impossible to relegate his materialist aesthetics to a "naïve realism" or simple-minded reflectionism. Kracauer's critique of totality and his concern for history have also inspired extended comparisons with such poststructuralist thinkers as Jean Baudrillard and Michel Foucault, and it would not be unthinkable to imagine future comparisons between Kracauer's conceptualization of modern culture as a "mass ornament" and the Situationists' description of their own era as "the Society of the Spectacle." That Kracauer's writings have now become readable from the vantage point of poststructuralism is undoubtedly related to the fact that the cinema itself has once again become a marginal sphere, dominated by television and the computer. It is nevertheless ironic that the reevaluation of Kracauer's career has involved elaborate appeals to the authority of French traditions in criticism and theory, and that Kracauer's later work continues to be criticized when it seems most overtly or most resolutely "German."

But it would be too easy to dismiss as ahistorical and disingenuous the recent characterizations of Kracauer as a proto-poststructuralist. And it would also be a mistake to underestimate the role played by what Edward Said has called "borrowed" or "traveling theory." As Said explains:

Cultural and intellectual life are usually nourished and often sustained by [a] circulation of ideas, and whether it takes the form of acknowledged or unconscious influence, creative borrowing, or wholesale appropriation, the movement of ideas and theories from one place to another is both a fact of life and a usefully enabling condition of intellectual activity. Having said that, however, one should go on to specify the kinds of movements that are possible, in order to ask whether by virtue of having moved from one place and time to another an idea or a theory gains or loses in strength, and whether a theory in one historical period and national culture becomes altogether different in another period or situation.[17]

This concept of "traveling theory" helps to illuminate the reasons for an epistemological shift in recent Kracauer criticism, as well as the shift in Kracauer's own thinking about film. Indeed, what attracts contemporary scholars to Kracauer's early work on cinema, and, moreover, to his final thoughts on history, is precisely his commitment to the feel and texture of experience, his critique of abstraction and totalizing theories of culture, and his investment in questions of the local, the ephemeral, and the everyday. Kracauer's early writings are fascinating for us today because they do not present a theoretically closed or coherent system but read instead like a phenomenology of everyday life, offering both an analysis of the sensory, perceptual apparatus of film viewing and a critique of its reified institutions. In the wake of the massive system building of structuralism and semiotics, Kracauer's materialist phenomenology represents a timely alternative to outmoded forms of conceptual thinking and an early historical precedent for what is now called cultural studies. While the movement of Kracauer's early theory into contemporary film studies has necessarily involved processes of representation and institutionalization different from those in Weimar Germany, it has also inaugurated a subtle approach to questions of cultural production and reception from the standpoint of a theory that, one would hope, will one day constitute a history of subjectivity in relation to everyday life.

In this regard, it is important to emphasize that Kracauer's less fashionable American work also merits serious rereading, since it clearly reframes the arguments originally posed in the 1920s and offers a compelling critique of abstraction and conceptual thinking, if often in highly abstract and conceptual terms. *Theory of Film,* for instance, provides a reading of mass culture in relation to the fragmentation and alienation of everyday life and levels a critique against intellectuals for attempting to preserve outmoded aesthetic values under changed cultural conditions. Focusing attention on peculiarly modern forms of subjectivity, *Theory of Film* thus takes up where "The Mass Ornament" left off, analyzing a culture dedicated to the play of surface in and through its representations. Whereas the early essays enlist Marxist theory and economic analysis more obviously and more thoroughly, lending equal weight to the manipulative character of mass culture as well as to its emancipatory potential, the later work preserves an interest in dialectical thinking, although it tends to take up either side of the dialectic in individual studies.

In *From Caligari to Hitler*, for example, Kracauer analyzes the cinema as an institution that functioned historically to paralyze social life, reifying it into ornamental patterns, and evacuating the possibility for individual judgment or critical thought. In *Theory of Film*, the reifying process of cinematic representation is interpreted more positively, as a force that energizes the unforeseen and potentially liberating possibilities of a technological medium in an abstract and modern age. This much is suggested by Kracauer when he writes, "We literally redeem this world from its dormant state, its state of virtual nonexistence, by endeavoring to experience it through the camera"; or, again, when he observes that "abstract painting is not so much an anti-realist movement as a realistic revelation of the prevailing abstraction."[18] Kracauer's final work on *History* then restates the dialectical relationship between critique and possibility in photography and in history, thereby restoring the complicated alternation of ideas that energize the early work.

The corpus of Kracauer's writing therefore suggests the difficulties in viewing his ideas as mere reflections of his time, as Adorno tended to do, for there is, in fact, no linear progression in his thinking about film, and no necessary movement from critique to embrace of mass culture as his theory traveled across time, or, indeed, across space. Kracauer's later writings, I would submit, actually reveal less an epistemological shift than a shift of emphasis, resulting in an overstatement and, in places, a simplification of the analysis of mass culture developed in the 1920s.[19] Taken together, *From Caligari to Hitler* and *Theory of Film* constitute a complex, dialectical view of the cinema such as one finds in the earlier writings. When read separately, however, these books tend to suggest a one-dimensional, one-sided, and impoverished account of the relationship between institutional constraints and perceptual possibilities in the cinema and in history. As Adorno might have reminded Kracauer, although here, in a celebrated passage, he is responding directly to Benjamin: "The reification of the great work of art is not just loss, any more than the reification of the cinema is all loss. It would be bourgeois reaction to negate the reification of the cinema in the name of the ego, and it would border on anarchism to revoke the reification of the great work of art in the spirit of immediate use values. Both bear the stigmata of capitalism, both contain elements of change. . . . Both are torn halves of an integral freedom to which, however, they do not add up." [20]

In typical fashion, Kracauer seems to have anticipated such a critique in the writing of *Theory of Film* and, as if to defend himself against it, offered a comparison of Marx and Freud that illuminates his own reasons for attempting to extend his theory of film beyond the early writings, precisely by underlining the ways in which the cinema helps us to overcome abstraction and reified thinking through a concrete mode of apprehending and understanding. "Freud probes deeper than Marx into the forces conspiring against the rule of reason," writes Kracauer. "But Marx, intent on widening that rule, could not well make use of discouraging profundities." As a kind of afterthought, and in a gesture that speaks both to his experience of exile in the United States and his own intellectual journey from "The Mass Ornament" to *Theory of Film,* and from Berlin to New York, Kracauer adds, "When you want to travel far, your luggage had better be light." [21]

AFTER SHOCK, BETWEEN BOREDOM AND HISTORY

Boredom is a very useful instrument with which to explore the past, and to stage a meaning between it and the present.

— FREDRIC JAMESON

HE title of this chapter proposes a rather unconventional relationship between modernity and the image by locating film and photography *after* the "shock of the new" and *within* what might be called an intermediary zone between boredom and history. By *after shock* I mean to suggest another side to modernity, when change itself had become routinized, commodified, banalized, and when the extraordinary, the unusual, and the fantastic became inextricably linked to the boring, the prosaic, and the everyday. The term *after shock* preserves an element of shock but nonetheless signals the fading of its initial intensity. Not unlike the term *afterimage,* it invokes an impression, or experience, or affect that persists long after an image or stimulus has passed from view.

The second part of my title, "between boredom and history," posits a relationship between terms otherwise kept separate, given their distinct temporalities and identification with either subjective or historical time. Boredom, for instance, is typically thought to describe a subjective experience—a time without event, when nothing happens, a seemingly endless flux without beginning or end. History, by contrast, is commonly understood to document that which happened—a series of events or, at least, moments thought to be eventful, which suggest that something occurred (rather than nothing at all). In locating film and photography *between* boredom and history and *after* the shock of the new—in other words, between the psychic and the social, after that which happens and that which fails to occur—I aim to provide a different framework and series of questions for thinking historically about film, photography, and discourses of subjectivity in modernity.[1]

Two sets of images will serve to ground this analysis. The first is a selection of photographs taken by the French-Hungarian artist Brassaï in the late 1920s and early 1930s, entitled *The Secret Paris* and *Paris by Night,* which document Parisian life in the streets, brothels, alleyways, cabarets, and gay and lesbian nightclubs of the period—what Brassaï himself called "Paris at its least cosmopolitan, at its most alive, its most authentic."[2] The second set of images is a contemporary remake of Brassaï's work in the pages of *Rolling Stone,* a series of photographs taken by the U.S. photographer Steven Meisel that features Madonna, entitled "Flesh and Fantasy."[3] By juxtaposing these two sets of images, and by exploring their views of sexuality and looking, I aim to stage an encounter between the past and the present, and thus to demonstrate the usefulness of the concept of boredom to an understanding of history and historical change. In the case of Brassaï, for example, the representation of sexual otherness remains a nonevent, precisely banal, located in the moment after shock and within the terms of everyday life. The Madonna remake, by contrast, reinvests sexuality with a sense of the eventful; as a result, sexual otherness reemerges in our time as both provocative and shocking, the purported proof that something (rather than nothing at all) is taking place.

Before proceeding to these images, I would like to say something about the difficulty of writing about boredom—a difficulty that has little to do with the risks of complicity with the object. The pressing and more serious difficulty involves writing about boredom as *historical,* precisely because boredom is often considered to be without event, an experience (of being) suspended in time. Just as it was once important to overcome the idea of history as mere reproduction of the past detached from the work of a writing subject, it is now important to overcome the idea of boredom as merely subjective, as somehow beyond historical forces or social change. There is, in fact, an extensive (if sometimes elusive) literature on boredom as a peculiarly modern experience, which encompasses romantic, scientific, psychoanalytic, and postmodern thought.[4] I therefore begin my analysis by providing a brief account of boredom theory that, not coincidentally, remains inextricably linked to modernity and to debates about the historical status of the image.

THE END OF HISTORY?

What were once vaguely apocalyptic pronouncements about photographic reproduction and "the end of history" have recently been reformulated according to a logic of cultural appropriation and cultural banality. In his book *Postmodernism, or, The Cultural Logic of Late Capitalism,* Fredric Jameson argues that the contemporary fascination with recycling past images and former styles merely fuels a pervasive sense of ahistoricity in the present. To counter this trend, he proposes—albeit briefly and rather tentatively—both a theory and an aesthetic practice of boredom. In the process, he makes three basic arguments about postmodernism and media that I would like to consider further here.

First, Jameson claims that the Hollywood nostalgia film, a genre that appropriates and recycles historical images and styles, actually responds to a genuine "craving for historicity," only to then block or paralyze any real historical understanding. As he explains in an interview:

> The increasing numbers of films about the past are no longer historical; they are images, simulacra, and pastiches of the past. They are effectively a way of satisfying a chemical craving for historicity, using a product that substitutes for and blocks it. . . . [N]ostalgia art gives us the image of various generations of the past as fashion-plate images that entertain no determinable ideological relationship to other moments of time: they are not the outcome of anything, nor are they the antecedents of our present; they are simply images.[5]

It is not, according to Jameson, simply historical consciousness that is lost in postmodernism. In a second and related argument, he further claims that such time-honored concepts as anxiety and alienation, much elaborated by philosophers of existence and the unconscious, "are no longer appropriate to the world of the postmodern."[6] This leads to his third and, for my purposes, final observation. Drawing upon his experience of reading modernist literature and of watching independent video, Jameson raises "the question of *boredom* as an aesthetic response and a phenomenological problem" in an effort to restore historical thinking and to refuse the (commodity) logic of postmodern practices. In one of the few extended passages about boredom in his book, he explains that, in the Freudian and Marxist traditions,

> "boredom" is taken not so much as an objective property of things and works but rather as a response to the blockage of energies (whether those be grasped in terms of desire or of praxis). Boredom then becomes interesting as a reaction to situations of paralysis and also, no doubt, as defense mechanism or avoidance behavior. Even taken in the narrower realm of cultural reception, boredom with a particular kind of work or style or content can always be used productively as a precious symptom of our own existential, ideological, and cultural limits, an index of what has to be refused in the way of other people's cultural practices, and their threat to our own rationalizations about the nature and value of art. (71–72)

One might argue with Jameson's own rationalizations about the nature and value of art, particularly his views of popular culture and high modernism. Of course, Jameson seems to anticipate this critique by attributing boredom with certain works and styles to a kind of (critical) paralysis, a reaction formation based as much on personal taste as on ideological grounds. One might nevertheless question Jameson's own nostalgia and personal taste for an aesthetic of self-alienation and anxiety (what Jacqueline Rose has called a nostalgia for "the passing of a fantasy of the male self").[7] I am more interested here, however, in exploring his all too brief, but nevertheless extremely suggestive, remarks about boredom as a mode of refusal, and boredom as a symptom of our existential, ideological, and cultural limits.

BOREDOM THEORY

To begin with the terms of Jameson's own analysis: How is boredom both an aesthetic response and a phenomenological problem? If it is an aesthetic response, to what does it respond? A blockage of energies? A situation of paralysis? In other words, is boredom a defense mechanism or avoidance behavior—an aesthetic response to the blockage or paralysis of our current situation—or, is it, in fact, the thing itself? Questions must also be raised with respect to the phenomenological problem of boredom and subjectivity. Is boredom a passing mood? A more lasting disposition or mindset? Or is it an emotion or, rather, the very opposite of an emotion, a lack or waning of affect? In this regard, boredom reemerges as both an aesthetic and a phenomenological problem, which is to say, boredom seems to be about both too much and too little, sensory overload and sensory deprivation, anxieties of excess as well as anxieties of loss.

These issues are further complicated by the slippage or semantic permeability of the term *boredom* itself—its ability to begin as one thing, only to turn into something else, usually some other particularly intense emotion, disposition, or mood. In philosophical, clinical, and scientific discourses, *boredom* seldom exists in isolation from another term or set of terms. For example, in eighteenth-century theories of the sublime, boredom is typically assumed to mask uneasiness, anxiety, or terror; as such, it is theorized as a reaction to privation or absence, a refusal to engage the unattainable or unrepresentable by remaining resolutely within the realm of the common, the ordinary, and the everyday.[8] In nineteenth-century romanticism, boredom takes on the quality of a negative passion, associated both with the nothingness and nonbeing of the sublime as well as the unbearable experience of being in the everyday (in other words, a negative passion is transformed into passion for negativity).[9] In the twentieth century, particularly in the discourses of psychoanalysis and clinical practice, boredom becomes inextricably linked to depression and to anger, grief, or loss as the source of a depression which must be experienced, overcome, and worked through.[10] (In this respect, the psychoanalytic cure of boredom is similar to that evoked by the romantics.) In critical theory, particularly German critical theory of the 1920s and 1930s, boredom is understood in relation to leisure, and also to waiting, to an expectation or future orientation of subjectivity devoid of anxiety or alienation.[11] Finally, in contemporary theories of the postmodern, boredom is associated with both frustration and relief, in other words, with the frustration of the everyday and with the relief from frustration in the gesture of aesthetic refusal; boredom thus becomes, as in Jameson's text, both a symptom and a cure.

What this points to, among other things, is that boredom has a history, which is as much a history of the subject as it is of cultural change. In a recent study of ennui and its discourses, French theorist Michèle Huguet refers to this "socio-cultural permeability" of boredom and its subjectivities when she writes:

There is not one psychology of boredom but many, the common feature of which betrays the way in which, when confronted with a void which

is painfully experienced, the subject can elaborate its defenses according
to an ideal that is perceived as absent, unsatisfying, or impossible. . . .
The subject experiencing boredom is not suffering from an absence of
desire, but from its indetermination, which in turn forces the subject to
wander, in search of a point of fixation.[12]

The notion of indetermination—of a desire, of an ideal, and of a void—
helps to situate historically the various permutations of boredom I have
already described. In his analysis of melancholy and European society, for
instance, Wolf Lepenies explains that boredom or ennui is at least in part
the expression of a social class that has lost or has failed to achieve public
significance. The French aristocracy in the eighteenth century and the
German bourgeoisie in the nineteenth century, for example, had been
cut off from acting in or influencing the world, and thus, according to
Lepenies, they articulated their powerlessness in literary forms of melancholy and ennui.[13] Thomas Weiskel similarly maintains in his study of the
romantic sublime that theories of boredom and anxiety assume their modern, secular quality only at the end of the eighteenth century; in other
words, at the beginning of the formation of the modern bourgeois state.[14]
The modern period, which witnessed the growth of technology and urban
spaces, the emergence of mass society and mass culture, and changes in
the understanding of sexual difference, also witnessed the proliferation of
literary discourses on boredom, which functioned to articulate the fading
of subjectivity and the cure for its relief: a sublime experience of terror
and astonishment, a romantic abandonment of self to negative passions, a
modernist vision that revels in its own operation and, hence, in its own
existence.

Importantly, both the fear and the lure—and the gendered connotations—surrounding the loss of self undergo significant changes in the
course of the nineteenth and twentieth centuries. These changes, moreover, are registered in contemporary dictionary definitions of *ennui* and
boredom.[15] *Ennui*, for instance, is defined as "a feeling of weariness and
discontent, resulting from satiety or lack of interest"; as such, it designates
a quality of spiritual malaise or inner migration produced by the difference
or the gap between an ideal and its realization. As understood by the romantics, the first moderns of the nineteenth century, ennui involved an
affective experience of anger and discontent, an anxiety of abundance and
absence, and a perception of both too much or of nothing at all—themes
that would later be taken up in emergent theories of psychoanalysis to

describe a specifically masculine subjectivity, and the threat of symbolic castration involved in the subject's encounter with a feminine body perceived as both excessive and lacking.

In contrast to the passive and pathos-laden term *ennui, boredom* is defined more actively; indeed, its primary definition takes the form of a verb: "to weary by dullness, tedious repetition, unwelcome attentions; a cause of ennui or petty annoyance." Notably undervalued in this definition of *boredom* are the affects of anger and discontent, and the anxieties associated with both abundance and absence. Although ennui is still a part of the definition of *boredom,* it is subordinated to a secondary clause, treated on the same level as a "petty annoyance." What is more interesting, however, is that the definition of *boredom* introduces a potentially *visual* dimension to the experience of repetition and tedium in the form of "unwelcome attentions." The term *boredom* thus anticipates a visual economy of repetition notably absent from ennui, and a displeasure in being seen while looking that simultaneously evokes the experiences of the classic male voyeur as well as the ostensible (feminine) object of his gaze.[16]

This kind of looking further suggests an important link between boredom and theories of the image. As several commentators have pointed out, theories of the image have long been split between spiritualism and science; in other words, between philosophical and theological traditions on the one hand and scientific studies and documentary practices on the other. The same could be said of boredom theory, of course, particularly given the way in which, in the nineteenth and twentieth centuries, boredom increasingly became a matter of visual perception, and therefore as much a scientific problem as a philosophical one. In his study of vision and modernity in the nineteenth century, Jonathan Crary explains:

From the 1890s until well into the 1930s one of the central problems in mainstream psychology had been the nature of attention: the relation between stimulus and attention, problems of concentration, focalization, and distraction. How many sources of stimulation could one attend to simultaneously? How could novelty, familiarity, and repetition in attention be assessed? It was a problem whose position in the forefront of psychological discourses was directly related to the emergence of a social field increasingly saturated with sensory input.[17]

The fading of subjectivity and loss of conscious agency registered in the term *boredom* and in other nineteenth-century discourses were thus similarly in evidence in empirical studies of the eye and its tendency toward distraction and fatigue. Indeed, in Crary's view, scientific studies of experience and mental life merely underscored changes taking place elsewhere in conceptions of knowledge, as a direct result of the subject's encounter with "a social field increasingly saturated with sensory input."

> [Vision,] rather than a privileged form of knowing, becomes itself an object of knowledge, of observation. From the beginning of the nineteenth century a science of vision will tend to mean increasingly an interrogation of the physiological makeup of the human subject, rather than the mechanics of light and optical transmission. It is a moment when the visible escapes from the timeless order of the camera obscura and becomes lodged in another apparatus, within the unstable physiology and temporality of the human body.[18]

BOREDOM, DISTRACTION, SHOCK

Early scientific studies of visual perception were soon complemented, and complicated, by an emergent sociology that interpreted the experience of boredom in far more critical, and less instrumental, terms. In his 1903 essay "The Metropolis and Mental Life," for example, Georg Simmel describes the effects of transportation and industrial production on the human sensorium and explains how overstimulation produces a peculiarly modern form of boredom in what he calls the "blasé attitude" or "outlook":

> There is perhaps no psychic phenomenon which is so unconditionally reserved to the city as the blasé outlook. . . . [For] just as an immoderately sensuous life makes one blasé because it stimulates the nerves to their utmost reactivity until they finally can no longer produce any reaction at all, so, less harmful stimuli . . . force the nerves to make such violent responses, tear them about so brutally that they exhaust their last reserves of strength and, remaining in the same milieu, do not have time for new reserves to form. . . . This psychic mood is the correct subjective reflection of a complete money economy to the extent that money takes the place of all the manifoldness of things and expresses all qualitative distinctions between them in the distinction of "how much."[19]

Although Simmel never uses the term *distraction* in this essay, the violent sense impressions he describes are clearly the equivalent of distraction—an experience of sensory stimulation as sensory overload that leads to boredom, exhaustion, and indifference—the perception of a universal equality of things. Significantly, Simmel suggests that boredom is no longer the sole possession of a particular class (as it was thought to have been in the eighteenth and nineteenth centuries, especially in the attitudes and practices of those who pursued "an immoderately sensual life"). Instead, he argues, by the turn of the century, boredom had become available to all through the leveling effects of a money economy, which had permeated leisure as well as labor time.

These ideas had a tremendous impact on the writings of Siegfried Kracauer and Walter Benjamin, two of the most important theorists of film in the twentieth century. It is well known, for example, that Kracauer and Benjamin extend the notions of distraction, sensory stimulation, and shock, initially elaborated by Simmel, to describe the aesthetics and reception conditions of photography and film. According to both theorists, film and photography rehearse in the realm of reception what Taylorism and industrial management impose on the human body in the realm of production; these media are, in Kracauer's words, "the aesthetic reflex of the rationality aspired to by the prevailing economic system."[20] Importantly, neither Kracauer nor Benjamin sees film and photography as symptoms of a general cultural or historical decline; instead, they celebrate the cultural negativity of the new media for subverting the bourgeois cult of art and its aesthetic of illusionist absorption. Reception in a state of distraction, they argue, allows for a complex kind of training, sharpening the senses and enabling the subject to parry the shocks of a new, and often antagonistic, reality.

While Kracauer and Benjamin are best known for their theories of modernity based on shock and distraction, what is less known, and less remarked upon, is their central preoccupation with boredom. As Heide Schlüpmann has argued in an extremely influential essay on early German film theory: "The relation between film and the end of bourgeois culture is not so much captured in the term *distraction* [*Zerstreuung*], in which, after all, capitalism protects itself from its loss of metaphysical elevation. It is captured rather in what are interruptions in the production process: in a boredom that protects itself against organization, in a form of leisure as waiting."[21] For Benjamin and Kracauer, boredom becomes a key concept for exploring subjectivity in modernity, not least of all because, in its German formulation (*Langeweile*, literally, "a long whiling away of time"), boredom captures the modern experience of time as both empty and full, concentrated and distracted. Whereas Benjamin tends to theorize boredom in relation to emptiness and ennui (typical of nineteenth-century formulations), Kracauer emphasizes the distracted fullness of a leisure time become empty (a twentieth-century view). The differences between these views on boredom are perhaps best illuminated by the images of modernity that emerge from their work: in Benjamin, the empty streets of Eugene Atget's Paris; in Kracauer, the crowded stadiums and picture palaces of 1920s Berlin.

Both theorists nonetheless agree that boredom retains a radical edge— not unlike that which is attributed elsewhere to distraction and the sensation of shock—in that it helps to sustain subjectivity rather than simply contribute to its loss. "Monotony nourishes the new," writes Benjamin in the note to his unfinished Arcades project, where he also remarks that "boredom is the threshold of great deeds." [22] Similarly, in a 1924 essay devoted to boredom, Kracauer criticizes the restless pursuit of novelty in modernity and extols the virtues of boredom as perhaps "the only activity that may be called proper, since it offers a certain guarantee that one will have, so to speak, an existence at one's disposal." [23] *Boredom* and *distraction*, in other words, are complementary rather than opposing terms, whose relationship might be stated as follows: reception in a state of distraction reveals cultural disorder and increasing abstraction; the cultivation of boredom, however, discloses the logic of distraction, in which newness becomes a fetish, and shock itself a manifestation of the commodity form. To reverse the slogan of the Russian formalists, *boredom habitualizes renewed perception*, opening up the potential to see differences that make a difference, and to refuse the ceaseless repetition of the new as the always-the-same.

In this regard, the relationship between boredom and waiting becomes especially important, for it is in a waiting without aim or purpose that the possibility of change might be sighted. "The more life is regulated administratively," writes Benjamin, "the more people must learn waiting." Or, as Kracauer put it, "He who decides to wait neither closes himself off from the possibilities of faith like the stubborn disciples of total emptiness, nor does he force this faith like the soul searchers who have lost all restraint in their longing." Otherwise expressed, hidden in the innovation of distraction and shock is a despair that nothing further will happen. Hidden in the negativity of boredom and waiting, however, is the anticipation that something (different) might occur. [24]

This becomes especially apparent when boredom, as a peculiarly twentieth-century experience, is refracted through the lens of sexual difference. It is not insignificant, for example, that Kracauer describes boredom in relation to Taylorized labor and rationalized leisure and chooses a twentieth-century female figure—a middle-aged, working-class woman, who stops outside a movie theater, to stand for "those who wait." Benjamin, by contrast, describes boredom primarily as a form of leisure and embodies this figure in a variety of heroic nineteenth-century male types: "the gambler just killing time, the flaneur, who charges time with power like a battery, and finally, a third type, he who charges time and gives its power out again in changed form—that of expectation."[25] If we recall that, for many intellectuals at this time, the boredoms of modern life included "the spread of democracy to women and the lower classes, the replacement of governmental authority by popular votes, [and] the liberation of sexual activity from state and church dictates," then we might reformulate the relationship between boredom and shock, and boredom and anxiety, along the lines of both historical and gender difference.[26] As Jean-François Lyotard has written, "Shock is, *par excellence,* the evidence of (something) happening, rather than nothing at all."[27] Boredom, in this view, might be seen as evidence of nothing happening—a nothingness that accounts for women's experiences of modernity (particularly in relation to the promises and failures of social change), and for men's perceptions of feminine excess and lack typical of nineteenth-century discourses on ennui.

Boredom, in other words, helps to describe a postshock economy— that moment after the shock of the new described by Simmel—when exhaustion and indifference are no longer the preserve of a particular class (or, indeed, the sole prerogative of men). This is a moment when the new ceases to be new and ceases to be shocking; when leisure as well as labor time becomes routinized, fetishized, commodified; and when the extraordinary, the unusual, and the unfamiliar are inextricably linked to the boring, the prosaic, and the everyday. Maurice Blanchot remarks of this relationship among boredom, perception, and everydayness that "boredom is the everyday become manifest: as a consequence of having lost its essential—constitutive—trait of being unperceived."[28] Or, in the words of Henri Lefebvre:

> The days follow one after another and resemble one another, and yet— here lies the contradiction at the heart of everydayness—everything changes. But the change is programmed: obsolescence is planned. Production anticipates reproduction; production produces change in such

a way as to superimpose the impression of speed onto that of monotony. Some people cry out against the acceleration of time, others
cry out against stagnation. They're both right.[29]

In contrast to eighteenth-century theorists of the sublime, who saw
boredom as a reaction to the indeterminate and the sublime as an antidote
to the ordinary and the everyday, twentieth-century theorists of boredom
locate the indeterminate precisely within the realm of the everyday—that
site of both change and stasis, identity and nonbeing, happenings and
nonevents.

In this respect, boredom shares important affinities with traditions of
the avant-garde, particularly those that come after political modernism
and refuse its aesthetics of distraction, sensory stimulation, and shock.
One thinks, for example, of the attitude of actively passive waiting in
Samuel Beckett's *Waiting for Godot* (where "nothing happens," twice), or
of Andy Warhol's notoriously esoteric and nearly unwatchable early films:
Eat (forty-five minutes of a man eating a mushroom), *Kiss* (one close-up
after another of people kissing), *Sleep* (six hours of a man sleeping), and
Empire (eight hours of the Empire State building).[30] To this, one might add
Chantal Akerman's *Jeanne Dielman, 23 Quai du Commerce—1080 Bruxelles*,
which explores the routinized, repetitious, and painful experience of time
between events in a day in the life of a middle-class housewife. As these
examples suggest, an aesthetics of boredom retains the modernist impulse of provocation and calculated assault. (How long must one watch
and wait until something actually happens? How much tedium can one
possibly stand?) It nevertheless abandons the modernist fiction of the self-
contained aesthetic object, precisely by exploring the temporal and psychic structures of perception itself. The tedium and irritation of perceptual
boredom, in other words, enable an awareness of looking as a temporal
process—bound not to a particular object but to ways of seeing—at once
historical and, as the examples just offered suggest, often gender specific.

BRASSAÏ, MADONNA

But if an aesthetics (or, rather, an anaesthetics) of boredom shares certain affinities with the avant-garde, it also shares characteristics with popular cultural practices, particularly those that attempt to render material
otherwise immaterial or ephemeral experiences of everyday life. My examples of aesthetic and phenomenological boredom are therefore taken

from photography and popular culture: Brassaï's 1930s photographs of *Paris by Night* (as well as previously censored photographs from his collection entitled *The Secret Paris*), and the remake of these images by U.S. photographer Steven Meisel in the pages of *Rolling Stone*, featuring Madonna and entitled "Flesh and Fantasy."

Brassaï was not only a photographer but also a painter, sculptor, and writer who photographed the prostitutes at the Bastille as well as the members of the Jockey Club, and who wrote a book about his housekeeper, Marie, as well as a book about Picasso. Although his intellectual affiliations were much closer to surrealism, Brassaï nonetheless earned a reputation as a "pioneer of documentary photography" as a result of having captured in images the underside of Parisian life in the 1930s, what he himself called "the cesspool cleaners, the inverts, the opium dens, the *bal musettes*, the bordellos, and the other seedy spots with their fauna." Brassaï nonetheless rightly rejected the title of "photojournalist" or "photo-reporter" for, as he put it, "it is not sociologists who provide insights but photographers of our sort who are observers at the very center of their times."[31]

Brassaï published his photographs of Parisian nightlife in two separate editions. The first book, *Paris by Night*, was published in 1933; the second book, *The Secret Paris of the 1930s*, was initially censored and formally published only in 1976, decades after Brassaï had attained recognition for his other artistic work. The images included in both books nonetheless provide a view of Paris as the site of sexual otherness, and as the capital of a modernity that exudes boredom, exhaustion, and petty annoyance. The city as represented by Brassaï, for instance, is no longer the source of sensory overload or sensory deprivation. It is rather the site of an unsettled heterogeneity, after the "shock of the new," when sexuality ceases to be shocking, and when boredom itself assumes the quality of a release from anxiety. The mythic metaphors of progress that had long permeated historical and philosophical discourses are here unmasked and exposed: whether the images are of graffiti, of empty streets, or of prostitutes in dull sleep, there is no material abundance, no surface glitter or glamorous appearance, to offer proof of progress before our eyes. The lure is that of depersonalization. As Brassaï himself once said: "In photography you can never express yourself directly, only through optics, the physical and chemical processes. It is this sort of submission to the object and abnegation of self that is exactly what pleases me about photography" (40).

Significantly, the photographs censored in the 1930s reemerge almost

Brassaï, *Lovers in a Small Café, near the Place d'Italie*, 1932. Copyright Estate Brassaï.

Brassaï, *In a Brothel, Rue Quincampoix,* 1932. Copyright Estate Brassaï.

Brassaï, *Kiki de Montparnasse—Kiki with her friends Therese Treize de Caro & Lily,* c. 1932.
Copyright Estate Brassaï.

Brassaï, *One Suit for Two, at the Magic City,* 1931. Copyright Estate Brassaï.

Steven Meisel, *Madonna and two friends,* 1991.

Steven Meisel, *Madonna with woman in restaurant,* 1991.

Steven Meisel, *Madonna and friends, in drag,* 1991.

Steven Meisel, *In a brothel, Madonna and her lover, in a mirror*, 1991.

Steven Meisel, *Draped in the American flag,* 1991.

fifty years later via a discourse that promises to reveal the "secrets" and "mysteries" associated with sexuality and the body. A closer look at the censored images themselves, however, suggests less the mystery than the banality of sexuality and sexual orientation—the everydayness of lesbian and gay life, for example—behind which there is no secret, no truth to be revealed or disclosed. Although sexual curiosity is undeniably part of their appeal, Brassaï's photographs do not exactly, or do not only, invite a voy-euristic gaze: within the confines of the carefully composed and studied compositions, the figures seem at once aware of the photographer's pres-ence and either mildly annoyed or entirely indifferent to his gaze.

It is, of course, this calculated stance of indifference—this cultivated boredom—that is notably missing from the remake, which dramatizes a longing for an active and unrestricted self at a mythical point in history. One immediately notices, for example, that the remake chooses not to en-vision a city, or a street, or, indeed, any social or historical milieu or mise-en-scène. There is only the untrammeled personality of Madonna played out across a series of photographs that remain much slicker, much more aesthetically stylized and sleekly calculated, than their prototype—in many ways closer to contemporary fashion photography than to Brassaï's repre-sentation of 1930s Parisian life. The remake, of course, is premised upon an internalized identification based on fantasy—not unlike other Madonna remakes of classic images, whether of Marlene or Marilyn, or of a film like *Metropolis*. The fantasy of sexual mobility, in other words, is confined to a single individual, and to the desire for a feminine identity that transgresses by incorporating traditional symbolic and social definitions.

This accounts in part for the very different structures of looking in the remake, and the distance it actually takes from Brassaï's work. Madonna's direct and knowing look at the camera, for instance, could not be further from the indifference of the female gaze registered in Brassaï. (Compare, for instance, Madonna's sultry look at the camera in the remake of Brassaï's *Kiki de Montparnasse . . . with her friends.*) Of course, one might wonder what prompted the remake of Brassaï in the first place. Madonna, somewhat disingenuously, explains: "For me, it was a great chance to re-create an era that I feel I would have really flourished in, that nothing I would have done would have been censored."[32] The appeal is to the apparently timeless secrets and mysteries of sexuality that allow Ma-donna to construct versions of herself as a way of acting out a narcissism across different subjectivities: the lover of women, the dominatrix, or the pin-up girl draped in the U.S. flag. To be sure, the remake discloses the disappearance of the photographer in a way similar to what occurs in Brassaï. Here, however, the disappearance of the photographer signals the reappearance of the performer. It is Madonna (and not the ambiguities of the image) that remains the ultimate curiosity.

To put this another way: whereas Brassaï admits to perceptual boredom in modernity, the remake aims to recuperate boredom as the fantasy of distraction and the sexualization of shock. As I have already indicated, the "shock effect" of the remake coincides with what Benjamin called "the phony spell of the commodity" in the artificial buildup of the personality of the star. In this respect, and in this respect alone, no image in the remake is boring. As Roland Barthes has put it, "You are not obliged to wait for the next in order to understand and be delighted; it is a question not of a dialectic (that time of patience required for certain pleasures) but of continuous jubilations made up of a summation of perfect instants."[33]

This is not to say that the remake is beyond boredom, whether of an aesthetic or phenomenological kind. Indeed, whereas the Brassaï images remain provocative in their utter banality (they seem to have been censored for their representation of sexuality in its everydayness), the remake is banal in its attempt to shock and provoke. The Brassaï images, moreover, revel in the sexually indeterminate as a source of relief from the anxieties of modernity, whereas the remake discloses a panic surrounding indeterminacy, and a certain anxiety of nonbeing outside of representation. (One recalls Warren Beatty's remark in *Truth or Dare* that, for Madonna, there seems to be no existence, or, perhaps, no point of existing, off camera. The figures who populate Brassaï's Paris, even the celebrated and infamous Kiki of Montparnasse, appear to have far less investment in the image and in photographic immortality, even though they have been immortalized—and depersonalized—by the camera.) For all its play with sexual difference and sexual orientation, the remake ultimately neutralizes and blocks the indeterminate in the realm of sexuality. Unlike Brassaï's images, which assume sexuality to be banal, precisely noneventful, a mask behind which "there is nothing at all," the remake stages sexual identity through shock and sensation—as proof that something, rather than nothing at all, is taking place.

This returns us to the question of nostalgia art and consumer culture, postmodernism and the possibility of historical knowledge in the present. In contrast to Jameson, however, I would argue that nostalgia art neither annihilates history nor completely effaces its ideological relationship to the past. The Madonna remake, regardless of its slickness, and despite its banality, nevertheless returns us to a specific past, and to a particular set of photographs, in order to retrieve a moment in history when it seemed possible to inhabit (if only in the realm of images) a world of sexual differences and unregulated ways of seeing. Given that much of Brassaï's early work was censored, this is, of course, a mythical past, and an imaginary solution, and yet no less historical or ideological for that. Indeed, the historical distance that separates the two sets of photographs—and the two visions of sexuality identity—reveals at once how much, and how little, has changed: whereas Brassaï makes visibly palpable the experience of a world and a subjectivity in fragments, the Madonna remake registers the desire to reinvent this particular past, only to cling to a subjectivity in the hope of surviving its historical shattering.

It would therefore be a mistake to dismiss the remake as merely imagistic or simply banal—or, as Jameson might have it, "effectively a way of satisfying a craving for historicity, using a product that substitutes for and blocks it." For there is a historical quality to the remake, even though this quality has more to do with repetition and duration—with a history in which nothing happens—than with transformation or change. The photographs that feature Madonna represent the relationship of a feminine self to the female body in terms of sexual provocation and self-display, thus reviving the conventions that give existence to a masculine economy of vision. The Brassaï photographs, by contrast, represent this relationship in terms of depersonalization, banalization, and loss—pleasures of a narcissistic self, to be sure, but pleasures that acknowledge, with neither the desperation nor the disingenuousness of the remake, that nothing happens in the realm of sexuality, and therefore that something happened after all, after shock.

HISTORICAL ENNUI, FEMINIST BOREDOM

It is particularly tempting to write a history of feminist theory—precisely because it is feminist—which stresses or even implies "progress." Yet, it is important to acknowledge that, even perhaps especially within feminism, there is the ever present potential of regression, uneven development, failure and disillusion, not to mention misunderstanding. For some, what had once been enabling is now perceived as a restrictive and tiresome paradigm, which generates analysis after analysis, but little new insight. There is a kind of ennui which haunts the project of feminist film criticism at the moment and which has become increasingly visible.

—JANET BERGSTROM AND MARY ANN DOANE

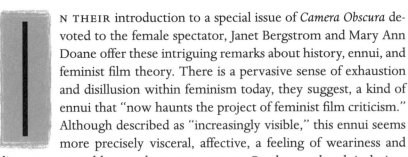

N THEIR introduction to a special issue of *Camera Obscura* devoted to the female spectator, Janet Bergstrom and Mary Ann Doane offer these intriguing remarks about history, ennui, and feminist film theory. There is a pervasive sense of exhaustion and disillusion within feminism today, they suggest, a kind of ennui that "now haunts the project of feminist film criticism." Although described as "increasingly visible," this ennui seems more precisely visceral, affective, a feeling of weariness and discontent traceable to at least two sources. On the one hand, it derives from a teleological, progressive, even generational view of history, one that sees feminist film theory (particularly in its Mulveyan or modernist mode of the seventies and eighties) as somehow exhausted or completed—merely a stage in the development of the next new thing. On the other hand, it results from the "ever present potential of regression, uneven development, failure and disillusion" to which, Bergstrom and Doane point out, "even perhaps especially" feminism is prone.[1]

Needless to say, Bergstrom and Doane at once acknowledge and reject the ennui they so aptly diagnose. (Not all repetitions are redundancies, they imply, given the potential within feminism for uneven developments, not to mention misunderstandings.) If, as they maintain, it is tempting to write the history of feminist theory in terms of progress—in other words, in terms of novelty or innovation that leaves the past behind—it is nonetheless important to also write its failures and regressions, since failures, like successes, both impede and generate change.

I would like to approach the question of the relationship between feminism and historical representation by introducing terms similar to Bergstrom's and Doane's; namely, *modernism* and *feminism, boredom* and *history*. I intend to show how modernism, like feminism itself, is best understood not as a *novel* way of representing history but as a *banal* way of representing novelty as well as gender difference. Thus understood, both feminism and modernism open up ways in which to historicize and destabilize gendered experiences of ennui as well as modern experiences of time. As I hope will become clear, the current state of feminist film theory—its sense of boredom, exhaustion, and fatigue—might be seen within this perspective as more enabling, less restrictive, and less novel than it does at first glance.

MODERNISM, POSTMODERNISM

It is significant, I think, that most discussions of ennui and boredom today take place within discourses of postmodernism (where the status of modernism, rather than gender, is usually at stake). From Jean Baudrillard's remarks about banality and fatality to Fredric Jameson's work on boredom and aesthetics to Jean François Lyotard's ruminations on boredom and the sublime, it would seem as though various postmodernisms evoke a language of exhaustion, repetition, and decline. To take but one example, in his book *The End of Modernity: Nihilism and Hermeneutics in Postmodern Culture* (1988), Gianni Vattimo sees the contemporary or postmodernist experience of history as the experience of the "end of history." By this Vattimo means the end of a certain sense of history, what he calls a "banal vision" of an "already articulated order" which he links both to

modernism and to the experience of modernity. For Vattimo, historical
ennui is the most enduring legacy of modernity, with its logic "of novelty
become obsolete and replaced by new novelty in a process that discour-
ages creativity in the very act of demanding it."[2]

Paradoxically, he claims, it is the modernist cultivation of the new that
inhibits novelty and produces a pervasive feeling of historical ennui in the
present—"the feeling that the weight of history would effectively suffo-
cate the possibility of any new creation in the culture at large," as one
critic has described it.[3] According to Vattimo, the only way out of this
condition is to deny historical novelty all meaning and to reject its vulgar
(i.e., progressive and cumulative) vision of time. Instead of novelty, and
against banality, Vattimo proposes a recollection and a rethinking of the
past—what he calls *Verwindung* (overcoming, getting over, recuperating)
and also *pietas* (devoted affection, respect).[4]

From a feminist perspective, Vattimo's diagnosis of both the condition
and the solution to postmodernity raises interesting issues and questions.
(The historical ennui he describes, for example, seems remarkably similar
to that described by Bergstrom and Doane). To begin with, what has banality meant for women modernists as well as for women more generally
in modernity? Is the sense of historical ennui Vattimo describes gender
coded? More to the point, what does a stance of "devoted affection" or
"respect" for the past have to offer feminist historians? And to what extent
do they need to get over, overcome, or recuperate from what has been
counted and recounted as history? Indeed, to what extent has the weight
of the past actually "suffocated" women's creativity and the very possibility of social and political change? Is it, in fact, the weight of the past or the
leaden quality of the present that inhibits feminist novelty and produces
ennui?

In her book *The Gendering of Melancholia* (1992), Juliana Schiesari poses
similar questions and argues that the politics of lack and loss, as articulated
in postmodernist discourses of "history at an end," themselves have a long
and venerable history:

> After two decades proclaiming new beginnings and new sciences of all
> sorts, contemporary theoretical discourse seems given over to a rheto-
> ric of loss and to a general sense that things are at an "end." . . . Where
> the "ends" of man, modernity, or Western metaphysics were once
> greeted with morbid glee and anarchistic celebration, now the apoca-
> lyptic tone of such pronouncements seems somewhat hollow, and even

tinged with a sense of defeat and anguish. . . . Of course, this is not the first time that melancholia has surfaced as a dramatic cultural phenomenon among a Western intellectual elite, even to the point of signifying what it means to be a thinker, scholar, or poet.[5]

Schiesari explains that the discourse of melancholy and historical ennui, a specific representational form of male creativity familiar to philosophy and literature, was "inaugurated by the Renaissance, refined by the Enlightenment, flaunted by Romanticism, fetishized by the Decadents, and theorized by Freud, before its current resurgence" (3). This discourse, moreover, functioned to convert feelings of disempowerment into privileged cultural artifacts: male losses were transformed into representational gains and, in the process, women's losses and disempowerment in culture were systematically devalued and excluded. "The great melancholic of yesteryear, would have been a tortured but creative male genius, but the stereotypically depressed person of today is an unhappy and unproductive woman," writes Schiesari. "Nothing more eloquently expresses what I call the gendering of melancholia than this split between a higher-valued form understood as male and a lower-valued one coded as female. . . . And not only is the male form empowering and the female one disempowering, but melancholia is romantically garbed in the past while depression is given only the banality of the present" (16). This analysis of melancholy underscores the ways in which banality and ennui are gendered in intellectual discourses of the "ends" of man, modernity, and Western metaphysics. There are, of course, important and historically continuous relationships among melancholy, ennui, and boredom, not to mention those among modernism, mass culture, and postmodernism. Nevertheless, in marked contrast to melancholia, which remains "romantically garbed in the past" in intellectual discourses of the present, boredom offers a peculiarly twentieth-century conception of self as well as a subjective, and less exclusively masculine, experience of history and the banality of time.

BOREDOM, MELANCHOLY, ENNUI

Throughout the nineteenth and into the early years of the twentieth century, a reasonably exhaustive study of boredom progressed in the West. . . . This philosophy put forth the idea that human suffering oscillated along a continuum between anxiety/privation and boredom/

satiety. The former carried a connotation of commonality, a quality abhorrent to post-romantic thought, while the latter had more of a connotation of nobility. . . . The modernist aesthetic takes the narrative in the other direction. Rather than having the connotation of nobility, boredom became an attack on the mundane aspects of fragmentation and redundancy. . . . It became a democratic affliction that affected everyone, . . . less a problem due to shortages of production (privation) than it was a problem of the monotony of production itself.[6]

Although various disciplines have recently contributed to the study of melancholy (including psychoanalysis, sociology, and literature), for the most part boredom remains somewhat undertheorized in contemporary scholarship, relegated to the status of an uninteresting subset of the more general phenomenon of ennui. For example, in an expansive study of Western fiction entitled *The Demon of Noontide* (1976), Reinhard Kuhn excludes four types of boredom from his analysis of melancholy because he believes they are tangential to the metaphysical concerns of a properly literary history. These are momentary boredom (what he calls *désoeuvrement*), psychosomatic boredom (which he describes in relation to the typical portrait of the female suburbanite), sociological boredom (or the boredom that results from industrialized labor and leisure), and anomie (or the "total loss of the will to life"). In what amounts to the virtual exclusion of every form of boredom known to twentieth-century life, Kuhn argues for the value of melancholy as a creative male condition that is grounded in the explicit exclusion of women. "It is a generally accepted interpretation that Flaubert's Emma Bovary presents symptoms similar to those felt by the bored suburbanite," he writes of one of the founding texts of literary modernism. "And yet to reduce her ennui to this level is to misunderstand the very complex condition to which she is victim. The former suffers from a metaphysical malady, and the latter only feels a superficial and vague disquiet. It is this difference in dimension that makes of the one a great literary figure and the other an undistinguished and uninteresting representative of a group."[7]

Kuhn's remarks confirm what Schiesari sees as central to the tradition of male melancholy: the way in which melancholia is made to represent— is literally represented as—a sensitive or exquisite male illness, which is then said to characterize representation itself, whereas the "lower" form of boredom is characterized by its materiality, by its associations with femininity, and by an incapacity to "translate symptoms into a language beyond its own self-referentiality as depression."[8] What Kuhn's example of *Madame Bovary* unwittingly reveals, however, is that the very "superficiality" of boredom links it to a more modern, more gender-specific, and female experience of self. Indeed, as Andreas Huyssen has argued, although "critics have gone to great lengths to show what Flaubert had in common with Emma Bovary—mostly in order to show how he transcended aesthetically the dilemma on which she foundered in 'real life'"—the novel itself became known in its own time as giving representation to a "woman who tried to live the illusions of aristocratic sensual romance and was shipwrecked on the banality of bourgeois everyday life."[9]

This is not to deny the misogyny of Flaubert's text or the way in which Flaubert fetishized his own sense of loss (through an imaginary identification with femininity) while simultaneously sharing his own period's hostility toward women. Nevertheless, if melancholy and boredom are both defined by a certain self-consciousness, in melancholy, self-consciousness is painful precisely because the perception of otherness comes at the cost of exclusivity. In boredom, by contrast, self-consciousness is more "vague" and "superficial"—in Kuhn's example, more apt to bring into representation women's experiences of everyday life. Whereas melancholia is about loss and about converting male losses into representational gains, boredom, at least in the twentieth century, is about excess, sensory stimulation, and shock (generated as much by the existence of others as by the media and overproduction). What is ever present in melancholia and seems palpably missing from boredom is thus an overriding sense of nostalgia for an exclusive fantasy of privileged suffering that separates self from others. In boredom, there is no sense of privilege or nobility. Indeed, in the twentieth century boredom becomes both a "democratic affliction" and a great leveler, bound up with changing definitions of work and leisure, art and mass culture, aesthetics and sexual difference.

Boredom, in other words, is at once an empty and an overflowing conceptual category—empty because it has no ultimate, transcendent meaning; overflowing and excessive because even when it appears fixed it still contains within it definitions that are denied or suppressed. In a sociological study entitled *Overload and Boredom: Essays on the Quality of Life in the Information Society* (1986), Orrin Klapp suggests that the transformation of everyday life in the twentieth century accounts for the variety of meanings attached to boredom as well as the proliferation of words that refer to boredom as a modern condition. "The following list," he writes, "may suggest that there is more to boredom than people recognize by that particular name":

Accidie (acedia), anhedonia, apathy, arid, banal, banality, blasé, burn-out, chatter, chatterbox, glazed eyes, hackneyed, harping, ho hum, humdrum, inane, insipid, insouciance, repetitious, routine, rut, sameness, satiety, soporific, stagnant, stagnation, sterile, chitchat, chore, cliché, cloying, dismal, doldrums, drag, dreary, dry, dull, dullness, effete, enervation, ennui, flat, irksome, jade, jaded, jejune, lassitude, listless, longwinded, monotony, museum fatigue, pall, platitude, prolixity, prosaic, prosy, stuffy, stupefying, surfeited, tedium, tedious, tiresome, torpor, trite, trivia, uninteresting, verbosity, weariness, world weary.[10]

Klapp concludes the list with the following speculation: "That we have so many words plausibly suggests that modern people have need for them just as the Eskimo has so many words for snow" (23). Otherwise expressed, if boredom is a signifier that fluctuates and resists interpretive closure, it is also a term that attests to broad-based cultural changes that are at once psychical and aesthetic, economic and political.

This very instability, moreover, confounds the oppositions—between work and leisure, nobility and commonality, inertia and action, excess and lack, fullness and emptiness, masculinity and femininity—that had once characterized the understanding of melancholia (and its difference from boredom) in the eighteenth and nineteenth centuries. With the rise of visual culture, mass society, mass production, and consumerism, boredom came to describe the modern experience of time as both empty and full, concentrated and distracted (the experience of temporal disruption in the sense of "dead time," as well as temporal duration in the sense of "killing time"). If the division of labor produced sensory deprivation in the overload of repetition, so, too, did mass culture produce boredom in the distracted fullness of a leisure time become empty. As contributors to the journal *Documents* have recently put it, the expansion of boredom in the twentieth century "breaks the boundary of nineteenth century narrative that separated boredom/satiety and anxiety/privation. There is a high velocity crash, and the two once separate qualities are twisted together in an inseparable entwinement."[11]

CONFORMITY AND SUBVERSION

Given the "inseparable entwinement" of opposing terms within twentieth-century boredom, it is not surprising that the politics of banality have been the subject of an intense and protracted debate. Is boredom about resistance and opposition, a refusal of the novel in the anticipation of something truly new? Or is boredom about conformity and repetition, the banalization of identity or of novelty in the very act of demanding it? In other words, does boredom involve an uncomfortable yet creative self-consciousness, or does it merely reinforce sameness, disinterest, and apathy—a resignation to the status quo? "Monotony nourishes the new," wrote Walter Benjamin in the notes to his unfinished Arcades project, where he also remarked that "boredom is the threshold of great deeds." [12] Some thirty years later, the Situationist International declared, "Boredom is always counterrevolutionary." [13]

Whether boredom and banality take on qualities of resistance or conformity obviously has much to do with historically specific and competing views of mass culture and mass society. But the political instability of the terms also has something to do with assessments about the inevitability and, indeed, the very desirability of the fragmentation of identity and of history. The role of gender is not innocent here, but neither is it obvious or self-evident. To be sure, a split persists in the twentieth century between a higher-valued form of boredom understood as male and a lower-valued form of boredom understood as female. But in the modalities of boredom that proliferate in the twentieth century (modalities that include ennui, resistance, subversion, conformity, dullness, nonidentity), women's losses and disempowerment in culture begin to come into representation, and thus into historical view.

This is especially true of certain modernist representations of boredom that, as I suggested earlier, are distinguished both from eighteenth- and nineteenth-century views of melancholia and from some current versions of postmodernism by their emphasis on the banality of the present, now understood in gendered terms. For instance, in her early journalistic writings as well as in her later novels and plays, Djuna Barnes performed a critique of fin de siècle attitudes toward women and heterosexual romance and in the process offered another way of understanding the banality of the present and its pervasive sense of historical ennui. For Barnes, *gender and sexual difference produce ennui.* She therefore focuses on the conditions of modern women in the city, where new freedoms prove to be only relative and contingent, and where gendered dichotomies limit and contain women's desires for sexual transformation and social change. The possibility of imagining a way out of this situation haunts all of Barnes's writings but is especially apparent in her early interviews with women whose activities exceeded traditionally defined feminine roles: Mother

Jones, the suffragettes who endured forced feeding, women boxers, a po-
licewoman who wrote poetry. Barnes's attempt to render the everydayness of these women's experiences in mass culture is, in part, an effort to
defamiliarize the familiar understanding of gender and sexual difference in
modernity—not by seeing things anew, but by seeing them as no longer
novel, thus perceiving difference in banality.

In her 1917 interview with stage actress Helen Westley, for example,
Barnes explores ennui from a woman's perspective and shows how the
estrangements and banalities of modern life are fundamentally bound up
with experiences of sexual difference. Barnes begins by asking Helen
Westley to offer advice to young women who aspire to work in the theater, to which the actress responds that there is no advice, only the experience of ennui:

> This history of the world has been one not of conquest, as supposed; it
> has been one of ennui. Why do we fall in love? Because we are filled
> with ennui. Why do we fall and break our limbs? Because of ennui. Why
> do we fall ill and remain unconscious for hours? Ennui, my dear. Ennui
> sends us to our death; ennui sends us to the battlefields; ennui sends us
> through the world, and ennui takes us out of it. If this were not so, do
> you suppose for a moment that we would permit ourselves to fall in
> love once we had heard of its effects? . . .
>
> Give me despair, and I am at my best. Give me sorrow, and only
> then are my shoulders worthy of me. . . . Where have I learned this
> trick of the half-turned shoulder, the cold, drooping eyes? Through sor-
> row and difficulties. There's nothing like it for developing the figure and
> making one supple; it's better than dancing or swimming. Oh, yes, I can
> face all things.[14]

At once serious and frivolous, provocative and self-mocking, Barnes's
interview with Helen Westley challenges the assumption that ennui is a
male condition and exposes its status as theatrical gesture or pose. This is
not to say that the pose is without reference to real suffering or disillusionment—or to real women. It is rather to suggest that women's suffering and disillusionment in the present have less to do with novelty than
with banality, with feelings of weariness and discontent despite (apparent)
sexual freedoms and social progress. In the middle of the interview,
Westley and Barnes break into laughter at the recognition of this fact and
admit the futility—and banality—of ennui for women:

WESTLEY: Well, let's stop.

BARNES: We can't, not yet; I have at least three more pages to fill. (258)

Here, as in her later writings, Barnes at once mimes and subverts the conventions that both demand and inhibit novelty and prevent the possibility of anything new. In this early interview, for instance, she targets the interview form and the traditional discourses on ennui; the former was historically in the business of selling novelty, and the latter was considered the preserve of a tortured but creative male genius. Paradoxically (or, perhaps, not so paradoxically) it is the acknowledgement of boredom that relieves anxiety through laughter. If melancholy had previously been the measure by which the novelty of historical ennui was assessed, Barnes destroys this measure by insisting on the significance of ennui for women and then by undercutting this significance and replacing it with laughter and boredom—the empty pages to be filled.

Barnes was not, of course, the only modernist writer to explore ennui in relation to modernity and sexual difference. T. S. Eliot—Barnes's editor, friend, and consistent critic—took up remarkably similar issues in a celebrated 1930 essay on Baudelaire, in which Eliot seems to speak of nineteenth-century France but is in fact referring to twentieth-century European and American culture. "The possibility of damnation," he writes of Baudelaire's poetry in this essay, "is so immense a relief in a world of electoral reform, plebiscites, sex reform, and dress reform, that damnation itself is an immediate form of salvation—of salvation from the ennui of modern life, because at least it gives some significance to living."[15] Glossing this quote, one literary critic explains:

> The list of modern life's boredoms is itself significant: it includes the spread of democracy to women and the lower classes, the replacement of governmental authority by popular votes, the liberation of sexual activity from state and church dictates, and the disappearance of rigid dress codes for men and women in public. Behind each of these threats is a breakdown in hierarchical differences, an unleashing of possibilities of relation and meaning.[16]

Whereas Eliot insists on ennui as the meaning of the modern age, Barnes opts for boredom in an effort to dislodge meanings that appear fixed in modernity. As the examples I have cited from their writings suggest, if ennui, melancholia, and boredom are all defined by a certain self-consciousness, this very consciousness involves an implicit notion of the gendered self. For Eliot, self-consciousness is painful because the perception of otherness comes at the cost of male exclusivity—the spread of democracy to women and the working class. For Barnes, self-consciousness remains more vague and superficial because it lacks this sense of privileged suffering that separates self from others. Whereas modernity and sexual difference are thus the explicitly named sources of Eliot's ennui, for Barnes they are the sources of boredom—a boredom that at once denies and asserts the novelty of historical suffering by acknowledging women's discontent, and thus a notion of a gendered self, previously denied representation.

MODERNISM AND HISTORIOGRAPHY

As the examples of Barnes and Eliot suggest, the relationships among modernism, ennui, and boredom must be reassessed if we are to understand what Hayden White sees as the dissolution of the historical event in the unrepresentability of such twentieth-century phenomena as two World Wars, the Great Depression, and the Holocaust. In his recent writing on modernism and historiography, for instance, White has drawn extensively on the work of modernist writers (notably Virginia Woolf and Gertrude Stein) in an effort to detail and defend the modernist tendency to unleash possibilities of relation and meaning, to de-realize the distinction between fact and fiction, and to dissolve the event into a specter of nonmeaning.[17] It is nonetheless significant that White never addresses the role of gender in historiography and fails to consider the way in which sexual difference is either represented or unrepresentable in the modernist experience of boredom—of a time without event.

As I have attempted to demonstrate, gender and sexual difference are central to this experience of time in modernity—the time between the event and the uneventful, between that which happens and that which fails to occur. If, as Fredric Jameson has claimed, "history is what hurts," then, as Djuna Barnes, Virginia Woolf, Gertrude Stein, and other women modernists have shown, history is also about what *fails to happen* (something about which female artists and feminist women in the twentieth century have long been painfully aware). This, it seems to me, is the significance of the modernist derealization of the historical event as something objective, discrete, teleological, and uncontested in twentieth-century feminisms. All too often, when history "hurts," pain is expressed in the tradition of male melancholia. This tradition, I have argued, not only excludes women's experiences of the noneventful—and thus their experiences of history—but also elevates male suffering as a sensitive or privileged illness that apparently characterizes representation and, in recent debates about post-modernism, the very possibility of history itself.

This is why boredom offers such a useful conceptual language to begin thinking about the fading of the historical event and the status of history in twentieth-century representational forms. Indeed, similar to modernism and like gender, *boredom* is a term that appears fixed and yet whose meaning remains contested, open-ended, always in flux. It is perhaps not surprising, then, that so much feminist work over the past decades—from the literary writings of Djuna Barnes to the experimental work of feminist filmmakers to the critical writings of feminist film theorists—has involved an aesthetics as well as a phenomenology of boredom: a temporality of duration, relentless in its repetition, and a stance of active waiting, which, at least in their feminist formulations, allow for redefinition, resistance, and change.

For women modernists, aesthetic and phenomenological boredom provided a homeopathic cure for the banality of the present—a restless self-consciousness (a "desire to desire") very different from the ideal of disinterestedness that characterizes traditional historiography. It seems to me that the same kind of self-consciousness is available to feminist film theorists today. Indeed, the ennui that currently haunts the feminist project (and that has haunted feminism in the past) may ultimately prove a creative and enabling force rather than a cause for ennui or despair. Boredom and repetition, of course, have long been central to feminist aesthetics as well as to mass culture and women's experiences of everyday life. And although some now find feminism (rather than the limitations placed on women) tiresome and repetitive, it is important to remember that dead moments and dead ends in the present have been the source of new ideas and new creations in the past. Feminist insights therefore bear repeating (not all repetitions are redundancies, given the ever-present potential for failure, not to mention misunderstanding) in the ongoing attempt by women to create spaces for reflection, renewal, and change.

In any event (and perhaps especially in this time without event for feminism), a feminist historiography that takes its inspiration from modernism must reject the tedium of conventional representation (including what has now become a conventional representation of feminism itself) in order to reclaim the banality—in the sense of the everydayness—of gender, sexuality, and sexual orientation. At the same time, however, it must refuse postmodern melancholy and its discourse of lack and loss, of "history at an end," if it is to represent women's (past) losses and imagine their (future) gains. To put it slightly differently, in this time of historical ennui, even (perhaps especially) within feminism, there remains an ever-present need to struggle against the everyday on behalf of the everyday. And this will involve, as it has always done, a struggle not simply against boredom, but also for it.

WORLD-WEARINESS, WEIMAR WOMEN, AND VISUAL CULTURE

INCE at least the 1930s, in both Germany and the United States, the Weimar "golden twenties" have been thought to constitute a range of new cultural affects, dispositions, or moods. Some scholars have located these new sensibilities in nihilism or cynicism or even linked them to discourses of cultural coldness, dissociation, distraction, or decline. What I would like to suggest is that boredom helps us to understand another dimension to Weimar culture—one that has gone largely untheorized in the scholarship on the period—insofar as boredom is bound up with the contending sensibilities, voices, and impulses clamoring for attention at this time.

Boredom, of course, is typically thought to describe a subjective experience, a time without event, when nothing happens, a seemingly endless and ahistorical flux without beginning or end. And yet, as I have written elsewhere, boredom has a history that is documented as a particularly modern experience, and that encompasses romantic, scientific, psychoanalytic, and postmodern thought.[1] Rather than trace this history here, I would like instead to think through what are now conventional views of Weimar culture, particularly as they circulate around images of sexual violence and otherness—androgyny, homosexuality, femininity, race— and the apparently shocking qualities associated with them. In this discussion, I will look at central images from the period: the paintings of Georg Grosz and Otto Dix, such key films as *Destiny*, *Pandora's Box*, and *The Blue Angel*, as well as photo collages by Hannah Höch.

FROM SENSATION TO MOOD

To the extent that film studies provides models of stylistic and narrative analysis, I believe it is important to raise a number of questions about certain key issues and developments in film theory regarding perception and representation, bodily sensation, and the history of the senses in cinema. I would like to begin, then, by offering some ideas about *affect, disposition,* and *mood,* for these terms suggest what one theorist has called "a coloration or passion" within which one's investments and commitments might best come into view.

This theorist is Lawrence Grossberg, and he makes an interesting distinction between desire and mood, or, rather, what he identifies as libidinal economies of desire and affective economies of mood. Grossberg argues that the two economies represent different ways of organizing psychic energy:

> If desire is always focused (as the notion of cathexis suggests), mood is always dispersed. While both may be experienced in terms of needs, only libidinal needs can be, however incompletely, satisfied. Moods are never satisfied, only realized. If desire assumes an economy of depth (e.g., the notion of repression), mood is always on the surface (which is not to be equated with consciousness). It is the coloration or passion within which one's investments in, and commitments to the world are possible.[2]

Desire, in other words, is object centered and goal oriented; mood, by contrast, arises out of a situation and gives to it a certain tone.

While this discussion of mood is meant to set a tone for this essay, I would also like to suggest how it helps to set a theory and practice of mood in historical context. As I hope to show, the turn to questions of mood also derives from my own investments in recent debates in film theory, which have increasingly embraced bodily sensation as antidote to the lingering Cartesianism in theories of vision and looking. Here, I am thinking of Linda Williams's recent work on genre theory and pornography, and particularly of her claim for the need to attend to bodily sensations as they are generated or induced by images. Once we attend to the relationship between images and sensation, she argues, we will be able to jettison "the baggage of a long tradition of mind/body dualism which tends to view all bodily sensation provoked by images as suspect." Williams contends that "without this baggage, it becomes possible to discuss the effects of images on bodies without invoking the judgment that has been in effect since Plato in apparatus theory and feminist film theory: that the senses are duped by images; that the image is a lure whose seductive resemblances to reality must be countered by exposing the reality effect that deceives the body."[3]

While I think Williams is right to critique a transcendent, ahistorical, and disembodied model of vision promoted by psychoanalytic theories of the apparatus, I wonder if her emphasis on bodily sensation, which aims to deepen and extend a radical politics of the visual, is not itself a well-meaning displacement of such politics. Certainly it provides us a vocabulary to describe the materialism of bodily sensation, but this also seems to compensate for certain more classical strains of materialism now in dire trouble. Indeed, for all the talk of shocks, thrills, and bodily sensation, there has been precious little attention to the relationship between the dulling of sensation and the laboring body. Or to the way in which cinema involved "a complex kind of training"—rehearsing in the realm of reception what Taylorism and industrial management imposed on the human body in the realm of production. In other words, if the cinema enabled viewers to accommodate themselves mentally as well as physically to the new technologies of urban culture, and hence to experiences of sensation and shock, such accommodation necessarily led to adaptation—and adaptation to repetition, banalization, and boredom.

The "shock of the new" or the thrills of bodily sensation seem to me inadequate and one-sided accounts of the complicated relationships between shock and boredom, or innovation and repetition, in the visual arts or in culture. They keep film theory locked into libidinal economies of desire, and they fail to address its affective economies of mood. Finally, and most importantly, the shocks and sensations of cinema—as well as its repetitions and boredom—are inextricably linked to women and to gender difference. Thus, most lamentable in recent body talk is the way in which the female spectator is considered a category now exhausted or superceded, not to mention the way in which feminism and feminist film theory are now seen as tiresome and repetitive.

Rather than continue to sensationalize sensation, I would like to suggest how sense perception in cinema and in culture might best be understood in terms of mood. To return to Grossberg: If sensation appeals to the body and libidinal economies of desire, mood refers to context and is more dispersed, "never satisfied, only realized"—and only then in a momentary, transitory, and fleeting way. Like classical narrative, desire is

object centered and goal oriented. Mood, by contrast, arises out of setting
and gives it a particular tone. Moods, in other words, are something we
are "in." They color our investments and commitments. They are, by
very definition, contextual, situational, and historical. Rather than suggest
how sense perceptions are duped by a reality effect, or how bodies are
provoked by images, I propose to think about film history according to
affect, context, and setting, in other words, according to aesthetic as well
as cultural moods.

MOOD, MISE-EN-SCÈNE, AND WEIMAR CINEMA

Weimar film and culture provide a useful place to begin this discussion,
since twenties German cinema has long been recognized for its atmospheric "moodiness," just as Weimar culture has long been thought to
constitute evidence of new cultural affects or dispositions. In the aptly
titled *The Haunted Screen,* for instance, Lotte Eisner celebrates Weimar
cinema for its aesthetic atmospherics—its slow and deliberate narrative
pace, its excessive and emphatic visual style, its propensity for violent contrast in both tone and style. She uses the German term *Stimmung* to capture this aesthetic propensity, which she describes as "an intensity of
expression that comes close to pantomime."[4] With this term, Eisner
means to signal her difference from a critic like Siegfried Kracauer (who
focuses, in *From Caligari to Hitler,* primarily on narrative structure).[5] She
emphasizes mise-en-scène over narrative, film style over ideological critique. And she justifies her aesthetic approach by appealing to Weimar
cinema's own preference for style over substance, composition over action, in addition to the generally static impression the films convey.

Eisner is certainly right to insist that the most enduring Weimar films
are those that create a palpable, almost visceral, atmosphere or mood.
When we think of F. W. Murnau's films, for example, we recall the dramatic intensity and visual beauty of the settings, the ominous and fore-
boding nature of landscape. (In the scene in which Faust first invokes
Mephisto at the crossroads, a full moon gleams in the darkness and two
dead trees frame the meeting place.) Similarly, when we think of G. W.
Pabst's films, we remember dizzying, almost disembodied close-ups as
well as settings drenched in fog, mist, steam, and smoke. On the occasion
of a recent Pabst retrospective at the Museum of Modern Art, one critic
writes that "the vapors that drift through [Pabst's] movies remind us of
impermanence, hinting that much of experience is ephemeral."

Sometimes the smoke means destruction, as it billows from a bombed house or over a battlefield. Or it can express dissipation, when it be-clouds a nightclub or rises from thick cigar butts abandoned in choked ashtrays. The haze may be romantic, as two lovers—soon to be sepa-rated by a political crisis—embrace in swirling mist and smoke. Many of Pabst's characters live in the moment: in love (which can evaporate), in war (in the midst of sudden death).[6]

Pabst's films, in other words, are not only imbued with an atmospheric "moodiness"; they are, more fundamentally, precisely about the transi-tory, fleeting, impermanent condition we call "mood." To recall Grossberg once again, moods are something we are "in"—like the most memorable and distinctive films, they put us into states of mind that evoke atmo-spheres and convey emotions. They exist, in other words, not only on the surface; they are fundamentally about surface. Dispersed and situational, they arise out of a specific context and give to it a particular coloration or tone.

Of course, it is not simply, or not only, the Weimar cinema that has been recognized for its distinctive moods. German society in the turbulent 1920s has itself been endlessly analyzed for its creation of distinctive, and distinctively modern, dispositions or moods. From Oswald Spengler to Martin Heidegger to Thomas Mann, these dispositions or moods have been variously diagnosed as nihilism or located in cultural decadence and decline. Most recently, Peter Sloterdijk has called the dominant mood of the period "cynicism" and argued that Weimar culture is its "essential founding period," for it was here that cynicism found its way into dis-courses of politics, medicine, religion, philosophy, sexuality, and gender. Sloterdijk further claims that this legacy of cynicism—what he calls "en-lightened false consciousness"—is very much with us today.[7] In a gloss on Sloterdijk's seemingly paradoxical conceptualization, theorist Stephen Brockmann explains that the two concepts—"enlightened" and "false consciousness"—would seem a contradiction in terms, since "false con-sciousness" is false precisely because it is not enlightened, and enlightened consciousness is, by definition, no longer a false consciousness at all. And yet, Brockman continues,

> What Sloterdijk is getting at is that the workers know better, that in fact everyone knows better. In other words, there is no point in trying to educate or agitate people, to bring them the facts so that they will

behave in their own best interests. They already know the facts. Modernity, Sloterdijk suggests, is already enlightened. People know the right thing to do and they still do not do it. . . . Strictly speaking, "enlightened false consciousness" is not defined by a lack of knowledge but rather by lack of action. Cynicism is theory without practice.[8]

Importantly, the cynicism Sloterdijk describes also involves a strategic, performative immorality that hinges on a rejection of the romantic idealism and corresponding sexual repression of an earlier era. As he explains it, cynicism entailed a modern sophistication, whereby not to be deceived meant to know that everything is deception. In the realm of the sexual, this involved a debunking not only of love, but also of women, with whom the ideology of love had been associated. To borrow from Brockman again, "The woman who is no longer rendered powerless on a pedestal as an object of adoration is now rendered powerless as a sex object. The liberation from the ideology of love reveals itself in an enslavement to an ideology of sex."[9]

Sloterdijk has been taken to task for his exclusive emphasis on masculinity and male subjectivity, and for his blindness where gender is concerned.[10] More recently, and in a different register, Helmut Lethen has attempted to distinguish cynicism from coldness or "the cold persona," and to situate this disposition within the culture and artistic production of *Neue Sachlichkeit.* For Lethen, coldness is related to cynicism, but in some ways distinct from it. Like boredom, it involves a lack of affect, a decided understatedness and distance, a disinclination to say what is on one's mind. But like cynicism, it is a calculated and calculating way of behaving, very much in keeping with urban modernity, where one constantly creates distance from other people and one's own emotions, not to mention the unpredictability of the times. Coldness, like cynicism and like boredom, involves a mode of anticipation and reservation, a mode of being present and yet not being there at all.[11] I will have more to say about these things in a moment. Suffice it to say here that there is plenty of textual support for Sloterdijk's claim of a sophisticated male cynicism—an acute self-consciousness and strategic immorality, a desire not to be deceived by knowing that everything is a deception, and this desire especially where women are concerned.

Maria Tatar's 1995 book *Lustmord,* on sexual murder in Weimar Germany, for example, shows how the obsession with sexual transgression in Weimar visual arts was itself the symptom of an extraordinary displacement—specifically, a displacement of war weariness and shell shock onto world-weariness and male violence against women. Tatar focuses particular attention on the work of Georg Grosz and Otto Dix—especially their numerous canvases entitled "Lustmord" or sexual murder, which provide vivid testimony of the sexual cynicism described by Sloterdijk, here revealed in an unprecedented dread of female sexuality and violence against the female body. In a wartime drawing from 1917 entitled *When It Was All Over, They Played Cards,* Georg Grosz sketches a group of card players, one of whom sits on a crate into which the hacked-up body of a woman has been stuffed. A year later, in 1918, Grosz had himself photographed in the pose of Jack the Ripper, emerging from behind a mirror in which the narcissistic woman—Eva Peter, who would later become his wife—remains unaware of impending danger, absorbed as she is in the image of herself. In a work from 1920, entitled *Sex Murderer: Self-Portrait,* Otto Dix similarly portrays himself as a "lady killer," literally slicing up female body parts in a moment of frenzy. Similarly, in his 1922 *Sexual Murder,* Dix depicts a veritable mise-en-scène of murderous violence, the aftershock of male rage. The eviscerated corpse, the gash in the wall, and the overturned chair, Tatar points out, "form a triangular space that contrasts sharply with the elaboration of a bourgeois social space marked by the hanging lamp, the table, and the window in a world of architectural order." [12]

For Grosz and Dix, the female corpse is literally the source of disorder and dis-ease. Their images reveal a pervasive sexual cynicism, a rejection of the romantic idealism described by Sloterdijk, as well as a strategic and self-consciously performative immoralism. This is a world in which men are violent killers and women are prostitutes or barely recognizable lumps of flesh. But this is also a world in which the male artist self-consciously performs his murderous rage. Tatar explains that such cynical representations of Lustmord are implicated in the psychic fallout of the war years: the sense of resentment directed against victors, noncombatants, and military leaders alike; the crisis of subjectivity occasioned by military defeat; the painfully acute sense of the body's vulnerability to fragmentation, mutilation, and dismemberment. Unlike Sloterdijk, however, Tatar emphasizes the way in which sexual cynicism has asymmetrical and gendered effects on fallen soldiers and fallen women. "While most critics have emphasized how images of seductive femininity can be read as symptoms of male anxieties about female libidinal energy," she writes, "they can also be seen as fueling those anxieties to a fever pitch" (10).

Georg Grosz, *When It Was All Over, They Played Cards,* 1917.

Georg Grosz, *Self-Portrait with Eva Peter in the Artist's Studio*, 1918.

Otto Dix, *Sex Murderer: Self-Portrait,* 1920.

Otto Dix, *Sexual Murder*, 1922.

In other words, the suspicion of romantic ideals and sexual identities encouraged male artists to masquerade as sexual murderers in a sophisticated display of the emptiness of ideals. But it also, and simultaneously, enhanced the popular image of the prostitute as femme fatale and engendered a culture of sexual suspicion, danger, and fear. Thus were battlefield experiences brought back to the home front, and symptoms of war weariness transformed into images of sexual pathology. As Tatar so convincingly demonstrates, women who had escaped the shells and shrapnel of the trenches and survived the war with bodies intact were at once imagined as omnipotent sexual and social subjects (with the newly acquired right to vote) and as faceless and anonymous victims of sexual assault. This dynamic can certainly be described as misogynist, but there is more to Weimar visual culture than this, as I would like to suggest by looking at several key films of the Weimar era that locate war weariness in boredom and repetition rather than in cynicism or fantasies of violent assault.

WAR WEARINESS, CYNICISM, AND BOREDOM

Perhaps the place to begin—or rather, the place where all histories of the Weimar cinema have begun—is in 1920, with the release of *The Cabinet of Dr. Caligari. Caligari* continues to fascinate scholars who wish to establish Weimar cinema's expressionist or avant-garde credentials, or to show how premonitions of national character are enacted in a fiction of tyrannical authority and the inevitable submission of the individual to larger forces and control. Kracauer's 1947 study *From Caligari to Hitler* is undeniably the point of reference here, but even film scholars today look to this film to understand Weimar culture and its continuing appeal. In a 1997 lecture at the Goethe-Institut in London, Tony Kaes proposed a new reading of *Caligari* by looking at it not as simply avant-garde or expressionist or allegorical, but as direct evidence of the trauma of the Great War. Rather than understand the film retrospectively, from the perspective of Nazism (as Kracauer does in his book), Kaes suggested that *Caligari* be understood as coming "after the shock" of war. The shaky and halting movements of the somnambulist Cesare, he argued, parallel those seen in images of shell-shocked veterans. The spatial disorientation, extreme angles, and anti-realistic settings of the film, he further claimed, were actually realistic reenactments of the soldier's view from the trench. The centrality of psychoanalysis and psychotherapy in the film, moreover, are for Kaes rather direct references to the supposed cures for war weariness and shell shock at that time—temporary cures that aimed to bandage the mental and physical anguish of soldiers and then return them to the front. *The Cabinet of Dr. Caligari*, Kaes concluded, locates death in murder, even mass murder. In his view, *Caligari* is thus a war film and an antiwar film, more indebted to the spirit of Dada than that of expressionism.

When I asked him about Fritz Lang's 1920 film *Destiny*, Kaes responded that while *Caligari* is progressive in its antiwar stance (and its understanding of death as murder), *Destiny* is reactionary in its fatalism (and in its view of death as fate). To be sure, this is a longstanding assessment of the film among scholars, who have often contended that *Destiny* confirms the Weimar cinema's (and Fritz Lang's) general obsession with fate in its various guises. It is seen as a film that relates in some ways to expressionist concerns (it has, in fact, many similarities to *Caligari*, including the same set designers and many of the same actors, as well as similar motifs, such as the power of tyrannical authority and petty bureaucracies). But is also considered to be a film that looks further backward to German Romanticism (in its preoccupation with death, alchemy, and the supernatural) and forward to the Nazi years (in its appeal to monumental architecture and its insistence on the necessity to submit to irrational authority). But if *Caligari* is a postwar film that reflects on trench warfare and shell shock, then *Destiny* is equally a film about the war years—not the military front but the home front; not the experience of fighting but that of boredom and waiting; not male identity and shell shock but female identity and the ubiquity of suffering and repetition.

Destiny begins by introducing a young couple who travel by carriage and stop at the inn of a small town, "lost in the past" (as the intertitles explain). An uncanny stranger joins them first in the carriage and then again at the inn. Via flashback, we learn that this stranger had long ago bought land bordering the nearby cemetery and surrounded it with a huge wall, with neither door nor gate. We then return to the inn, a veritable male preserve populated by various dignitaries of the town. At one point, the woman gets up to pay a visit to the kitchen (where she plays with kittens). When she returns, her lover has disappeared, as has the stranger. Terrified, she hurries to the huge wall, where she swoons and then faints. Soon after, she is found by the town's aging pharmacist, who takes her to his home. There he prepares a tonic, but the woman, in her despair, lifts a poison cup to her lips. Just before she drinks it, however, she seems to dream a long dream, in which the huge wall reappears.

This time there is a door, and behind the door a seemingly endless flight of steps. At the top of the steps, the woman meets the hooded stranger, whom she now recognizes as Death, and implores him to reunite her with her lover. He leads her to a dark room filled with burning candles, each representing a human life. Her wish will be granted, he says, if she can prevent three burning candles from being extinguished. What follows are three separate stories that show Death triumphing over the woman in various places and times: a Moslem city, Venice of the Renaissance, a fantastic China. Three times she is given narrative agency and three times she fails to reverse the catastrophic course of events. Again, the woman implores the mercy of Death, whereupon he offers her a last chance: if she can bring him another life, he will return that of her lover. At this point, the woman's dream ends, with the pharmacist snatching the poison cup from her.

The pharmacist intimates to the woman that he himself is weary of life; when she asks him to sacrifice his life for her lover's, he throws her out. A beggar and several old women in a hospital likewise refuse to make such a sacrifice. Fire breaks out in the hospital and after the adult patients take flight, they learn that a baby has been left behind. The woman fights her way through the flames to save the child. Death, keeping his promise, extends his arm to take the child, but the woman hands the baby to the happy mother, who waits at the window outside. Death then guides the woman through the blaze to her dead lover and, via superimposition, the lovers take leave of their bodies and wander off together, spiritually united in a dreamscape—literally an empty space— and with this, the film ends.

Destiny's German title—*Der Müde Tod* or "weary death"—led at least one contemporary critic to title his review "The Tiresome Death." *Destiny* is without question indebted to an earlier, less classical style of film-making, marked by a slowness of pace, requiring a different mode of attention on the part of the viewer. But if it is a boring film, its tedium is especially interesting for us, since the woman's fate is bound up in tedium and in traditional notions of femininity and the maternal (a moral and spiritual superiority not limited to biological mothers). Throughout the film, the woman is at the center of attempts to destroy and create community. And only through her death is community reestablished in the little village, precisely as it was in the various framed tales, which are only resolved by expelling a variety of dangerous and exotic others (including, of course, the woman herself). The narrative thus insists that female desire and volition are not only impossible but quite literally beside the point: Death cannot be avoided, history and narrative cannot be rewritten, and Love is only stronger than Death in fantasies of self-destruction.

Destiny, it would seem, is therefore a very different kind of document of Weimar culture. It is devoid of the physical violence and cynicism of the Lustmord paintings by Grosz and Dix. And it lacks the liberated, openly sexualized female protagonist we have come to associate with so many other Weimar films. While *Destiny* might appear, at first, to offer premonitions of fascism (or rather, premonitions of women's place in fascism), it also seems, at least in narrative terms, quaintly old-fashioned, indebted to an earlier, less modern, at least, less urban, age. But when we consider a later Weimar film, like *Metropolis,* also directed by Lang and released in early 1927, we can see the persistence of *Destiny*'s influence as well as the irresistible pull of a counter-force of erotic provocation. Of course, both films ultimately contain the exoticism and otherness they nevertheless evoke. In *Metropolis,* however, we see traces of the modern cynical consciousness Sloterdijk describes—the sophisticated, knowing wink that acknowledges that "not to be deceived means to know that everything is deception"—and the way this cynicism is put to rest in fantasies of spiritual renewal.

I refer here, of course, to the split and doubled character Maria: the false, seductive, and decadent Robot who winks at the camera at the success of her deceptive performance as a real, sexualized woman, and her human, nurturing, maternal counterpart who preaches the virtues of patience, perseverance, and self-denial. Much has been written about this film, particularly concerning its treatment of sexuality and technology, and not only in relation to the Robot Maria but also as figured in the Luddism of the workers who turn into a raging—and ragingly feminine— machine-destroying mob.[13] As is well known, the workers' wives are seen for the first time in the film once the riot is underway; the Foreman tries to stop them, saying, "You fools, don't you know that by destroying the machines, you destroy yourselves?" He refers to the collapse of the central powerhouse, the flooding of the workers' homes, and the danger posed to their children as a result. But the Foreman's words—and the film's Luddism—have much wider significance than this.

Just as the real Maria's sexuality is drained to fuel the erotic deceptions of the Robot-machine, so, too, are the workers drained of energy, affect, and will. They emerge in the film's closing moments as an ornamental, hierarchical wedge, an aesthetically pleasing part of the mise-en-scène, organized to witness the formation of the couple and the healing of the breach between capital and labor. But ironically, in destroying the

machine, it is they who have become machinelike, deceived by the deception of this pseudo-unity and community. In what would appear to be the
absolute limit case of cynical reasoning, the final sequence of Metropolis
leaves us with the image of a faceless mass whose revolutionary impulses
have been purged, just as the real Maria is purged of sexuality, volition,
and control.

But if Metropolis can be described as a cynical film, it is also a film about
waiting—about workers who wait and then revolt in the name of change
and renewal, and who experience the passing of time as mere tedium and
duration. (Recall the ten-hour clocks, the night and day shifts, and the
relentless repetition of industrial routine.) This notion of waiting was in
fact analyzed in great detail by theorists in the Weimar period, most notably by Kracauer, who described the postwar years in Germany as ones
of exhaustion and indifference, involving the experiences of both shell-
shocked veterans and supposedly liberated working women.

In an essay entitled "Those Who Wait," he explains that "those who
decide to wait neither close themselves off from the possibilities of faith
like the stubborn disciples of total emptiness, nor do they force this faith
like the soul searchers who have lost all restraints in their longing." What
he means to signal here, I think, is precisely what I have been trying to
analyze: the relationship of cynicism and boredom to the capacity for recognizing and producing change. Kracauer sees in boredom both the "total
emptiness" of cynicism and the "loss of restraint" in spiritual renewal.
Both are trajectories of the modern age, and both are present as potenti-
alities in the cultural moment after the shock of war and before the institution of National Socialism. Importantly, Kracauer suggests a third
alternative or strategy for thinking through the boredom of the present
in its relationship to stasis and change, "waiting," which alone offers what
he calls "a certain guarantee that one will have, so to speak, an existence
at one's disposal." [14]

What might this mean in the context of the world-weariness and the
supposed sexual decadence of the Weimar years? More precisely, what
might this mean for Weimar women, who were certainly not guaranteed
any existence or subjectivity in the work of postwar artists like Grosz and
Dix, or even in the films, like Destiny and Metropolis, that were ostensibly
(or at least in part) addressed to them?

In an essay on Pabst's Pandora's Box, Mary Ann Doane acknowledges
the pervasiveness of the sexual cynicism analyzed by Sloterdijk but nonetheless asks a question similar to the one I raise here: "Where is the place

of the female subject in such a configuration? Can she share in the cynicism whose function is to bandage a wounded male identity? Or does she act, instead, as the symbol of all the losses and catastrophes afflicting modern consciousness?" Through close analysis of the Pabst film, Doane ultimately comes to the latter conclusion. Modernity and self-conscious modernist strategies, she says, "do not necessarily promise anything to the woman; or, if they do, that promise is always already broken. *Pandora's Box*, fairly classical in much of its design, does not, in its modernist moments, escape the power-knowledge relations of the problematic of sexual difference." [15]

Interestingly, the pivotal sequence for Doane's analysis of *Pandora's Box* resonates with the Georg Grosz photograph with his wife-to-be Eva Peter (both texts, of course, reference the Jack the Ripper story). To be sure, Doane typically fastens on metacinematic moments in her film analyses. But, in her reading of *Pandora's Box*, the assessment of the place of the female subject in sexually cynical structures depends precisely upon an interpretation of a purposely ambiguous and fleeting mise-en-scène, the setting of Schon's death. Similar to the Grosz–Eva Peter photograph, this sequence evokes a scenario of the female subjectivity and narcissism in the mirror. Lulu gazes admiringly at her own image, begins to take off her wedding gown, and starts to remove her necklace. As she bends down to set it aside, the ghostly, clearly tormented, and horrific image of Schon appears in the mirror. "The free and joyful sexuality represented by Lulu," Doane points out, thus "seems to call forth in response its weighty, cumbersome other, signaled by the presence of Schon and his problematic of sexual guilt" (159). In a self-consciously modernist gesture, the film thus reveals that the woman is there by virtue of the other, that she is a projection of male desire, and that male desire is dependent on a certain image of female sexuality.

The film's cynicism is therefore inextricably linked to its modernism—to its self-conscious revelation of the device. Its "knowing sophistication" or "enlightened false consciousness" is thus bound up with its knowledge about the libidinal economies of desire, and its failure to do anything different with them. Doane says that "the film seems to recognize and even attempt to analyze the dialectic of subjectivity and objectivity which underpins sexual desire" (161). And yet, given the sudden appearance of Jack the Ripper in the film's final sequences, it ultimately succumbs to a story about a man's internal struggle with himself. At the beginning of her essay, Doane asks, "Is not cynicism a necessary moment in the development of feminist theory? Insofar as cynicism involves an active suspicion of romantic ideals and the sexual identities they dictate and an interrogation of the mores and moralisms of a patriarchal order, it would seem to ally itself with the feminist enterprise." But the feminist enterprise is about practice as much as theory, she concludes, and since cynicism is about resignation to the status quo, "cynicism as an operational strategy for feminist theory has its limits" (144).

If cynicism has its limits, and I agree with Doane that it does, the self-conscious, knowing sophistication of the Weimar era—wherein not to be deceived is to know that everything is deception—nonetheless has wider permutations and dispositions, especially for women and for feminism— in both Weimar culture and our own. I would argue, in fact, that boredom as much as cynicism or coldness helps us to understand the knowing sophistication of Weimar representation—representation often made for and by Weimar women, which existed alongside and yet outside of the Lustmord legacy.

TRANSITORY MOODS: SEXUALITY, RACE, BOREDOM

It might at first seem counterintuitive, even perverse, to describe Weimar culture in terms of boredom, particularly given the view of this time registered in the Lustmord images as well as in popular culture. Louise Brooks, the U.S. star of *Pandora's Box*, refers in her memoirs to Berlin nightlife, with "girls in boots advertising flagellation," clubs that displayed "an enticing line of homosexuals dressed as women," another with "a choice of feminine or collar and tie lesbians," and the "collective lust which roared unashamed at the theater." [16] It is perhaps begging the obvious to say that Berlin in the 1920s would hardly seem to warrant the epithet *boring*—especially in view of such inflated and exorbitant claims for its sexual decadence outside the constraints of law or convention.

And yet another observer, writing in the 1920s, provides us with a different view. In his Weimar diaries, Bertolt Brecht wrote, "How this Germany bores me," lamenting his lot of living in a mediocre land with a languid intelligentsia. He then asks: "What's left?" only to answer: "America!" [17] For Brecht, Weimar was a culture in which everything seemed to have happened—war, civil war, inflation, depression—and yet, it was a culture in which, simultaneously, nothing at all seemed to have fundamentally changed. Importantly, in this passage Brecht links Weimar culture dialectically to the United States. If America is what's left, and what's truly new, it will nonetheless become, in his later writings, much like the Weimar culture he lamented earlier: a curious mixture of old and new, of rapid change and nearly unbearable stasis, as much a source of stimulation as of boredom. Historian Peter Gay frames the issue in a different, if related, way: "In August of 1914, the Western world had experienced a war psychosis: the war seemed a release from boredom, an invitation to heroism, a remedy for decadence."[18] The postwar period released Germans from this boredom, returning them to decadence, which persisted in being figured, from the twenties to today, almost exclusively in sexual terms.

There are reasons for this, of course, which become apparent in theoretical, avant-garde, and popular cultural texts by and for women. Many of these texts reject cynicism and coldness to reclaim boredom as an aesthetic and affective mode with a critical edge and resistant potential, particularly where sexuality and gender are concerned. In this regard, it is important to reference perhaps the single most significant essay for contemporary feminist and queer theorists who want to call attention to the construction, indeed, the constructedness, of femininity for women. Joan Rivière's 1929 essay "Womanliness as a Masquerade," written in the context of Berlin psychoanalytic debates, seems to partake of the same kind of knowing sophistication theorized as cynicism by Sloterdijk. For example, it is well known that Rivière theorizes femininity as a performance of sexual difference by women who wish for masculinity and who then "put on a mask of womanliness or femininity as a defense to avert the anxiety and retribution feared by men."[19] Like Sloterdijk, Rivière thus acknowledges that identity resides not in biology or sexual essence but in the mask, the game, and the deceptiveness of performance.

But is this really cynical reasoning? It is, in part, if we focus solely on the "enlightened false consciousness" of Rivière's patient, a woman who wishes for masculinity (for power and intellectual authority), only to mask that wish through the performance of femininity. And yet, as a psychoanalytic text, Rivière's essay is not really about strategies of *conscious deception* at all, even though its status as a historical document reveals much about conscious and unconscious strategies of self-deception and denial. Rivière's essay in fact marks a moment in German history (as early as 1929) when the decade-long experimentation with gender roles—which involved women's appropriations of masculine styles, gestures, and prerogatives—was in the process of being reversed and superceded in a performance of womanliness in all aspects of cultural life.

This returns us to questions of setting, context, and mood—to the affective (rather than the libidinal) economies that surfaced briefly in the German 1920s. In this regard, it is interesting to compare cynicism or even coldness (which are associated with German culture in the 1920s) with discourses of "cool" (which are often linked to African American subculture, particularly bebop jazz and Miles Davis and the United States in the 1940s). Like "coldness," "cool" has been theorized as an adaptive mechanism and form of self-armoring, an expression of bitterness, anger, and distrust, and a reaction against years of mistreatment and discrimination. "Cool" is also typically described as a "mask" (not unlike Rivière's masquerade), and yet, unlike the feminine masquerade, coolness is specifically masculine, even a form of macho posturing, linked to African American male outsider culture of the post–World War II period. Significantly, elements of African American cool found expression earlier, in the years following World War I. Weimar culture in particular was fascinated with questions of race deriving from U.S. as much as German culture—and the Nazis were later able to channel this fascination and obsession into both racist discourses (about Degenerate Art, for instance) and murderous practices.

In the 1920s, however, discourses on race in Germany were far more contradictory and complex, involving both the racist hysteria during and after the Rhineland occupation (in which French colonial troops were popularly represented as "weapon-toting gorillas in French uniforms") as well as a protest against it. In the realm of avant-garde art, moreover, the weariness with European civilization, especially following the war, as well as the satiation with Western art on the part of many cultural thinkers, led to an interest in exotic art, including that of Africa.[20] It also led to a demand to take that art out of the ethnographic museums and grant it the aesthetic recognition it deserved. Along with this retrieval of African art, there was also an intense interest in popular culture on the part of many Germans, who were especially drawn to the energy and modern sensibility they experienced in African American jazz.[21] This popular cultural phenomenon was also a by-product of war, since jazz had been imported to Germany when the United States deployed black troops in Europe during World War I, still segregated into their own units.

It is in this context—in this setting and within this momentary cultural mood—that we can perhaps best appreciate many of Hannah Höch's Berlin photomontages of the 1920s. As is well known, Hannah Höch was the only woman among the group of artists who made up the legendary Dada circle in Berlin (which included Grosz as well as Raoul Hausmann and

John Heartfield). Her work, moreover, is quite distinctive and notably different from that of her male contemporaries, particularly in its incisive,
playful, and often ironic treatment of gender roles.[22] This can be seen in
what is perhaps her most complex and undeniably most famous photomontage, *Cut with the Kitchen Knife Dada through Germany's Last Beer Belly
Epoch*. This work depicts a cross-section of German culture circa 1920,
bringing together representatives of the former empire, the military, and
the new moderate republican government in the "anti-Dada" section in
the upper right, while grouping communists and other radicals together
with the Dadaists in the lower right. These mostly male figures are paired
with image fragments of women—indeed, New Women—women in
movement (dancers, athletes, actresses, artists) who animate the work
both formally and conceptually. This is, after all, the work of a thoroughly
modern female artist, aware and yet outside of the Lustmord tradition,
cutting through what she hoped would be the last beer-belly cultural epoch, and with a kitchen knife, no less.

Höch's work is without question both fascinating and complex. But it
is her 1925 collage entitled *Love in the Bush* (*Liebe im Busch*) that resonates
most profoundly with the moods of Weimar culture I have been describing. *Love in the Bush* features a hybrid image of a black man-child as well
as a composite image of Weimar's New Woman that blurs traditional male-
female distinctions. Arguably, this work condenses several art and entertainment forms, such as cabaret, tribal art, ethnographic museums, and
jazz, that were extremely popular in Berlin of the 1920s. But, as art historian Maria Makela points out, this collage doubtlessly references the
French occupation of the Rhineland and the ensuing "bastard controversy" of the 1920s. This controversy, she explains, brought with it "racist
propaganda about 40,000 'black savages' roaming the Rhineland at will,
raping the women, infecting the population with all manner of tropical
and venereal diseases and—worst of all—fathering 'mischlingskinder' or
children of mixed race." The controversy reached its height in 1923,
when territorial forces also occupied the Ruhr and President Friedrich
Ebert denounced their presence as an "injury to the laws of European
civilization."[23]

In this context, Makela sees *Love in the Bush* as a truly radical work,
since it suggests not only that "the white woman enjoys the embrace
she is receiving but that she may have initiated it" as well. And this "at a
time when many Germans were describing all liaisons between black men
and white German women as rape" (85). Interestingly, *Love in the Bush*

Hannah Höch, *Cut with the Kitchen Knife Dada through Germany's Last Beer Belly Epoch*, 1920.

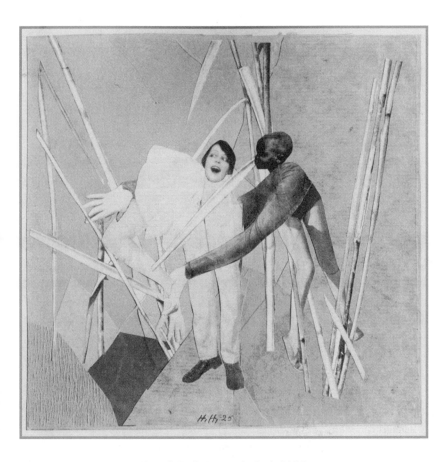

Hannah Höch, *Love in the Bush*, 1925.

anticipates a fantasy in which racial fear and desire—and identification—
lead to an exaggerated performance of sexual difference. As a woman and
an artist, Höch obviously empathized and identified with the disrespected
and exoticized Other of non-European culture. In her work, moreover,
she consciously employed an aesthetic strategy that fuses seemingly incompatible images into hybrid figures so that all we are left with is the
residue of that conflation. Needless to say, this residue cannot be easily
unified or simply explained, since it arises out of a particular situation and
gives to it a certain tone.

 This brings me to my final examples, involving Hannah Höch but also
referencing the cinema and perhaps Weimar Germany's most enduring
female star. To begin this conclusion it is important to emphasize that
Höch's work reveals not only highly charged and complex compositions
but also a striking change in form and tone over the course of the 1920s.
For example, in its density of references and complexity in style, *Cut with
the Kitchen Knife* exhibits a sense of anticipation about women's mobility
and the possibilities of collaboration and solidarity between men and
women of the Left. By the end of the decade, however, Höch's own
mood, and the mood of her work, had undergone profound change, as we
see in her 1930 collage entitled *Mother*. Here, Höch features a listless, over-
worked proletarian woman in an advanced state of pregnancy. She borrowed this image from John Heartfield's photomontage of the same year,
which was published in the *AIZ*, a popular left-wing illustrated magazine.
Heartfield's montage features the same pregnant proletarian woman but
also includes, above her image, a photograph of a dead boy with his rifle.
The caption to Heartfield's montage reads: "Forced supplier of human
ammunition! Take courage! The state needs the unemployed and soldiers!" Heartfield's work clearly refers to the broad-based battle then taking place in Germany over an act called Paragraph 218, which outlawed
and criminalized abortion. In his address to working-class readers, he positions the working-class mother as both addressee and victim—the mere
vessel for producing human fodder for war.

 In contrast to Heartfield, Höch covers the woman's face with a primitive mask, eliminates her swollen belly, deletes the photograph of the dead
boy and rifle, and titles the work simply *Mother*. Interestingly, she also
adds a New Woman's eye to the side of the face—an eye that, in the
context of this montage, lends an aura of dissociation to the masked face.
Höch aims here, I think, to employ aesthetic means of simple forms and
the reduction of elements she adapted from African art. She thus forces

Hannah Höch, *Mother,* 1930.

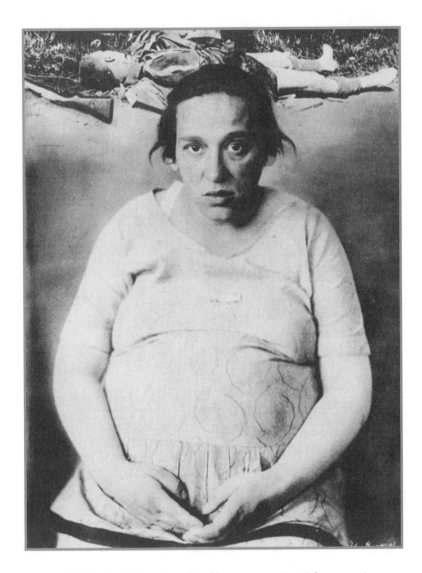

John Heartfield, *Forced supplier of human ammunition! Take courage!*
The state needs unemployed and soldiers! 1930.

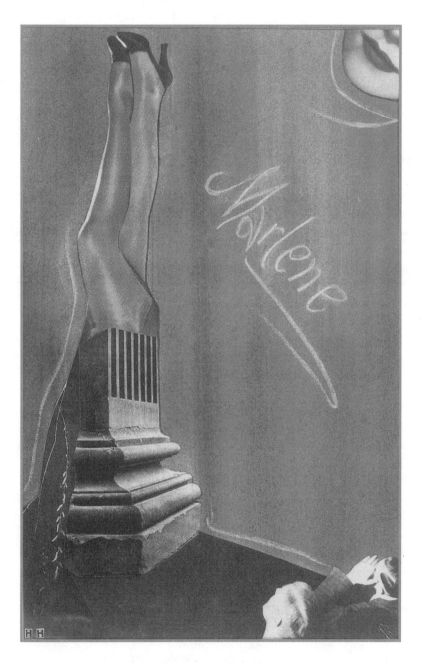

Hannah Höch, *Marlene,* 1930.

into abstraction, even emptiness, the stereotypical view of the working-class woman in the left-wing press, thereby presenting her own image of exhausted maternity simply by focusing on the figure's drooping shoulders and mouth. This image is not sensational nor does it attempt to sensationalize the issues. Instead, it gives us a haunting image of the laboring (rather than the sexualized) female body. The mood here is not one of coldness or cynicism, but one of boredom and ennui: there is no dead male body or rifle to motivate its meanings, merely the countenance of the masked proletarian woman.

Another of Höch's photomontages, also from 1930, includes the same brightly striped papers of coral pink, peach, and gray that serve as the background in *Mother*. The title of this work is *Marlene*—an obvious reference to Marlene Dietrich, who played the leading role in Josef von Sternberg's 1930 film *The Blue Angel*, which established Dietrich as an icon of Weimar Germany's sexually liberated woman and sexually decadent star. With Sternberg's film, Dietrich quickly gained a reputation for sophisticated and knowing self-consciousness, one that involved a play with sexuality and gender identity, but one that also, more importantly, seemed to break with the ideology of love as well as that of sex. In *The Blue Angel*, Lola's blasé sexuality—her seeming lack of affect, often described as coldness, but perhaps better understood as boredom—suggests that sex, as much as modernity, promises nothing to the woman; or, if it does, that *this* promise is always already broken.

This is a knowing self-consciousness, and Höch was obviously drawn to it as a compelling, if never fully realized, ideal. In this photomontage, Höch literally puts Dietrich's legs on a pedestal; significantly, she also depicts a woman's smiling face in the upper left corner as well as two men's faces looking up at this monument to feminine allure in the lower left corner. She therefore seems to reference the appeal of the Dietrich image to both male and female audiences at the time. This appeal, moreover, was dispersed not merely across gender but also across other categories of difference, in what Gertrud Koch has called "a projective topography of nations, races, and sexes." "The coincidence of [Dietrich's] departure for Hollywood with the rise of National Socialism," Koch writes, "turned her portrayal of Lola . . . into an image iconic of both memory and leaving: the image of a woman as openly sexual and lascivious as she is motherly; an image that died, along with the Weimar Republic, in National Socialism." [24]

What are we to make of the photomontages, one of a proletarian mother, the other of Germany's most celebrated female star? Created in the same year, and linked by their settings or colored backgrounds, these images bespeak a provocative destabilization of identity that is the very signature of the Weimar era. Here, though, destabilization has less to do with the shock effect of sexual otherness than with its very banality and everyday recognition. As a female artist who began her career in the immediate postwar period, Höch was in a unique position to document at once how much and how little had changed for women at this time. Whereas the Left continued to imagine women as mothers in need of didactic reproach, and whereas the film industry proceeded to capitalize on the female fetish, Höch drew attention to both the didacticism and the fetishism as strategies in her own work. And yet her attitude toward her subjects (whether abortion or the release of a popular film) seems neither bitter nor resigned, but perhaps merely cool rather than cold, not cynical but only bored. Bored with the Left's representation of working women, tired of the view of sexual decadence (which assumed women were sexual objects rather than self-knowing sexualized subjects), fed up with the hype surrounding the illusion of change.

Hannah Höch's changing views of Weimar women are only one instance of what I have attempted to describe as part of a more diverse range of cultural and aesthetic dispositions or moods. Obviously, there were those, like Höch, who actively waited for change, and who refused to succumb to the kind of cynicism described by Sloterdijk or imagined in the work of Grosz and Dix. But there were many others, women as well as men, who refused to wait, and who looked to National Socialism for a release from decadence and boredom in an invitation to heroism and spiritual renewal (an invitation that, in its racism and misogyny, represented cynical reasoning at its most extreme). The ideal of female self-sacrifice, of course, was as central to Weimar as to Nazi Germany, as was the idea of sexual murder. Both were tested for acceptability during the 1920s by less violent but no less virulent means than would be enacted a decade later. While some of the most memorable images of the Weimar years are drawn from this legacy, the most fascinating and enduring images remain, for me, those that challenge both the cynicism and the self-denial surrounding sexuality and race and gender in a self-conscious and sophisticated knowing I have called boredom.

NAZI CINEMA AT THE INTERSECTION OF THE CLASSICAL AND THE POPULAR

T HE PAST few years have seen a great deal of scholarly activity and interest in the cinema of the Third Reich, especially in the United States and Britain. In 1996, not one but two scholarly books on Nazi cinema were published in the United States: Eric Rentschler's *The Ministry of Illusion: Nazi Cinema and Its Afterlife* and Linda Schulte-Sasse's *Entertaining the Third Reich: Illusions of Wholeness in Nazi Cinema.*[1] Essays on individual films as well as the broader political and cultural context of Nazi filmmaking have appeared in the pages of *Screen* and *Sight and Sound.*[2] November of 1997 saw two international conferences devoted, at least in part, to Nazi film: at Dartmouth, a conference on the career of Detlef Sierck / Douglas Sirk, and in London, a day-long symposium (sponsored by the Goethe Institut and the British Film Institute) on Weimar and Third Reich cinema.

What are we to make of this recent interest in Nazi cinema among British and U.S. intellectuals? As Rentschler and others have pointed out, there has long been a devoted and specifically national audience for these films, spanning the 1930s and 1940s and continuing throughout the postwar years and up until today. Nazi cinema, in other words, may be experiencing a resurgence of sorts among English-speaking intellectuals, but its appeal is not new to German audiences, who are accustomed to seeing Nazi films stocked on video shelves and shown as staples on television, matinee, and festival programs. To phrase the question in a slightly different way (and to borrow from Rentschler's evocative title): Why has Nazi Cinema taken on a particular "afterlife" in the context of British and U.S. film studies, and why now?

One answer, of course, can be found in larger trends in German cultural and political historiography. Here, I refer not only to the *Historikerstreit* and the acrimonious disputes among West German historians about the place of the Holocaust in German history, but also to more recent histories that chart continuities as well as discrepancies between National Socialist policy and everyday culture in the Third Reich.[3] For example, rather than focus on German anti-Semitism from the perspective of the policy making of Nazi leaders or the initiatives of the so-called "banal" bureaucrats, historians have turned instead to the choices faced, the emotions felt, and the coping mechanisms employed by ordinary people. Not simply a history of everyday life, but also and explicitly a history of *everyday fascism,* even this *Alltagsgeschichte* has raised suspicions and concerns (most notably, that the focus on everyday life in the Third Reich will have the effect of normalizing and depoliticizing our view of the Nazi years). Nonetheless, it is curious (or perhaps not curious at all) that historians of "everyday fascism" have rarely looked to cinema for evidence of the mundane, everyday aspects of life within which Nazism and its crimes unfolded. Indeed, what better place than the cinema to find traces of the choices, emotions, and coping mechanisms of ordinary Germans? This, of course, is the entry point for recent work by film historians on Nazi cinema. As Linda Schulte-Sasse puts it, "Nazi movies, regardless of genre, need to be studied in themselves and anchored in the context of their culture's moral and aesthetic values. To begin understanding these we have to consider the anxieties and fantasies that find their way into aesthetic products like movies."[4]

But in order to fully consider aesthetic products like movies, it is helpful to have some model of the aesthetic as well as some understanding of the cultural function of entertainment and the structures of desire that make film viewing both pleasurable and difficult to analyze. While recent research on Nazi cinema certainly reflects trends in German historiography, it also responds to wider debates within film studies—the discipline that has been historically engaged with examining cinema's political, cultural, and aesthetic forms. The best new work on Nazi cinema intervenes in these debates, especially those that have animated the field for a decade and more, namely, the relative status of classical (Hollywood) narrative cinema and popular (European) film. The stress here, as marked by punctuation, is on the classical and the popular (which is not to say that the Hollywood/Europe opposition has lost its force or currency, as I will suggest later on). Put simply, Nazi cinema raises questions about the peculiar continuities within the discontinuities of film history—and not only German film history—and urges a rethinking of what have now become commonplace terms and categories in the field of film studies. Was Nazi cinema merely a version of the classical Hollywood cinema? What makes a cinema "classical" in the first place?[5] Is Hollywood merely a synonym for "U.S." consumer culture or a covering term for an aesthetic that is "conventional" or "norm establishing"? Furthermore, if films of the Third Reich "appear readable in terms of classical narrative in much the same way as Hollywood films of the 1930s"[6]—and film scholars have certainly claimed this to be true—to what extent did the popularity of Nazi film promote distinctly national preferences and designs?

These questions move us beyond Theodor Adorno and Max Horkheimer's high-modernist equation of the U.S. culture industry with German fascism. But they don't take us much beyond the perennial issues about the status of Hollywood classicism and of alternatives to it that have vexed film scholars. Indeed, ever since the inception of film studies as an academic discipline, theorists and critics have attempted to find "alternatives" to Hollywood (as a style and as an economic system)—sometimes within Hollywood (auteur criticism, for example), sometimes in independent and avant-garde practices (Laura Mulvey in "Visual Pleasure and Narrative Cinema"), and sometimes in European art cinemas (the list here is certainly long, but the New German cinema or Weimar cinema serve as excellent examples).

And yet, for all the effort to find alternatives, Hollywood cinema remains privileged as much in international markets as in the marketplace of ideas. As film theory developed in the 1970s and 1980s, Hollywood cinema and U.S. culture remained the central focus of study.[7] Virtually every major theoretical formulation over the last thirty years has taken Hollywood film as a model and U.S. culture as the starting point for discussion of any number of issues, whether narrative conventions, sexual difference, spectatorship, audiences, genres, or stars (from Christian Metz and Raymond Bellour and Laura Mulvey to David Bordwell and Kristin Thompson, Mary Ann Doane, Linda Williams, and others). But the urge to find alternatives to Hollywood persists unabated in film studies, as seen in the proliferation of appeals to a "cinema of attractions" as well as in approaches to "popular European film."

Indeed, just as Laura Mulvey's essay on visual pleasure inspired a veritable industry in feminist film criticism and theory in the 1980s, Tom Gunning's "Cinema of Attractions" essay has encouraged and sustained a wealth of new research in film history in the 1990s.[8] According to Gunning, the cinema of attractions marks both a historical period (filmmaking between 1895 and 1907) and an alternative aesthetic based on showing rather than telling, exhibitionism rather than voyeurism, visual spectacle and its display rather than psychological narrative and its strictures of dramatic motivation and closure. While notably oblivious to gender (Gunning says little about the way in which the female body functions as a main "attraction" in the cinema of attractions), Gunning's essay has nonetheless been taken up by feminist and traditional film historians alike.[9] Part of the reason is that Gunning's model appears to offer a way out of the negative view of pleasure advanced by Mulvey—and a way of replacing abstract concepts of visual pleasure (as well as psychoanalytic concepts) with historically grounded studies of popular entertainment forms. More than this, however, the "cinema of attractions" provides an alternative to Hollywood "classicism" by locating visual effects precisely *within* Hollywood classicism. As Gunning explains, "The cinema of attractions . . . dominates cinema until about 1906-1907. . . . [It] doesn't disappear with the dominance of narrative, but rather goes underground, both into certain avant-garde practices and as a component of narrative films, more evident in some genres (e.g., the musical) than in others."[10]

This parenthetical reference to the musical is especially interesting for historians of German cinema, given the commercial longevity and popularity of this genre in German culture and its prominent position in Nazi film. Interesting, too, is the way in which the cinema of attractions both challenges and preserves (or preserves by challenging) a view of Hollywood classicism. After all, if attractions go "underground" after 1907 in certain avant-garde practices, they simultaneously remain front and center in what was a staple of the U.S. cinema and emblematic of Hollywood-style entertainment worldwide; that is to say, the classical Hollywood musical.[11]

While the cinema of attractions model has proven to be remarkably influential, it is not the only approach that challenges the dominance of Hollywood cinema in recent histories and theories of film. Since 1989,

Richard Dyer and Ginette Vincendeau have been active, organizing conferences, writing essays, and editing books devoted to "popular European
cinema." By this they mean an indigenous and often local commercial
European cinema, as against the standard understanding of European film
history, with its focus on art movements, "golden eras," and films made
by accomplished and world-famous auteurs. As they explain, "Part of the
existing map of cinema is coloured in quite clearly: there is America,
which is Hollywood, which is popular entertainment, and there is Europe,
which is art. Critics and historians of film have started to put new shades
into the picture. . . . Yet one aspect of the equation has remained stub-
bornly unacknowledged: popular entertainment cinema made by Europeans for Europeans." [12]

Obviously, there is more at stake than film history in this endeavor "to
make the popular in European cinema visible beyond national boundaries." Research on popular European film attempts, in its own way, to
forge a European Union of scholars dedicated to analyzing a transnational
media culture (by no means exclusively led by the United States) and pro-
moting a place for national media within it (as against the importation of
popular entertainment from Hollywood into Europe). "Europe has never
appeared a more contested notion, as the European Community seeks to
engineer a new economic and political (and cultural?) unity into place,"
write Dyer and Vincendeau. "We don't know what the prospects for
popular European cultures are and we shall not make much headway on
that front until we know what those cultures are and have been" (2).

The essays collected by Dyer and Vincendeau under the rubric of
"popular European cinema" achieve this fundamental objective. Taken
together, they demonstrate convincingly that there is more to European
film history than "art cinema" and auteurs, and that any European cinema
is also local and national (i.e. Italian, Polish, German or Soviet)—in other
words, more heterogeneous than film scholars have hitherto assumed.
And yet, as Nataša Ďurovičová points out in a review essay that considers
the Dyer/Vincendeau volume, "While the objects of study brought to
light do seem to be in some cases new, in some cases renewed, the modalities and formats by which they are approached are quite predictable:
individual star/theme studies, genre studies, genre/gender, stylistic influences, genre/economic approaches, and so on." [13] The same could be said
of the terms *classical* and *popular* in this volume, particularly as they circulate in studies of popular German cinema.

Among the eighteen essays in the Dyer/Vincendeau collection, two serve to represent the case of Germany. The first, Heide Schlüpmann's analysis of melodrama and social drama, focuses on early German film (with reference to Gunning's "cinema of attractions"). The second, Thomas Elsaesser's study of Reinhold Schünzel's career as popular comedian-director-producer in the tradition of Hollywood film, focuses largely on the Weimar period.[14] Both essays reflect changing views of the relationships between popular culture and national cinema in Germany, and both make reference to the classical/popular divide. In Schlüpmann's essay, early German film emerges as popular, nonclassical, and still able to resist the (bourgeois) imposition of classical (Hollywood) narrative form. In Elsaesser's essay, twenties German film emerges as firmly conventionalized, if not yet fully Americanized—evidence that popular taste was in the process of being captured by Hollywood norms.

Thus, even within the context of popular European film—of "popular entertainment cinema made by Europeans for Europeans"—Hollywood looms large as a classical narrative system and as a popular entertainment form. To be sure, the German cinema remains a special case, primarily because it was able, unlike other European film industries, to compete successfully with Hollywood in the 1920s both domestically and in Europe. By the late 1930s, the German film industry achieved nearly complete dominance of its home market and, at the same time, secured exclusive rights to manufacture, use, sell, or lease sound recording technology in central Europe and Scandinavia. As Ďurovičová explains, "It is clear that the strength of its base guaranteed Germany an unprecedented linguistic parity: indeed, with respect to the smaller European nations, the threat German sound film posed to other national cultures was analogous to that of the USA as perceived in Europe."[15] In the early part of the decade, the consolidation of UFA (Universum Film A.G.) therefore assured financial viability, while the coming of sound promoted the expansion of the German market in Europe and erected a language barrier that made Hollywood films less attractive to German audiences and exhibitors. At the end of the decade, moreover, Hollywood films were banned outright as the Nazi film industry redirected its energies toward the war effort. Thus, it is entirely appropriate that it was Nazi cinema—not Wilhelmian or Weimar cinema—that finally achieved the economic status that put an end to Hollywood dominance and extended German influence in Europe, making it perhaps the most emblematic and most successful popular European cinema of all time. Film historian Thomas Saunders puts the matter succinctly: "The simultaneous transition to talking motion pictures and realization by German cinema of its long-standing aspiration to national primacy appear causally related. . . . In the language of the mid-1920s, Germany finally had spawned a national cinema."[16]

It is understandable that scholars have had difficulties in adequately explaining the peculiar status of Nazi cinema at the intersection of popular culture, national traditions, and classical forms. Indeed, the German cinema has long served as a litmus test for several contradictory approaches to film history, as scholars attempt to account for the discontinuities within the continuities of German history (and not only film history), and to find ways of explaining the continuities that override obvious historical breaks. Thomas Elsaesser, for instance, has written extensively about Weimar cinema as an "art cinema"— a modernist-inspired "author's cinema" that was part of a deliberate industry policy of differentiating German cinema from Hollywood.[17] In analyses of individual, exemplary films, he shows, consistently and persuasively, that Weimar art cinema provided an aesthetic counterpoint to Hollywood classicism. Most recently, Elsaesser has turned his attention to Nazi film, arguing that, if Weimar cinema was artistic and modernist rather than popular or classical (in the Hollywood sense), Nazi cinema was consumerist as well as classically narrative and codified, closer to Hollywood than to the German cinema that preceded it.[18]

One could, of course, take issue with this reading of Weimar film. Weimar cinema, like the commercial cinema more generally, hardly existed as anything but a popular medium, always striving for expansion into ever wider markets.[19] Yet Elsaesser's approach to film "classicism" in this context is even more intriguing. How, for instance, do we understand Hollywood classicism in relation to German filmmaking traditions? Elsaesser's answer is to align the Third Reich with the steady growth of a "lifestyle modernism" whose characteristics of material well-being and conspicuous consumption were basically American. The problem with this formulation, of course, is the slippage between "classical cinema" and "lifestyle modernism" or consumer capitalism, which tends to elide significant differences between Nazi Germany and Depression America as well as their respective cinemas. It is important to emphasize, moreover, that in this period the German industry actually faced two sources of competition: not just Hollywood but also Moscow. In viewing Nazi cinema solely through the lens of Hollywood influence, what gets lost is Nazi Germany's distinctiveness—its own self-image as a "third way" between U.S. capitalism and Soviet communism.

In an effort to account for this distinctiveness, the November 1997

Goethe Institut/British Film Institute (BFI) conference held in London aimed explicitly to link the study of Nazi cinema to research on popular European film. Organized by Erica Carter (of the University of Warwick, where Richard Dyer and Ginette Vincendeau also teach) and Margaret Dériaz (of the Goethe Institute–London), this conference was entitled "Weimar and Third Reich Cinema: A Different Take." The event featured four talks and two responses, ranging from the representation of the trauma of the Great War to the treatment and reception of stars, gender, and race in the Third Reich. Participants included Tony Kaes, Erica Carter, Stephen Lowry, Ginette Vincendeau, Richard Dyer, and myself. Moreover, the conference was organized to coincide with two London film seasons: the BFI's "Divine Decadence" series (a presentation of Weimar classics at the National Film Theatre) and the Goethe Institut's series "Zarah Leander and Ferdinand Marian: Two Stars in the Third Reich." The flyer for the conference made clear its revisionist intentions. Dividing the major themes into three categories (history, stars, and art versus popular cinema) it asked: "What is gained—or lost—by recent shifts in German film history from a focus on auteur cinema, to reception and popular film? Can a rediscovery of popular film help us rethink the relation between Weimar and National Socialism, tracing continuities where before there was only the radical break of the Nazi takeover? And how does German cinema appear in the broader context of popular European cinema?"

The most interesting and controversial research presented at the conference involved the status of the star system in the Third Reich and the politics of historical periodization involved in such designations as "Weimar" and "Nazi" film. Erica Carter argued for the persistent influence of Weimar cinema on Nazi films as well as the pressures of Nazi ideology on the popular reception of film divas like Leander. German film stars, she explained, were seen to complement and compete with the real stars of the nation, namely, Adolf Hitler and Joseph Goebbels and other politicians. It is well known that Hitler and Goebbels were fans of cinema and followed its progress carefully, insisting on its popularity as well as its profitability in the Third Reich. It was nonetheless fascinating to see the ways in which the film industry managed to negotiate governmental pressures on the star system, and how the government attempted to make its political leaders into stars. (The tobacco industry, for example, included stamps in cigarette packs that could be pasted into various books. Some stamps were of popular stars like Leander; others were of Hitler and Goebbels themselves.) Carter emphasized the performative excesses of a star like Leander and the exotic locales of films like *La Habanera* that served at once to quote, and then to cancel out, the sexual and racial provocations of the Weimar cinema. The larger issue here, of course, was not the revelation of a lifestyle modernism or the marketing strategies and media tie-ins of a U.S.-style consumer capitalism. Rather, it was the persistence of Weimar styles and themes (the centrality of female characters; the evocation of sexual and racial differences; the tensions between materialism, individualism, and community) and their incorporation—and eventual containment—in Nazi fictions about national identity.

At stake in this and in other presentations at the conference was therefore an argument about fundamental continuities in German film history. These continuities themselves raised questions, moreover, about how to approach and integrate Nazi cinema into the broader context of popular European film (itself part of a larger task of integrating Germany and the Nazi past into the broader context of a unified Europe). Much was made of the politics of periodization in German film history, particularly regarding the problems involved in understanding this history according to traditional, political frameworks, i.e., Weimar and Nazi cinema, instead of, for example, Weimar and Third Reich cinema. This latter designation, of course, was signaled in the conference's title—"Weimar and Third Reich Cinema: A Different Take." But it was also evident in the emphasis on *popular cinema* (along the lines suggested by German film historian Klaus Kreimeier) in the sense of a cinema of formula fare and escapist diversion, rather than a purely propaganda cinema, intent on ideological control and indoctrination.[20] Throughout the day, there were some who argued for dispensing with the terms *Weimar* and *Third Reich cinema* altogether in favor of reference to twenties, thirties, and forties German film. This seemingly more neutral, decade-by-decade approach, it was argued, would help to discourage the automatic and inevitable tendency to equate German films with right-wing ideologies and extremist politics, and thus to enable scholars to see German film within a continuum of European as well as national traditions.

The problem here, of course, is that the decade-by-decade approach is no more neutral and no more "historical" than earlier conceptual frameworks. When it does occur, historical change does not automatically coincide with the turn of the decade, and, in any case, historical designations are never merely neutral—they do not exist "in" history, but rather in historiography, often in the form of an explicit (or implicit) polemic. As we have seen, the history of German cinema can be read against, and in relation to, any number of histories: German political and social history, the history of consumer capitalism, the history of aesthetic forms as well as economic and technological change. Spanning and encompassing all of these, moreover, is the history of the coming of sound and its profound impact on conceptions of national identity, audiences, genres, spectators, and stars.

One might argue, then, that the problem of periodization simply requires a subtler and more finely tuned temporal framework. Histories of the Weimar cinema, for example, typically divide the decade according to economic and aesthetic trends, such as the growth of UFA and the impact of inflation (1920–1924), the Hollywood invasion (1923–1927), Hugenberg's bailout and the Film Europe strategy (1927–1933), and so on. But even the subtlest temporal ordering does not solve the problem of how to understand film history within an international, let alone local or European, context or of how to conceptualize relationships among audiences, industries, national preferences, and styles. The history of Nazi cinema, moreover, is not simply a history of Hollywood's aesthetic imperialism or of "Hollywood in Berlin." It is also, and equally, the history of Berlin in Hollywood and of the tremendous exodus of German talent (directors, actors, actresses, and technicians) to several points west (including France and England as well as Southern California) and east (the Soviet Union). Thus, while it is misleading to assume that the propaganda ministry exercised absolute control over film production and popular taste, it is patently absurd to think that the *Entjudung* decrees of 1933 had no effect on film production or reception (as these required that no Jewish personnel be employed in any position in either German or German-owned media industry). In any event, as I suggested earlier, it is a mistake to locate Nazi cinema solely within the nexus of Hollywood/Berlin relations. For if Hollywood exercised a kind of aesthetic imperialism in Germany once its economic dominance there subsided, Germany exercised its own aesthetic and economic imperialism in Central and Eastern Europe (even if the history of this constellation of aesthetic, economic, and popular influences has yet to be written or fully explored).[21]

For all of the recent research and renewed interest, Nazi cinema remains an only partly charted territory. To date, the best histories are those that acknowledge the agendas, assumptions, and pitfalls of Nazi cinema's complicated historical status. By way of a conclusion, let me offer some final remarks about the state of Nazi cinema within the field of film studies in an effort to reflect on what has been gained—and lost—in the encounter. To begin, it is instructive to compare Eric Rentschler's recent book on Nazi cinema with Karsten Witte's earlier essays on popular film genres in the Third Reich, particularly Witte's work on the musical revue.[22] Rentschler's book is not only dedicated to Witte's memory but also devoted to extending some of Witte's most groundbreaking early insights. Writing in the 1990s, Rentschler is acutely aware of the revisionist risks implied in considering German film history from the perspective of popular culture and "everyday fascism." He is also aware of his own position as critic (explaining in his introduction that he writes "as a child of the Allies and not, like Witte, as a German coming to grips with and critically confronting a collective legacy").[23] Significantly, Rentschler approaches his subject from the vantage point of more than twenty years of debates within film studies—debates that were only just emerging when Witte first wrote about Nazi film.

In chapter after chapter, Rentschler therefore takes pains to adapt and adjust key terms that have defined the field in recent years (e.g., classical Hollywood narrative, conformist ideology versus resistant or subversive formal strategies). He also dispenses with the dubious entertainment/propaganda distinction (once favored by historians of Nazi cinema) to explore the "attractions" of a popular cinema. Unlike Gunning, however, who suggests that "attractions" go underground in thirties narrative cinema and become "tamed" by classical narrative, Rentschler argues that such attractions, in their encounter with Nazi cinema, were not only "tamed" but proved to be positively fatal. Describing the narrative development of *The Blue Light,* for example, he shows how the female lead is divested of independent life, her sexual energy transformed into legend, fetish, and commodity form. Drawing on Susan Sontag's influential ideas about Nazi art, Rentschler further claims that Nazi film spectacle is invested with an excess of narrative meaning (e.g., the celebration of death, the containment of physical desire, and inhibition of female volition). "The fascist ideal," Sontag famously wrote, "is to transform sexual energy into a spiritual force for the benefit of the community. The erotic (that is, woman) is always present as a temptation, with the most admirable response being a heroic repression of the sexual impulse."[24]

Here, as elsewhere in Rentschler's book, it is fascinating to see how Nazi cinema imbues cinematic spectacle and its attractions (especially the attractions of the female body) with meaning quite different from what theorists of early film have proposed. But what is even more interesting is that Nazi cinema might be perhaps the most classically coded cinema of all time. Rentschler puts the case this way: "Film theorists have often speculated about the ideological effects of the 'dominant cinema,' proposing that classical narratives seek to mesmerize and mystify viewers by means of imaginary seductions. The Nazi cinema offers a strikingly concrete example of such a theoretical construct put into practice."[25] The Nazi cinema, in other words, represents the theory (of classical Hollywood narrative) put into practice rather than the practice (of Hollywood filmmaking) put into theory. Neither a failed version nor poor imitation of Hollywood models, it exhibits the strategies of visual enticement and narrative containment that we have come (often too hastily) to associate with the classical Hollywood film—the subordination of space, time, and movement to the strictures of dramatic development and closure.

It was Witte's achievement, of course, to have demonstrated how visual pleasure was at once awakened and inhibited in Nazi films. Drawing on Richard Dyer's early and extremely influential essay on the Hollywood musical, Witte compared Nazi musical conventions—particularly the relationship between narrative and number—to those of Hollywood films (many of which involved the talents of German emigrants and exiles).[26] Significantly, Witte aimed to underscore the differences, rather than the similarities, between the two national traditions. "What was mobility in the Hollywood musical freezes into hierarchy in the German revue," he explains. German revue films aimed for coolness, clarity, and an economy of motion; above all else they exhibited a marked "aversion toward merely untamed ecstasy." In Nazi film, spectacle is put in the service of narrative, rather than the other way around (as suggested by the cinema of attraction argument). In this way, the German cinema developed its own approach to film classicism, which, in the context of the Third Reich, necessitated that narrative evince a "deeper meaning" and seriousness than mere (Hollywood) spectacle would allow.[27] When Witte published his essay on the German revue film, of course, the "cinema of attractions" model had not be fully formulated, the movement for "popular European film" had not yet taken hold, and Laura Mulvey's analysis of visual pleasure and narrative cinema still held sway. His conclusions nonetheless warrant our renewed attention, not only for what they have to tell us about spectacle and narrative beyond Hollywood, but also, and more importantly, for what they have to tell us about a national (or, rather nationalistic) cinema at the intersection of the classical and the popular.

THE HOTTENTOT AND THE BLONDE VENUS

ERHAPS the single most significant essay for contemporary theorists who want to call attention to the construction, indeed, the "constructedness" of femininity for women, is Joan Rivière's 1929 essay "Womanliness as a Masquerade." As is well known, Rivière was English by birth but studied and trained to be a psychoanalyst in Germany. It is also well known (having now achieved the status of a cliché) that Rivière theorizes femininity as a performance of sexual difference on the part of women who wish for masculinity, and who then "put on a mask of womanliness or femininity as a defense to avert anxiety and the retribution feared by men" (35).[1]

Now, what seems to me especially interesting is that most debates within Weimar culture concerned the *masculinization* of women—women who engaged in a "masculine" rather than a "feminine" masquerade—women who put on the mask of masculinity to reveal it as a construction, as precisely unreal.[2] Rivière's essay thus emerges from a moment in German history (as early as 1929) when the decade-long experimentation with gender roles—which involved women's appropriation of masculine styles, gestures, and prerogatives—was in the process of being reversed and superceded by a performance of womanliness in nearly all aspects of cultural life. This becomes obvious, for example, when we compare twenties and thirties images of the New Woman that appeared in *Die Dame*, a popular woman's fashion magazine in Germany of the time. In the mid- to late 1920s, for instance, *Die Dame* represents versions of the New Woman on a continuum of realism and stylization, versions that connote masculinity and lesbianism, as well as a quintessentially feminine (and implicitly heterosexual) play with gender roles. By the early 1930s, by contrast, images of the modern woman in the magazine reveal that this earlier experimentation with gender styles has given way to a different, but no less emphatic, fashion trend: neoclassicism in hair and dress design, maternity and motherhood as ideals.

It is significant, however, that Rivière's essay deals with issues of national identity and race as well as those of sexual difference. Indeed, the patient that most preoccupies Rivière in her essay in not identified as German but rather as a woman who spent a great deal of her youth in the "Southern States of America." Interestingly, there was an intense identification with the American South, and with African Americans, on the part of many Germans at this time.[3] Many historians have attributed this identification to a shared sense of recent history among Germans, particularly after 1923, following the French deployment of African troops in the Rhineland. Stripped of its colonies by the Treaty of Versailles, Germany experienced an overturning of the colonialist paradigm, as the so-called savages they had once dominated now occupied *their* territory, just as they imagined was the case after Reconstruction in the American South.[4] But to return to Rivière: her patient who exaggerates the gestures of womanliness also repeatedly had dreams of being attacked and seduced by (and of seducing) a black man, whom she would then turn over to the authorities. This patient's racial anxieties obviously fascinate Rivière, but she doesn't do much with them, except to say that the dream is an expression of the woman's fear of reprisal for her fantasy of having "killed her mother and father"—a fear that leads her to perform womanliness with a vengeance.

Very few theorists have commented upon Rivière's brief account of her patient's dream, nor have they remarked upon how such racial and national anxieties impact on and perhaps revise Rivière's claims about femininity. The few who have, moreover, tend to suggest that race, like gender, might also be seen as a kind of "masquerade."[5] This view of course fails to take into account that race is not simply, or not only, constructed and performed. It also fails to address how gender inflects and is inflected by race, and how racial fantasy and identification involve much more complicated processes of projection and introjection, displacement and overdetermination, precisely because they take shape in specific cultural and historical contexts.

In an effort to explore these issues, I would like to reconsider a much discussed and analyzed film, Josef von Sternberg's *Blonde Venus* (1932), in relation to feminist film theory and German cultural studies, particularly as they engage with theories of gender, race, and international film culture. In my view, any analysis of this film must include a wider assessment of gender and race in the twenties and early thirties, especially with respect to the much celebrated and maligned "New Woman," who was as much a racialized as a gendered ideal. Much has been written about the German importation of and fascination with U.S. culture during this time.[6] And yet little has been said about the intersections between the New Woman (in both New York and Berlin) and the New Negro (itself a product of the Harlem Renaissance), which had an impact in Germany as well as the United States. Marlene Dietrich is a key figure here, as is the film *Blonde Venus,* particularly insofar as the film acknowledged Dietrich as an icon equally of Berlin and Hollywood.

Indeed, *Blonde Venus* is a film that self-consciously comments on Dietrich's move from Berlin to Hollywood, although her transgressive sexuality remains fundamentally linked to her "German-ness," to an exotic and fundamental foreignness at once acknowledged and denied. Like the character she plays, Dietrich / Helen Farraday is explicitly German. Much of the dialogue is in German in the opening sequences of the film, which establish how Helen meets her American scientist husband in the Black Forest (as she swims naked with a group of other female performers, who are taking a break from their next appearance on stage). *Blonde Venus* is thus literally about bringing Helen/Dietrich from Germany to the United States, where she conquers its capital (in this film, of course, America's cultural capital, New York) as well as the cultural capital of Europe (Paris).

Importantly, Dietrich's persona in this film, particularly her identity as "the Blonde Venus," was drawn from many sources, among the most important of which is Josephine Baker, whose all-black revue was a sensation in Europe of the 1920s.[7] As one of her biographers explains, Baker was an overnight sensation in Paris in September of 1926, when she first performed "The Dance of the Savages" to a distinctly jungle rhythm, wearing nothing but a bright pink feather tucked between her legs and rings of feathers circling her ankles and neck.[8] Critics at the time were equally fascinated and perplexed: "She's horrible, she's wonderful," wrote one, "Is she black? Is she white? Is that her hair I see or is her skull painted black?" Three months later, Baker traveled to Berlin, where she was similarly celebrated and reviled. One critic admitted she was supple and sensuous but

Josephine Baker in Berlin, 1926.

also called her performance a "lamentable transatlantic exhibition, which brings us back to the monkey much quicker than we descended from the monkey." Some saw in her persona "the black Venus that haunted Baudelaire." Picasso called Baker "the Nefertiti of Now."

To be sure, Baker was different from Dietrich in many ways, not least of all in her reputation for comic as well as sexual excess and in the source of her performance style in African American traditions. But Baker aspired to perform with the same kind of elegance and sexual sophistication that we now associate with Dietrich, and Dietrich clearly drew upon Baker's performances of sexual knowledge and sensual abandon, without, of course, taking this to the same extremes. (At times Baker performed completely naked, other times wearing only a banana skirt, and still other times in full male formal dress. Although a number like "Hot Voodoo" in *Blonde Venus* quotes directly from Baker's routines, it simultaneously erases the source of that quotation, in a less explicit, yet no less outrageous, play with sexual and racial identity.) Historian Nancy Nenno points out that, for the German public, Josephine Baker was not merely "the primitive but also the elegant, well-dressed, modern American woman who conquered its capital. Baker's persona and her performances coincided with Berlin's own image as both highly elegant and exceedingly decadent, as combining both American and European elements. During the 1920s, Berlin was fascinated with America and actively sought to model itself as the most 'American' of European cities."[9]

In light of Nenno's remarks, the ironies abound when we consider how the German Dietrich copied the African American Baker, quoting from her performances and career trajectory (from the stages of Harlem to the nightclubs of Paris) in her role as the "Blonde Venus" in the film of the same name. Thus was the German "New Woman" in America but a copy of an ultramodern primitivism, itself a product of an imaginary African American culture in Berlin, which evoked racial distinctions and oppositions only to push them to an uncomfortable and volatile extreme. To put this another way: at her most "American" (*Blonde Venus* is Dietrich's only film with von Sternberg where she plays a German American housewife, rather than, say, a Russian empress), Dietrich is also portrayed as "foreign" and fundamentally "German." (She meets her American husband, played by the English Herbert Marshall, in the Black Forest and never loses her accent or her propensity toward German "motherliness" in the course of the film.) And at her most "German," Dietrich imitates the performance style of an African American artist (after all, what is this

Josephine in banana costume.

Josephine in full formal attire.

German housewife doing performing in a Harlem nightclub?), whose own career flourished in Europe but foundered in the United States. Indeed, when Baker returned to the United States, searching for the success she had found in both Paris and Berlin, she was told that U.S. audiences weren't ready for a black woman who embodied both sexuality and sophistication. By that time, Dietrich was finishing her seventh and final film with von Sternberg, which firmly established her in Hollywood as both legend and star.

This brings us back to the masquerade and to representations of the New Woman, which involved a play with gender identity that was always—in Weimar as well as in Hollywood—inflected by other marks of difference: nation as well as race, sexual orientation as well as gender. In the twenties and early thirties, Hollywood and Berlin were equally part of a vital, and highly competitive, international film culture, which involved trade wars and quotas as well as the exchange of personnel (including German directors like Murnau and actors like Emil Jannings as well as U.S. actresses like Louise Brooks and directors like von Sternberg).[10] *Blonde Venus* was very much a part of this international film culture, even if it is now typically considered a classically Hollywood film, part of the Dietrich / von Sternberg cycle, or an early example of the "fallen woman" cycle or genre of the "maternal melodrama." Whereas German film scholars consider *Blonde Venus* to be a Hollywood film (and thus outside of their particular purview), Anglo-American feminist film scholars assume that the film has nothing whatsoever to do with Weimar film culture. In the pages that follow, I challenge this separation of Anglo-American feminist film theory and German cultural studies, bringing them together in a discussion of the complex intersections of race and gender and national identity in *Blonde Venus*.

It is significant, I think, that *Blonde Venus* has been central to the development of feminist film theory in Britain and the United States—and remains at the center of debate even today. In the 1970s, Laura Mulvey's thesis about visual pleasure and narrative cinema took Hitchcock's and von Sternberg's films as central examples to explore the way in which Hollywood cinema constructed the man as agent of the look, the woman as object of the gaze. Ann Kaplan also wrote about *Blonde Venus* in the wake of Mulvey's essay, in an attempt to refine ideas about female spectatorship and particular film genres, in this case, the maternal melodrama. Following this, Lea Jacobs challenged both Mulvey's and Kaplan's approach to von Sternberg's films and to the specific example of *Blonde Venus*. Turning from psychoanalytic theory to film history, Jacobs located

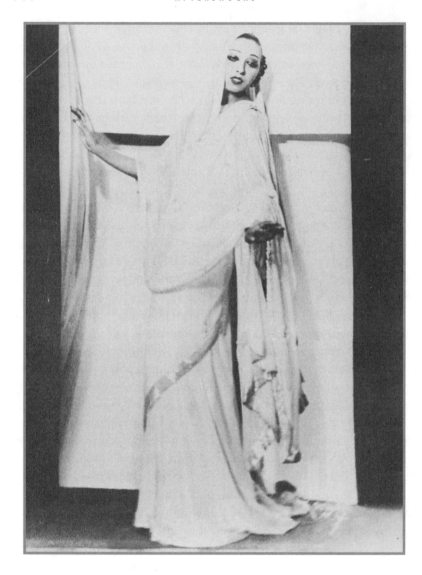

Classical elegance.

the film within the fallen-woman cycle of films in early Hollywood, and within the pressures of film censorship, analyzing the negotiations surrounding the film's production. More recently, Andreas Weiss has written about *Blonde Venus* from the perspective of its popular consumption, discussing Dietrich's status as queer icon among lesbian audiences in the 1930s. Finally, in the most recent piece published on *Blonde Venus*, Janet Staiger similarly focuses on the film's reception in an effort to demonstrate that its contemporary audiences read the film in several contradictory ways. These audiences, according to Staiger, were aware of the star discourse surrounding Dietrich's persona, such as her long-distance marriage with Rudolf Seiber, her relationship to her young daughter, her affair with von Sternberg, and her sexual relationships with women as well as men.[11]

While there is thus plenty of evidence to support the view of the centrality of *Blonde Venus* for feminist film theory, I would submit that much of this criticism misses a fundamental aspect of the film, which is precisely its direct and explicit representation of ethnicity and race. Even a most casual viewing would suggest that *Blonde Venus* presents us with a multiethnic, multicultural New York. Its cast alone sustains a range of ethnic and racialized characters, such as Irish Dan O'Connor, who runs the Harlem nightclub, or the English (although apparently "American") Ned, played by the very English Herbert Marshall, or the equally "American" Nick, played by the English Cary Grant. There is even the young Hattie McDaniel, who plays Cora in this film, introduced in the border town of Galveston, Texas, appearing as the stereotypical black "mammy" as well as the helpmate and double of the white German mother, who is similarly down on her luck. Featuring the German Dietrich, *Blonde Venus* also provides a wealth of references to both Berlin and New York culture.[12] There are, for instance, the multiple cabaret and nightclub settings, populated by a host of "decadent" and marginal figures, such as the lesbian proprietress, who advises Dietrich's Helen to get out of town, since she, too, has a child and a vengeful husband, and therefore knows of what she speaks.

But it would not be entirely accurate to claim that feminist film theorists have completely ignored issues of ethnicity and race in this film. Lea Jacobs and Mary Ann Doane, for example, each discuss *Blonde Venus* in relation to institutionalized racism and representations of race. It is suggestive, however, that Jacobs bypasses the issue of race almost as soon as she raises it, and that Doane, in her desire to show how Hollywood excluded and marginalized the black woman, can see *Blonde Venus* only as a racist text. Thus has the film been imagined as racist, even though it was a film that troubled southern racists at the time of its release.

This much is clear from Lea Jacobs's analysis of *Blonde Venus* in relation to its production context. In a chapter devoted to *Blonde Venus* in her book *The Wages of Sin,* entitled "Something Other Than a Sob Story," Jacobs suggests that the film departs from principles of narrative continuity through strategies of narrative indirection and visual ambiguity—a result of a complex series of negotiations between the director, the producers, and the censors. In analyzing the production context of the film and the multiple discussions between censors and producers, Jacobs attempts to show how the visuals of the film undermine the morality of the narrative—and how, in the process, they destabilize and undermine the film's promotion of a domestic and romantic ideal. In analyzing the censors' reports, Jacobs points out that the censors objected to three basic problems in the script, namely: (1) the representation of adultery, (2) the representation of prostitution and, (3) the representation of race. With respect to the third problem, Jacobs explains: "There is a very brief memo in the case file which indicates that Harold Hurley of the Paramount legal department was worried because Helen works in a Harlem nightclub and performs for blacks. The memo states, 'Mr. Hurley seems to share our [the Studio Relations Committee's] feeling that this would be questionable, especially in the Southern States where such equality is frowned upon.' There are several references to blacks, as well as a reference to Harlem, which are eliminated in the second and third versions of the script." [13]

Significantly, Jacobs writes at length about the negotiations surrounding the film's representation of adultery and prostitution (the two other "basic problems" in the censors' reports) but only touches upon the problem of race. Near the end of the chapter, Jacobs describes "Hot Voodoo" as a number that "verges on self-parody." "Sexuality is constructed as exotic," she explains, and is "allied with 'cannibals,' the jungle, voodoo. In performance, this set of associations is accentuated by the costumes—the chorus wears body-length primitive masks—and the music, which is decidedly percussive." According to Jacobs, Dietrich "is thereby associated with the primitive, at the center of a symbolic constellation which links female sexuality, animals, and blacks" (100). Although narrative indirection and visual ambiguity are central to her argument about the film's transgressive view of female sexuality, motherhood, and marriage, Jacobs does not detect any such indirection or ambiguity in the film's representation of race.

In her essay "Dark Continents: Epistemologies of Racial and Sexual Difference," Mary Ann Doane takes up where Jacobs leaves off, precisely by exploring the symbolic constellation of female sexuality and racial otherness. Doane argues that the term "dark continent" in Freud's writings and in psychoanalytic feminist theory has been stripped of its history, which she then attempts to restore by showing how femininity was linked to colonialist discourses of the nineteenth century. "A metonymic chain is constructed which links infantile sexuality, female sexuality, and racial otherness," she writes. "The 'lower' races, with their free sexuality and lack of neuroses would be, in a sense, unpsychoanalyzable and hence constitute the limits of psychoanalytic knowledge. . . . Just as Africa was considered to be a continent without a history, European femininity represented a pure presence and timelessness." [14]

According to Doane, there was thus a kinship between the white and black woman in the nineteenth-century imagination, but a kinship that was nonetheless limited. The civilized white woman remained the exemplar of culture, racial purity, and refinement, and hence the polar opposite of the Hottentot and the black woman, who was on the side of nature, not culture. (As Doane points out, there was, of course, an abiding fear that the white woman might "slip back" into her nature and into "blackness"—which was comparable to prostitution.) She then extends this argument through a discussion of *Blonde Venus,* situating the film itself within a larger argument about changes in nineteenth- and twentieth-century representations of racial and gender difference. If, in the nineteenth century, race was understood as an "essence," something innate and biological, in the twentieth century race was understood as a "mask," something performed and performative—significantly, however, only for the white woman. As Doane writes of *Blonde Venus:*

> In Josef von Sternberg's 1932 *Blonde Venus,* Marlene Dietrich does cross over the line separating respectable femininity from prostitution (whiteness from blackness in the nineteenth century imagination). Yet, within the maternal melodrama, the figure of the prostitute is not the target of an unambiguous censure but of sympathy manifested in the textual organization of pathos. Revised sexual mores connected with the emergence of the New Woman in the 1920s required a more flexible understanding of white female sexuality, which weakened the polarization between the respectable Victorian lady and the prostitute. Marlene Dietrich is, in fact, recuperated by the nuclear family at the end of the film. (214)

Directly following this statement, Doane suggests that *Blonde Venus* may in fact transgress racial boundaries: "Yet, the near collapse of the

moral opposition between types of white femininity threatened to collapse certain racial distinctions as well. If the white woman's excessive
femininity cannot be contained within that subclass, the status of the
upper-class white woman as guarantee of racial purity is seriously threatened." In a curious move, Doane then steps back from this view to argue
something else entirely. Near the end of her essay, she claims: "When
Marlene Dietrich emerges from the ape costume in the 'Hot Voodoo'
number, blackness is transformed from [an] essence into a disguise which
can be easily shed. . . . It is as though white femininity were forcefully
disengaged from blackness once and for all in the process of commodification of the image of white female sexuality. . . . Blackness functions here
not so much as a term of comparison (as with the Hottentot and the
prostitute), but as an erotic accessory to whiteness. The black woman . . .
becomes the white woman's mise-en-scene" (215).

For Doane, then, *Blonde Venus* demonstrates how nineteenth-century
views of racial essence and purity were transformed into a discourse that
commodified "race" as a performative style (a disguise, a mise-en-scène, a
mask) available only to whites. Marlene Dietrich, she claims, forcefully
disengages herself from blackness in order to become "a placeholder,
seemingly deprived of meaning in the racial schema." For Doane, Dietrich's performance as the Blonde Venus does not function to collapse
racial distinctions, but instead shores up and "exemplifies whiteness."

But is Dietrich's performance in *Blonde Venus* really an unambiguous
representation of whiteness, seemingly deprived of meaning in a racial
schema? And does blackness function here as mere accessory to whiteness,
or does it indeed remain a term of comparison (as with the white and
black woman, the prostitute and the Hottentot)? Finally, to what extent
does Dietrich "forcefully" or entirely disengage herself from blackness in
the course of the film? To put this another way, how might we account
for a more flexible and expansive understanding of the Dietrich persona
in this film as well as issues of race and gender in early cinema?

As I suggested earlier, a good place to start is with histories and theories
of the New Woman in both Germany and the United States, since the
"new" or "modern woman" was never simply an emancipated woman or
protofeminist icon but always (and simultaneously) a national and racial
ideal. In her research on debates in Weimar science and popular culture,
historian Lynne Frame makes this point powerfully when she writes of the
German biologists and medical practitioners of the time who worried that
modern women were losing sight of their obligation to propagate the race.

As Frame explains, these practitioners increasingly called for "the pro-
grammatic education of individuals to acquire 'biological conscience' . . .
or a personal sense of biological responsibility to society and the race,
which would govern their sexual behavior and choice of marriage part-
ner." [15] Thus did medical practitioners make the fundamental connection
between gender, nation and race, and in advocating the cultivation of a
"biological conscience," they likewise popularized pseudoscientific profiles
or taxonomies that came to identify not one, but three "New Women" or
conventionalized female types: the Gretchen, the Girl, and the Garçonne.
    What is especially interesting is the way in which these categories de-
pended upon stereotypes of national as well as gender differences. The
Gretchen, for example, was imagined to be a German woman, "the young
naïve German girl with braids," who is sexually powerless, personally passive, allied with the church and tradition. The Girl, by contrast, was considered to be an American import to Europe, the child of pioneers and
immigrants, the daring athlete, who is "sexy but without sizzle, [and]
rather coolly calculating." Finally, there was the Garçonne, the European
woman whose decadence required a French derivation, who was both
sexual and intellectual, combining a "male entrepreneurial sense" with
feminine devotion, signaling a character-type at once androgynous, artistic, and independent (12). As Frame points out, these three female types
populated the pages of German illustrated magazines in both image and
prose. In the context of a discussion of Marlene Dietrich and international
film culture, a question immediately emerges: Where would we locate
Dietrich within these categories?
    At first glance, it would seem as if Dietrich traverses all three apparently
competing categories: the German hausfrau, the coolly calculating American girl, the androgynous and independent French Garçonne. (Such a
range of roles is certainly supported by Blonde Venus, a film in which Dietrich plays herself as well as a character named Helen who traverses settings in Germany, the United States, and France. In the course of the
narrative, moreover, Dietrich/Helen takes on—indeed, performs—several female identities: water nymph, actress, devoted mother and wife,
glamorous star, outlaw, and prostitute, who, significantly, in view of my
earlier remarks about Rivière's patient, both finds her way and loses herself in the American South.) And yet, an American star like Janet Gaynor,
whose role as "wife" in Murnau's American film Sunrise would seem more
accurately to capture the (imaginary) image of the German "Gretchen":
the naïve girl with braids, who is heroic, sexually powerless, and allied

Josephine in the nude.

"Hot Voodoo" number, from *Blonde Venus*, 1932.

Marlene/Helen in full formal attire, from *Blonde Venus*, 1932.

Marlene/Helen in a border town, from *Blonde Venus*, 1932.

with church and tradition. If Dietrich was never quite the "naïve girl with braids," she was not exactly an American girl, "sexy but without sizzle," dazzling and bewitching, lacking in womanly warmth. That description appears more appropriately captured by the reception of Louise Brooks in Berlin, a U.S. actress who sparked controversy when she played the part of the German Lulu in Pabst's *Pandora's Box*. The American "Girl," moreover, was never simply imagined, in either Germany or the United States, as wholly or one-dimensionally "white." Indeed, Josephine Baker drew upon constructions of American Girl culture in Europe, representing herself as an innocent jungle "child" and daring athlete whose "African" sexuality she knowingly constructed for her sophisticated and world-weary European audiences.

It is impossible to examine the twenties and thirties—in either the United States or Germany—without understanding the complex and important role that African American culture played at this time. There was, first and foremost, the rejuvenating quality of African American jazz, which came to be figured as the absolute opposite to European intellectualism and its obsession with the past. Then there was the wider context of the Harlem Renaissance, spanning the immediate postwar period and up until the Great Depression, as Harlem reigned as the unrivaled center of African American culture. Harlem witnessed the flowering of African American literature, music, dance, art, and social commentary in the neighborhoods newly transformed by the Great Migration of African Americans to the North. Never before had so many people embraced the African American community's productions, expressions, and styles. And never before had the qualities of the "primitive" been inflected by the qualities of what was then considered the "ultramodern": jazz, certainly, but also cinema, dance (especially the Charleston), and theatrical performance.

It is within this context that we might best understand a film like *Blonde Venus,* and particularly the notorious "Hot Voodoo" number, which has either been ignored by feminist film theorists (or, rather, passed over in embarrassed silence) or dismissed as thoroughly and unredeemably racist. As both Lea Jacobs and Mary Ann Doane have argued, the sexual charge of "Hot Voodoo" derives from a series of oppositions that simultaneously overlap, collapse, and recombine: Dietrich is both animal and human, white and not white, primitive and modern, but finally, ultrawhite and ultramodern in her performance of a modern primitivism. Significantly, however, such ultramodern primitivism was Josephine Baker's legacy, too. While some critics have decried Baker as an agent of minstrelsy, she was nonetheless, and quite undeniably, the first modern international black star.

This point is made forcefully by Fatimah Tobing Rony in her recent book *The Third Eye: Race, Cinema, and Ethnographic Spectacle*. Rony argues that Baker, as an African American woman in Europe, was placed in an almost impossible position. "Baker believed that she was making strides for African Americans as a black star in a white entertainment world," Rony writes, "even as she understood that Euro-American culture constructed her as 'nothing but a body to be exhibited in various stages of undress.'"[16] According to Rony, Baker was trapped by an "Ethnographic spectacle" created by the media—neither man nor woman, neither human nor animal—she was also acutely aware of her predicament and directly responded to it. "Since I personified the savage on the stage," Baker once remarked, "I tried to be as civilized as possible in daily life."[17] Racialized "as a sign of the Primitive, contained by a discourse that could only read her as ethnographic spectacle," Rony concludes, "Baker in her extraordinary use of masquerade appears to be winking at the viewer."[18]

Although Dietrich was racialized in a different way, as a sign of the decadent European, could the same ironic self-conscious also be attributed to her performance as the Blonde Venus? Mary Ann Doane, it will be recalled, locates Dietrich's "Hot Voodoo" number within the context of the commodification of blackness as an "accessory" for white women—a mask or costume to be worn and removed at will. Obviously, as I suggested earlier, *Blonde Venus* is fundamentally about performance (in which Dietrich/Helen masquerades as a water nymph, a dutiful wife and mother, a nightclub performer, a prostitute, a bag lady, and so on, with no performance, and no presence, stronger or more palpable than Dietrich's own). But does Dietrich disengage herself from blackness, as Doane suggests? Or is her position in this film much more ambivalent, as suggested, for instance, by the dizzying fusion of incompatible images in the "Hot Voodoo" number, or even by Helen's friendship and identification with Cora / Hattie McDaniel, who helps her protect her child and elude the long arm of the law?

Rather than an uncomplicated example of the commodification of race or of notions of whiteness, *Blonde Venus* remains, for me, the site of a complex discourse about race, nationality, and gender in early U.S. cinema. This discourse, moreover, is indebted as much to Weimar as to U.S. culture, as well as to wider international debates about performance, sexual difference, and masquerade. In its play with racial distinctions and oppositions, *Blonde Venus* undeniably pushes racial and gendered stereotypes to an uncomfortable and highly volatile extreme. And yet, the Helen/Dietrich character remains as much a "foreigner" as a "white" woman, more German than American, a variation on the ethnographic spectacle, which, like Baker, she also attempted to shape and control. Instead of a one-dimensional figure of whiteness, lacking in irony, the "Blonde Venus" might therefore be more usefully seen as a kind of hybrid figure—one that intentionally fuses seemingly incompatible images that cannot be easily unified into a cohesive whole. In this regard, we would do well to recall the throwaway line given to the detective, who traces Helen/Dietrich to Galveston, only to fail to recognize her, as they sit together, over a beer, in this racially mixed border town. "You don't look like the other women in this place," he says. To which she responds, "Give me time."

FILM FEMINISM AND NOSTALGIA FOR THE SEVENTIES

N A recent article in the Sunday *New York Times,* included in the Arts and Leisure section, I read about the shift from film to video technology that occurred in the television news business around 1975. Film was laborious and expensive, the author explained. Hence, the welcome convenience and speed of videotape, despite the inevitable "generational deterioration" that resulted from its widespread use in television newsgathering. "Generational deterioration," the author remarked, "describes what happens when you make copies of copies of copies, an effect common in videotape (and the genealogy of Europe's royal families). By the fourth or fifth generation the loss of quality is obvious and one is left with only a dim facsimile, a blurred and colorless rendering of the original." [1]

A similar phenomenon might help describe what is now called "seventies film theory" or rather what is now dismissed as a thoroughly outdated and theoretically arcane tradition of Lacanian film semiotics. And yet, for all of the bad press and inevitable generational deterioration, seventies film theory has recently become the source of much debate and even more nostalgia among feminist women. In book-length autobiographies and essays rooted in personal reflection, women who lived through this period now reflect back on it with mixed feelings of pride and sadness, pleasure and displeasure—and with an overriding determination to defend its legacy and expose its conceits. To my mind, this is an immensely interesting development that raises all kinds of questions especially relevant for us today. For this reason, I would like to focus on this feminist nostalgia for seventies film theory. I want to suggest how we might better understand this nostalgia, and how this nostalgia, in turn, might enable us to better reflect on the past, present, and future of feminist film theory.

SPACE, PLACE, SCREEN

To begin, I want to turn to the site of a large gathering of international scholars at the 1999 Society for Cinema Studies Conference, held in West Palm Beach, Florida, and organized around the large and inclusive theme of "Media Industries: Past, Present, and Future." As with any national conference, this supposed "theme" functioned mostly as a broad rubric for an array of very different kinds of work, spanning film and television and video and internet studies as well as formalist and cognitive and feminist approaches to them. What was new this year, however, were two large plenary sessions, the first devoted to "Film and Media Theories," the second to "Film and Media Histories." Both plenaries were scheduled to take place near the beginning of the conference, and in their own time slots, outside of the regular conference schedule, so that all SCS members could attend. As a consequence, both plenaries generated a great deal of anticipation and excitement and were extremely well attended.

As a member of the audience at both events, what struck me immediately was the time-honored practice of separating "theory" from "history"—or, more to the point, the practice of separating feminist work (which, no matter what its approach, is considered "theory") from the work of history proper. I have written about this before, almost ten years ago, in fact, in a special issue of *Camera Obscura* dedicated to feminism and film history. In that essay (which is included as chapter 2 in this volume), I began with a quote from Australian cultural critic Meaghan Morris, who explained: "It's now too easy to assume that if a text is labeled 'feminist' theory, then it can't properly 'count' or 'figure'" as anything else ('woman's sphere,' again)."[2] If nearly ten years ago, it was all too easy to relegate feminist work to the specialized realm of gender criticism or speculative theory, it now seemed, in the context of a major film conference on the edge of the millenium, all too banal and excruciatingly familiar to witness the same old institutional division of labor—in which "historians" pursued the realm of the industrial, the quantifiable, the concretely known, while "feminists" explored the more intangible realm of theoretical speculation.

To be sure, the history plenary was given second billing to the theory event (thereby emphasizing the esteem with which the discipline treats its theorists, as opposed to its historians). Nevertheless, what struck me in the history plenary was not simply the absence of feminist historians (indeed, the feminist theorists on the theory plenary had quite a bit to say about film history). It was rather the stunning neglect of any feminist work in film history and, indeed, the absence of any reference whatsoever to feminist filmmakers or critics or any other trace of women's presence in forging film studies as a discipline or in establishing alternative modes of filmmaking. Not surprisingly, Tom Gunning presented the very best paper on the history plenary. He argued that film studies must maintain its position as an avant-garde discipline, in the tradition of Jack Smith and Jonas Mekas and, even further back, that of Joris Ivens, whose work Gunning had recently viewed while doing archival research in Amsterdam. All of this was compelling and persuasive, but as I sat through the other three talks, which ranged markedly in quality and interest and tone, I kept thinking about Gunning's remarks. Most of all, I kept thinking about the absence of any reference to feminist filmmakers and the way in which Gunning defined film's "avant-garde" tradition in rather traditional terms (which, for all that, ultimately seemed that much less "avant-garde" to me).

If the history plenary was disappointing, the theory plenary proved much more intellectually challenging and engaging. Of the five plenary speakers, three were major U.S. feminist film scholars: Teresa de Lauretis, Linda Williams, and Mary Ann Doane. All three addressed the conference theme of "Media Industries: Past, Present, and Future." But only de Lauretis and Doane took on this theme directly, expressing what seemed to many to be a disturbing "nostalgia" for seventies film theory, but what I heard as a lament for the loss of its urgency and excitement and political purpose. De Lauretis sounded this argument most forcefully (with the title of her talk, "Out of the Past," marking both the mood and tone of forties film noir as well as de Lauretis's own assessment of her ambivalent presence on the panel). She intended, I think, to be a voice from the past, coming not only "out of the past," but also in the name of the past—a past she specifically named as "seventies film theory." Within this project, she included an array of theorists, such as Christian Metz and Stephen Heath and Jean Louis Baudry, whose names, she pointed out, are rarely even mentioned anymore.

Mary Ann Doane's remarks were, as always, rich and complex and

often exceedingly abstract. In her talk, "The Object of Theory," she re-
flected on the end of cinema as well as on the end of certain trends in
cinema studies. If cinema is indeed an invention without a future (as
Lumiere claimed nearly a hundred years ago), Doane seemed to suggest
that the object of its theory is equally so. At a time when the accelerated
proliferation of media culture creates a kind of signifying environment or
space, in which individual media instances are not texts to be read but
instances to be celebrated or appropriated or resisted, then the object of
seventies film theory has indeed come to an end. And for Doane, this
sense of an ending is the source of considerable frustration and regret, as
evidenced by her comments in the question-and-answer period, which
emphasized the primacy of the film text, the necessary abstraction of film
theory, and the fundamental importance of psychoanalysis.

If I have lingered too long on these presentations, I have done so, at
least in part, in an effort to capture the tone and mood of the plenary and
of the audience response that followed. There were a few questions from
the floor, largely from established feminist film theorists who focused precisely on the nostalgia—on the sense that film theory, and especially,
given the reputations of the speakers, that feminist film theory was somehow at an end. How could feminist film theory be at an end, asked Maureen Turim, given the stature and longevity and the esteem in which it is
still held (as evidenced by the presence of the three plenary speakers)? I
myself raised a question about the understanding of history implied in
both de Lauretis's and Doane's talks. Rather than assert the force of a
chronological, linear, or homogeneous temporal schema—past, present,
and future, and in that order—in which seventies film theory and the
cinema itself are progressively abandoned and elided, why not focus on
the discontinuous and non-homogeneous structure of historical time?[3] In
other words, why not shift the emphasis from what feminist film theory
is (or seems to be) now in an effort to recall and redeem its failed opportunities and unrealized promises? Why not name and thus call into existence that which otherwise might be lost to history and to contemporary
thought? Perhaps my question would have been more appropriately addressed to the speakers on the history plenary.

In any event, what transpired next was even more intriguing. In the
corridors and at the reception following the theory plenary, I talked about
the session with younger scholars and many graduate students, several of
whom were attending the SCS for the very first time. Most, if not all of
them, were absolutely turned off by what they had heard; some were even

literally dismissive, if only mildly contemptuous, of the remarks made by
this generation of scholars, whom they otherwise respected and admired.
But what was all this talk about the past, they said? And why the seventies?
Why was this time singled out for its bold innovations and political purpose? Wasn't the present, the 1990s, also a time of innovation and political
energy and new directions in film and media studies, particularly in terms
of questions of sexuality, not to mention race? Why did this older generation of scholars insist on clinging to the past (a past that marked the child-
hood of many of these younger scholars and students, who seemed to
resent the implication that, by accident of birth, they were barred from
understanding what could only be experienced firsthand)?

My own reaction to these reactions of a younger generation was initially one of irritation. I identified with and thought I understood what
the speakers were talking about, and I had little patience for what seemed
to me a rather uninformed and indifferent attitude toward the plenary
speakers' desire to sustain the cinema and historical knowing against the
complex erosions of time. After all, it seemed to me, they were talking
about a time and a theoretical project that are worthy of our nostalgia. As
for the feeling among younger scholars—a feeling that they were somehow excluded from a past they never experienced—I could only respond:
just because you didn't live through a historical moment doesn't mean
you can't know anything about it. As someone who has long been drawn
to German culture of the 1920s—and as someone who is neither German
nor a contemporary of that time—I know there is much to be learned
from a past we haven't experienced directly. Indeed, historical hindsight
allows us to see what contemporaries of the time sometimes cannot,
namely, that particular decades—the seventies just as much as the twenties—are not so much unified "periods" but rather precarious conglom-
erates of tendencies, aspirations, and activities. In other words, they are
complex cultural spaces, much like the audience for the two seemingly
unrepentantly "nostalgic" talks.

But the more I thought about the plenary, the nostalgia, and the resistance to the plenary's nostalgia among younger scholars, the more I felt
uneasy about my own position. Certainly the younger scholars were right
to insist that the 1990s were a time of innovation and change and exciting
new directions in the field. More than this, I kept wondering, why were
the speakers (and why was Teresa de Lauretis especially) nostalgic for
the 1970s? To be sure, the feminist movement emerged and expanded at
this time, but it was also embattled from all sides, and even within its

ostensible ranks, there were significant intergenerational hostilities, contradictory constituencies, lots of disagreement, and potentially volatile
coalitions. So why the nostalgia? When I thought about it further, and
when I thought especially about feminist film theory (rather than the
feminist movement more generally), I wondered, why not the eighties as
well? After all, it was only in the 1980s that feminist film theory truly came
into its own, with a host of major publications that set the agenda for a
range of new work and new questions and new avenues for research, and
that included, among many other titles, de Lauretis's own book *Alice
Doesn't* and Mary Ann Doane's *The Desire to Desire*. Why, then, would de
Lauretis focus on the prehistory of feminist film theory and the debates
and discussions engendered in dialogue with Metz and Heath and Baudry,
whose work was itself hardly (or at least not obviously) feminist at all?

In one of those fortuitous moments, I decided to visit the book display
before I left for the airport for the long trip home. There, at the Duke
University Press table, I was encouraged by a young African American
woman, who was also looking for something to read on the plane, to
purchase B. Ruby Rich's new book *Chick Flicks: Theories and Memories of
the Feminist Film Movement*. This young woman told me that it was a really
good read: "Skip the essays themselves," she said, "what's really worth
reading is the author's autobiographical remarks—about people, about
conferences, about major fights and other gossip—that put the essays
themselves into context." I immediately flipped through the book, only to
open it midway to a place where Rich was talking about *New German
Critique*, the Center for Twentieth Century Studies, *Camera Obscura*, and
Milwaukee film conferences in the seventies. She wasn't exactly positive
about each and every one of these entities, but her remarks hit home, and
I found myself unable to put the book down. Ruby Rich was talking about
my intellectual history and both my past and current institutional affiliations. Some of my first essays were published in *New German Critique*, a
journal I have always admired. In the early 1990s, I coedited a special issue
of *Camera Obscura* on feminism and film history. Since 1986, I have been a
faculty member at the University of Wisconsin–Milwaukee, the site of the
infamous Milwaukee film conferences, most of which were organized by
my friend and colleague Patricia Mellencamp. Finally, I myself have organized a conference, "Film, Photography, and History," at the Center for
Twentieth Century Studies, a research institute on the UWM campus that
sponsored some of the earlier and more controversial film conferences in
the 1970s.

Reading *Chick Flicks* was therefore like reading about places and people and events I knew very well. At the same time, it defamiliarized those places and people and events and, more importantly, it underscored exactly why feminist film theorists might be nostalgic for the seventies. In the early part of the decade, as Rich explains, film feminism engaged women from all sectors of film activity: filmmakers, distribution collectives, journalists, scholars, and festival organizers. Emerging in tandem with and in relation to the antiwar movement and New Left politics, film feminism was imbued with the spirit of political activism, a belief in the possibility of change, and a profound internationalism. It was a global rather than a narrowly U.S. movement, and its internationalism provided the wellspring for a great part of its theoretical energy. Finally, and most significantly for Rich, film feminism in the seventies was not yet an academic area or specialty. In these years, the academy was not the only or even the most important site for feminist work, since this work emerged within discussions and debates across several places simultaneously: on campuses, certainly, but also in screenings, retrospectives, and festivals, and in the pioneering work of international women filmmakers.

Although I, too, was a film student in the 1970s, I was just that much younger than Rich and the others she mentions as part of the seventies generation. So although I knew about many of the events and debates and debacles she describes, I experienced many of them belatedly or second-hand. (I attended a Milwaukee film conference in 1982, for instance, when I was a doctoral student at the University of Iowa, but I was neither an established nor even a vaguely recognizable academic at the time, merely a curious member of the audience.) My own response to Rich's narrative of the feminist film movement, in other words, was at once one of recognition and agreement as well as difference and variation. We inhabited a shared historical and social environment, less a unified period than a precarious mixture of tendencies, aspirations, and activities that, more often than not, manifested themselves independently of one another. Rich anticipates this response to her book: "In truth, any number of women who lived through these times could spin out entirely different narratives in which they appear as central players. And we'd all be right. They were exciting times."[4]

OUTSIDE/INSIDE

Despite this gesture of historical inclusion, I have heard that many feminist scholars, especially those who appear in the pages of Rich's book, are deeply angered by her version of the feminist film movement and particularly by her characterization of academic feminism as it emerged in the 1980s. Rich herself seems to rely on George Santayana's famous dictum—"Those who cannot remember the past are condemned to repeat it"—in her repeated emphasis on the need for younger women to understand and embrace the activism of the 1970s. "For the younger generations that have come of age in the academy over the past two decades," she writes in her introduction, the "historical amnesia [about the early years of the seventies] has canceled out a birthright that would have been helpful in terms of avoiding the repetition of certain errors, learning how to negotiate across differences, and reconciling the personal with the professional—if not always the political" (1). For her detractors, Rich's remarks about academic, especially psychoanalytic feminism, recall another of Santayana's quotable remarks: "History is a pack of lies told about events that never happened told by people who weren't there."

But from a historical perspective, where, exactly, is "there"? I have heard a few of my feminist colleagues claim that Ruby Rich situates herself at the center of the history of film feminism, thereby implying that her version of history is *the* version of history, that her vision of the past is *the way it really happened*. *Chick Flicks* is in large part an autobiography, so it is not surprising that Rich herself features centrally in the book. But *Chick Flicks* is also a polemic, a kind of call to arms, which aims to speak to a nineties generation in order to restore a sense of "lived experiences now forgotten, shelved, or denied by those who went through them" (1).

In Rich's estimation, the seventies were a time of enthusiasm and inclusion and political activism, in which a broad and international coalition of feminist women struggled to invent new forms, new forums, and new theories. In the 1980s, however, film feminism as a *movement* evolved into film feminism as an *academic discipline,* a field entirely captivated (or so says Rich) by psychoanalysis, textual analysis, and academic concerns. Gone were the broad coalitions and contradictory communities that so defined the 1970s. And in their place, there was now an academically hierarchical, heterosexist, party-line feminist film theory, with its own conferences, its own journals, its own "professionalized, parochial, self-absorbed, and deracinated writing" (6). For Rich, it is no wonder that feminist cultural work hit an impasse in the nineties. As she explains: "What sprang up in the seventies and was institutionalized in the eighties has been stagnating in the nineties, its vigor bypassed by queer culture, on the one hand, multiculturalism on the other, and cultural studies in general" (5)

As is obvious from this brief summary, Rich heaps much of the blame for the current malaise on *academic* feminists, particularly those who promote the values of semiotics, textual criticism, and psychoanalysis. Unlike these women, who, according to Rich, became preoccupied in the eighties and nineties with tenure and promotion and the rewards of an academic career, Rich herself remained an unrepentant seventies radical, an "itinerant critic" and often bemused observer of trends within university life. One can only be impressed by the range of Rich's achievements and inspired by her efforts throughout the past three decades "to think," as she puts it, "creatively and rigorously outside of the university" (209). (It has also occurred to me, as former coordinator of a large graduate program, that her words and example have special resonance in the nineties, when academic jobs are scarce and job security is quickly becoming a thing of the past.)

But while Rich tells an interesting and compelling story about the academy from a position on its margins, her characterization of academic feminism does not always, or does not entirely, ring true. For instance, she criticizes the psychoanalytic feminism that emerged in the late seventies for its homophobia, its orthodoxy, and its theoretical jargon, claiming that it single-handedly determined theoretical agendas in the eighties and thereby closed down possibilities for real debate or change. This polemic leads to troubling generalizations and overstatements, as is obvious from the following passage:

> I think that the influence of psychoanalysis as a hegemonic theory with a singular world-view has been a disaster as a literary device and critical tool in literary analysis and feminist studies. . . . Lesbian culture is going strong in the nineties. It is heterosexual feminism that has lost its way, at least in the world of film theory. The psychoanalytic and poststructuralist agendas, once dominant, fostered a closed-shop atmosphere with an excess of homogeneity, inbred self-referentialism, and a tendency toward stasis and atrophy. (379–380)

Rich's characterization of psychoanalytic feminism here sounds as monolithic and authoritarian as that of the feminists she accuses. (Did de Lauretis or Doane or Modleski or Silverman really practice the same kind of psychoanalytic criticism?) Indeed, in Rich's narrative of the movement of film feminism into the academic mainstream, white heterosexual women emerge as the enemy of feminism, and psychoanalysis becomes the most potent source of homophobia and racism. This kind of argument, of course, is not entirely new; Rich had made similar (if less exaggerated) claims about the dangers of psychoanalysis for feminism throughout the seventies and eighties (as is documented in the essays included in her book). But coming from a self-proclaimed "outsider" to the university and academic disputes, Rich's version of the demise of film feminism seems overly partisan and one-sided. I sympathize with her critique of the opaque language and narrow assumptions of overly specialized psycho-analytic discourse. But I am less convinced by her recourse to blaming white, heterosexual, middle-class women for the failure of radical politics (an old ploy by the old Left) and by her wholesale dismissal of eighties film theory.

I am hardly alone in this view and, as an academic feminist myself, I suppose that's not surprising. And yet, in what might be seen as a compel-ling counter-statement to Rich's book (if it were not written nearly ten years earlier), Janet Bergstrom has provided another kind of history of feminism in the seventies, in a 1990 essay entitled "American Feminism and French Film Theory," to which I would like to turn now. Much like Rich, Bergstrom captures in this essay the sense of urgency and excitement that initially fueled the feminist film project. But speaking as someone from inside the academy, she takes pains to trace the movement from activism to theoretical reflection—and underscores the reasons why such a movement became necessary in the first place. The "dominant cinema," she points out, initially meant Hollywood cinema, which was seen as an insidious adversary, an institution that had produced not only racism and sexism but also the Vietnam War. "Throughout this period," Bergstrom explains, "two questions were raised again and again: How to analyze existing cinema? How to create a new, radical cinema? To begin with, it was necessary to establish a position from which to speak at all, in the most literal sense. The question: who speaks? had become highly politi-cized in the early 1970s. The answer was obvious in the sixties: men spoke. . . . Then, the question was *how* to speak, with what conceptual tools to go beyond sex roles and the common practice of condemning films as sexist."[5] For Bergstrom, potential answers to these questions emerged in British and French ways of speaking about the cinema, notably semiotics and psychoanalysis, which cut through the seeming naturalness of visual representation, which had hitherto seemed resistant to analysis.

Although important new work appeared early in the decade (for in-stance, Claire Johnston's pamphlet *Notes on Women's Cinema* was published in 1972), the emergence in 1975 of several groundbreaking works literally transformed the questions that feminists were asking. As Bergstrom points out, the year 1975 saw the publication of the famous "Psychoanalysis and Cinema" issue of the French journal *Communications,* which included work by Metz, Raymond Bellour, and Thierry Kuntzel. The British journal *Screen's* own "Psychoanalysis and Cinema" issue, which focused on Metz's "Imaginary Signifier" appeared shortly thereafter, and its next issue, also published in 1975, featured Laura Mulvey's epoch-making "Visual Pleasure and Narrative Cinema." Bergstrom describes her own efforts, as coeditor of the new U.S. feminist journal *Camera Obscura,* to bring French and British theoretical material to a U.S. audience. She emphasizes the general feeling at the time of a shared, international project, and the importance for feminism of forging a more complex understanding of textual codes and conventions as well as sexual difference, understood to be within the realm of ideological analysis. Bergstrom says: "We felt that the most important articles *for* feminism were not necessarily those written *as* feminist or from a feminist point of departure. Likewise, we thought that analysis of sexual difference was central to contemporary film theory, not restricted in its consequences to a feminist sub-section" (187).

   Much like Rich, Bergstrom also traces an unfortunate decline in the feminist project, which began in the late eighties and early nineties. But because she was centrally affiliated with the project that Rich deems responsible for this decline, Bergstrom necessarily provides us with another point of view. To be sure, she does acknowledge (in fact, she anticipates by almost a decade) the critique of academic feminism advanced by Rich. In an introduction to a special issue of *Camera Obscura* that she coauthored with Mary Ann Doane, she asks: "How has feminist film criticism, which was marginal and controversial at the outset, come to be seen so quickly as an orthodoxy, a monolithic enterprise?"[6] To which she answers:

To some extent, this is undoubtedly linked to its alliance with psychoanalysis, which has always been confronted by the spectre of orthodoxy. But it is also a function of feminist film criticism's academic entrenchment. Critical and theoretical texts which conveyed a political and intellectual urgency in the 1970s have become part of a canon which graduate students must master for their oral exams or dissertation projects. . . . There is a feeling among many, whether they were veterans of the sixties or not, that feminist film and media theory has been cut off from its original sense of bold innovation and political purpose. It is time to reexamine our priorities and to remember a sense

of shared goals in the light of our history over the past fifteen years, in
order to renew the sense of vitality that once kept film studies from
the self-perpetuating careerism that inevitably invades any academic
(publish-or-perish) discipline. (15–16)

When I read these words, I was struck by the way they resonated with
the central argument of *Chick Flicks*. Like Rich, Bergstrom emphasizes the
need for film feminism to renew its sense of purpose and underscores
the pitfalls of an enterprise that has only to do with careerism or academic
status. Also like Rich, Bergstrom stresses the need for feminists to forge
bridges between generations and to reclaim their contested and variegated
history. Significantly, however, Bergstrom does not dismiss feminist film
theory's success as an academic enterprise or malign its institutionalized
status. As she points out, "It would be a mistake to presume that the term
'institutionalization' automatically implies that which is politically and
ideologically reprehensible. We all inhabit institutions of one sort or another (the family, the press, legal, educational, governmental institutions)
and persistently work within, on the border, and outside of these institutions" (16). Finally, from her perspective from within the academy, Bergstrom argues that what has been lost in the nineties is not so much the
history of feminist *activism* as the history of its *intellectual formation*. Feminist film theory, in other words, emerged from extensive debate with film
theory more generally, and what we have lost in nineties is a sense of this
extensiveness and the context of that debate. "The elimination of a historical understanding of contemporary film theory," Bergstrom writes a
year later, in 1990, "often goes hand in hand with the charge that "film
theory" has failed, in one way or another."[7] She continues:

We have witnessed a number of attempts to by-pass its most difficult
conceptual problems by replacing it with something else. The "something else" is sometimes film history or aesthetics; sometimes it is a new
object, such as television, popular culture, video; and sometimes it is a
question of new methodologies, which may resemble dusted off methodologies from the social sciences, such as audience questionnaires or
interviews, procedures that haven't benefited from the literature in the
social sciences that has interrogated its own methods and limitations.[8]

For Bergstrom, most egregious in this regard is the virtual erasure of
seventies film theory from recent books and textbooks. And as she points

out, this is itself a result of the tendency on the part of scholars and critics (and even feminists like Ruby Rich) to dismiss anything produced from a psychoanalytic analysis or an ideological analysis that depends on its insights.

At this point, it should be clear that, taken together, Ruby Rich and Janet Bergstrom provide us with a complex and ultimately more nuanced account of a time that has recently inspired mixed feelings. Whereas Rich argues for a return to nonacademic feminist film activism, Bergstrom aims to restore the theoretical context for so much feminist film theory. Although they speak from different institutional places and champion different causes, both argue against the current lapse of historical memory and aim to recover a sense of the past that seems on the verge of being forgotten. Perhaps their remarks have everything do with the kind of reflection that comes with aging, with the efforts on the part of an older generation to look back in time in an effort to make sense of where it is now. Perhaps their similarities are more important than their differences, in any event. But maybe this is especially so in this time that seems without event for feminism.

FINAL THOUGHTS

By way of a conclusion, allow me to offer some final thoughts about the spaces and places for feminist film theory today, particularly in view of the many claims that seventies film theory has failed, or that feminist film theory is over, or that the cinema itself is at an end. As Bergstrom points out, these kinds of claims often go hand in hand with the elimination of a historical understanding, especially our understanding of the history of contemporary film theory. But perhaps we need to ask what makes film theory "contemporary" in the first place. Does *contemporary* mean "relevant" or "up-to-date" or, even more narrowly, "written in the last five years"? Or does it refer rather to the "ability to resonate," in the sense of having the capacity to speak to us today? On one level, of course, all of film theory is contemporary, just as the cinema is an invention of relatively recent date. On the other hand, it is precisely this longer duration of film history and theory that gets lost, I'm afraid, in our own time of accelerated obsolescence, which affects both our technologies and our theories.

Let me cite as an example a passage from an introduction to a recent collection of essays entitled *Viewing Positions: Ways of Seeing Film,* edited

by Linda Williams, whose work I otherwise very much admire. As someone for whom the seventies were formative, Williams nevertheless takes
her distance from its traditions in an effort to stress new developments in
the field, especially with regard to questions of spectatorship. She begins
by describing recent challenges to the transcendent, ahistorical, and disembodied model of vision that she associates with Laura Mulvey and seventies film theory more generally. She then writes: "[Tom] Gunning's
timely description of the difference between early cinema's spectatorial
relations and those of classical narrative has recently begun to vie with
Laura Mulvey's classic formulation of the spectatorial relations of classical
cinema as one of the most frequently cited concepts in the field."[9] Williams continues:

> The reason, I suspect, relates not only to the undeniable importance
> and relevance of this concept to the attractions of early cinema, . . . but
> also to its ability to point to aspects of spectatorial relations that have
> been ignored under the dominance of the gaze paradigm and that are
> perfectly applicable to all forms of spectatorship, not only those early
> sensations. Gunning's notions of *attraction* and *astonishment* have caught
> on, in other words, because, in addition to being apt descriptions of
> early cinema, they describe aspects of all cinema that have also been
> undervalued in the classical paradigm. (11–12)

After reading this passage, it is clear why Williams would want to revise
theories of looking in relation to bodily sensation—and why she deems it
important to get beyond the generic predictability of what she now calls
"gaze theory." At the same time, I could only think, when exactly did
seventies film theory become "gaze theory" and when did Mulvey's critique of classical narrative come to represent this "classical" (as opposed
to "contemporary") tradition? Is it "classical" in the sense that Sergei
Eisenstein's writings are classical? Or Rudolf Arnheim's? Or André Bazin's?
(In other words, is it classical because it is now over and we are past it?)
Perhaps the answer is too obvious: "Visual Pleasure and Narrative Cinema" is classical because its ideas have had a pervasive and lasting influence. But then I wondered, why would Williams say that Gunning's
descriptions have begun to "vie" with Mulvey's as the most frequently
cited concepts in the field? To suggest that film theory has become (or
perhaps always was?) a contest over most-cited or most-fashionable concepts? Because Gunning's model allows for more variable, less psychoanalytic, models of viewing? Because it is not focused on women or men or

the male gaze for that matter, it is therefore inherently more historical and concrete? Williams says none of these things but argues instead that Gunning's work attests to "the hunger for a new paradigm of spectatorial relations" (20n14).

While the hunger is no doubt real, I am nonetheless troubled by this description of the development of theories of spectatorship in the field. To say that concepts of attractions and astonishment have begun to vie with notions of classical narrative and the gaze is not simply to cast film theory as a contest or game of one-upmanship. More importantly, it is to miss the way the discourse of thrills and attractions says as much about spectatorship as it does about our own uneasiness, less with the conditions that gave rise to Mulvey's analysis, than with the boredom and repetition of an earlier feminist model.[10] Needless to say, the specter of orthodoxy is not limited to psychoanalysis, since any theory—Gunning's as much as Mulvey's—runs the risk of being appropriated and homogenized, taken out of context and reduced to a series of catchphrases to be appropriated and applied in a repetitive series of analyses.

Perhaps it is inevitable that new ways of thinking will quickly become models of what to think, rather than how to think, about intractable problems in the field. But I think it is important to emphasize that while there are differences between what Williams calls "gaze theory" and theories of "attractions" or thrills, there are also deeper connections between them, which must be recognized as well. Indeed, to emphasize only their differences is to miss the striking similarities between Gunning's and Mulvey's essays and the larger traditions of which they are part.

To be sure, the differences are as obvious as they are significant: Mulvey's approach is psychoanalytic; Gunning's is historical. Mulvey emphasizes voyeurism and scopophilia and unconscious mechanisms of viewing; Gunning insists on exhibitionism and curiosity and the viewer's highly conscious awareness of the image. More than this, Mulvey talks about narrative and analyzes individual films, whereas Gunning emphasizes the role of spectacle and dismisses what he calls "text-obsessed film criticism" in favor of an attention to exhibition practices and reception contexts. Finally, Mulvey's essay is polemically feminist, whereas Gunning's is not. In fact, Gunning says very little about the way in which the female body functions as a main "attraction" in the cinema of attractions, which is not to say, however, that feminists have not found his ideas useful or engaging or productive for their work.

Part of the reason is that Gunning, who draws on Eisenstein as well as early French film theory, champions an avant-garde or alternative cinematic tradition—alternative, that is, to a classical Hollywood model. In this, his work is very much within the tradition of seventies film theory, which undoubtedly shaped his intellectual formation as well. It is nonetheless remarkable that both Mulvey's and Gunning's work has tended to inspire, not further analyses of independent films or the avant-garde, but extended discussions of Hollywood cinema itself. In fact, just as Mulvey's polemic encouraged scholarship on women's films and soap operas and female spectatorship in classical texts so, too, has Gunning's work on "early cinema" inspired discussion of preclassical and postclassical cinema (as well as the so-called classical cinema, no longer understood in entirely classical terms). In all of this, film theory today seems more than ever before to be wedded to a model of culture that begins and ends in the United States. Indeed, I think it is fair to say that virtually every major theoretical formulation over the last thirty years has taken Hollywood film as a model and U.S. culture as the starting point for discussion of any number of issues, whether narrative conventions, sexual difference, spectatorship, audiences, genres, or stars.[11]

So where does this leave feminist film theory, and not only seventies film theory, today? At an end, or merely at a loss? For Ruby Rich, as I have suggested, what has been lost in the nineties is the sense of inclusion and collaboration and internationalism that energized feminist women in the early seventies. For Janet Bergstrom, it is the loss of a once vibrant intellectual tradition that was also international or, at least, one that attempted to think beyond the borders of U.S. culture. Both of them are right, of course, and it is not a contradiction or an easy way out of their differences to say so. Indeed, from our vantage point today, in the year 2001, it is no longer helpful or productive to pit practice against theory, or activism against scholarship, for, by now, we certainly know that feminist thought remains as crucial to the academy as to the institutions within and outside it.

Feminist film theorists are aware of this fact, I think, and their nostalgia for the seventies does not stem from a desire for some imaginary Edenic time of political activism or theoretical purity. After thinking long and hard about what Ruby Rich and Janet Bergstrom have written, and what Mary Ann Doane and Teresa de Lauretis had to say at the SCS plenary, I am convinced that what they yearn for, and certainly what I yearn for, is community. Not a unified, originary, or uncontentious feminist unity—but what I would call *a community of the question:* a community dedicated to a shared sense of what matters, of what questions need to be asked, of what issues need to be thought, of what battles remain to be fought.

A community of the question would not involve a series of agreed-upon answers or approaches or the establishment of cliques or orthodoxies to determine *what to think* about particular issues. A community of the question would instead involve a shared sense of *how to think* about questions and how to think about them in a profoundly historical manner. It would therefore not be bound by space or, indeed, by time. It would require dialogue, with thinkers past and present (not only Sergei Eisenstein and Bertolt Brecht, and Siegfried Kracauer and Walter Benjamin, but also André Bazin and Maya Deren, Christian Metz and Stephen Heath and Raymond Bellour and so many others, only some of whom I have mentioned in the course of my remarks here). It would also demand an international community and an international response, which would, in turn, allow for a more searching reflection on where we are now and where we have been.

Ruby Rich argues that "the early seventies were very much a continuation of the late sixties."[12] I take her point but would only add, then the nineties are very much a continuation of the eighties, which were themselves a continuation of the seventies, which were a continuation of the sixties (and so on). As I have pointed out before, Bergstrom argues that the elimination of a historical understanding goes hand in hand with the charge that film theory has somehow failed or come to an end. This historical understanding, it seems to me, must extend beyond the 1970s. (Seventies film theorists, after all, were engaged with sixties and fifties and forties film theorists—would we have had Metz without Bazin?) Indeed, I would argue that what now goes under the banner of "seventies film theory" was in fact developed through extended conversation with film theory of the twenties and thirties—not only Wollen's dialogue with Eisenstein but also *Screen*'s with Benjamin and Brecht. If it is to account for the non-homogeneous, discontinuous nature of historical time, feminist film theory must similarly embrace a wider, more international history of filmmaking and theory. And this especially since the most pressing issues for us today—about perception and representation, ideology and subjectivity, affect and bodily sensation—remain as elusively complex as they have been throughout this century. I would therefore like to conclude, not on a note of nostalgia for any particular past, but rather with a sense of anticipation for the future—a future that not only remembers its past more forcefully, but that also champions its lost causes.

NOTES

INTRODUCTION: AFTERSHOCKS OF THE NEW

1. A related and fascinating project, focusing on the history of attention in the late nineteenth and early twentieth centuries, is Jonathan Crary's recent book, *Suspensions of Perception: Attention, Spectacle, and Modern Culture* (Cambridge: MIT P, 2000).

2. Central in this regard is B. Ruby Rich, *Chick Flicks: Theories and Memories of the Feminist Film Movement* (Durham: Duke UP, 1998). Other recent work that assesses the history of film studies includes Dudley Andrew, "The 'Three Ages' of Cinema Studies and the Age to Come," *Publications of the Modern Language Association* 115, no. 3 (May 2000): 341–351; Alison Butler, "Feminist Theory and Women's Films at the Turn of the Century," *Screen* 41, no. 1 (spring 2000): 73–78; E. Ann Kaplan, *Feminism and Film* (New York: Oxford UP, 2000); Patricia Mellencamp, *A Fine Romance . . . Five Ages of Film Feminism* (Philadelphia: Temple UP, 1995); Tania Modleski, *Old Wives' Tales: Feminist Re-Visions of Film and Other Fictions* (New York: New York UP, 1998); Robert Stam and Toby Miller, eds., *Film and Theory: An Anthology* (New York: Blackwell, 2000); Robert Stam and Toby Miller, *A Companion to Film Theory* (New York: Blackwell, 1999); as well as Robert Stam, *Film Theory: An Introduction* (New York: Blackwell, 1999).

3. Siegfried Kracauer, *History: The Last Things Before the Last* (New York: Oxford UP, 1969), 4.

4. Gertrud Koch, *Siegfried Kracauer: An Introduction*, trans. Jeremy Gaines (Princeton: Princeton UP, 2000), 13.

5. See, for example, Koch's book on Kracauer, ibid., and the range of recent translations of Walter Benjamin's writings, as well as his correspondence with Theodor Adorno. Walter Benjamin, *Selected Writings, 1913–1926*, trans. Marcus Paul Bullock and Michael William Jennings (Cambridge: Harvard UP, 1996); Benjamin, *Selected Writings, 1927–1934*, trans. Marcus Paul Bullock, Michael William Jennings, Howard Eiland, and Gary Smith (Cambridge: Harvard UP, 1999); Benjamin, *The Arcades Project*, trans. Howard Eiland and Kevin McLaughlin (Cambridge: Harvard UP, 1999); Theodor Adorno and Walter Benjamin, *The Complete Correspondence*, trans. and ed. Henri Lonitz (Cambridge: Harvard UP, 1999), and Theodor Adorno, *Notes to Literature*, vols. 1 and 2, ed. Rolf

Tiedemann, trans. Shierry Weber Nicholson (New York: Columbia UP, 1991, 1992).

6. Laura Mulvey, "Hollywood Cinema and Feminist Theory: A Strange but Persistent Relationship," *Iris* 26 (1998): 23–32.

7. Ibid., 26.

8. Ibid., 27.

9. I owe this insight to Giuliana Bruno, who made this comment in response to a version of chapter 9, "Film Feminism and Nostalgia for the Seventies," presented at the Harvard Film Seminar in April 2000.

10. The most important thinkers for my own work have been Miriam Hansen, Heide Schlüpmann, Gertrud Koch, Mary Anne Doane, Linda Williams, and Tania Modleski, whose writings I list in the Works Cited section of this volume.

11. The original title of this essay, "Kracauer's Epistemological Shift," was intended to resonate with David Bordwell's earlier and influential essay, "Eisenstein's Epistemological Shift," published in *Screen* in the 1970s. Its title was intended, in other words, to address a film studies audience. Although I argue quite polemically for *continuities* in Kracauer's work over time (against the view of discontinuities, which is argued forcefully by Thomas Elsaesser and Schlüpmann, among others), this essay has nonetheless been interpreted otherwise, leaving me to wonder whether critics have read only the title. In this regard, see Thomas Levin's introduction to the English translation of Kracauer's Weimar essays, *The Mass Ornament: Weimar Essays* (Cambridge: Harvard UP, 1995). Levin actually seems to have read the essay, for he paraphrases the argument I make there; he then footnotes the essay itself, however, as evidence of a misguided attempt to see discontinuities in Kracauer's work. Hence, I have changed the title for republication in this collection.

12. Mulvey makes this point as well in the conclusion of her 1998 essay "Hollywood Cinema and Feminist Theory":

Although I have emphasized the importance of French ideas as an influence on British intellectuals, the late 60s to early 70s saw an enormously influential revival of interest in the politics and aesthetics of the 20s. It was then that artists had begun to [be] interested in psychoanalysis, that critics and theorists took up semiotics, that artists and theorists connected Marxist politics with avant-garde aesthetics. The movements associated with these intellectual trends were, of course, driven underground, dispersed and forgotten during the decades that saw the rise of fascism, the Second World War and the Cold War. But, with an archeological enthusiasm, similar, perhaps, to the spirit behind the women's film festivals of the 60s, intellectuals in Britain identified themselves with these 20s movements. (30)

13. Felicity Collins, review of *Chick Flicks* in the online journal *Screening the Past*, http://www.latrobe.edu.au/www/screeningthepast/shorts/reviews/rev 1199 (12 November 1999), 1.

14. Rich, *Chick Flicks*, 6, 5.

1. THE "PLACE" OF TELEVISION IN FILM STUDIES

I would like to thank Caryl Flinn for her critical and close reading of this chapter. The chapter epigraph is from Leslie Fiedler, "The Middle against Both Ends," in *Mass Culture: The Popular Arts in America*, ed. Bernard Rosenberg and David Manning White (New York: Free Press, 1957), 547.

1. For an elaboration of this argument, see Rick Altman, "Television/Sound," in *Studies in Entertainment: Critical Approaches to Mass Culture*, ed. Tania Modleski (Bloomington: Indiana UP, 1986), 39–54.

2. See, for example, the collection of essays edited by E. Ann Kaplan, *Regarding Television*, American Film Institute Monograph Series, vol. 3 (Frederick, Md.: University Publications of America, 1984), and especially Kaplan's introductory essay.

3. Hélène Cixous, "Castration or Decapitation," trans. Annette Kuhn, *Signs: Journal of Women in Culture and Society* 7, no. 1 (autumn 1981): 44.

4. Tania Modleski, "The Terror of Pleasure: The Contemporary Horror Film and Postmodern Theory," in Modleski, *Studies in Entertainment*.

5. I am referring here to Beverle Houston's analysis of television spectatorship in "Viewing Television: The Metapsychology of Endless Consumption," *Quarterly Review of Film Studies* 9, no. 3 (summer 1984): 183–195.

6. See, for instance, the collection of essays on early German film theory included in *New German Critique* 40 (winter 1987).

7. Donald Young, "Social Standards and the Motion Picture," *Annals of the American Academy of Political and Social Sciences* 128 (November 1926): 147, qtd. in Robert Sklar, *Movie-Made America* (New York: Random House, 1975), 123. Henry James Foreman, *Our Movie-Made Children* (1933), 64–65; qtd. in Sklar, *Movie-Made America*, 137.

8. "Early Silent Cinema: Whose Public Sphere?" *New German Critique* 29 (spring–summer 1983): 175. I am merely summarizing part of Hansen's argument here. For a more complete, illuminating discussion of German mass cultural debates, see the complete essay.

9. Alfred Döblin, "Das Theater der kleinen Leute," in *Kino-Debatte: Literatur und Film, 1909–1929*, ed. Anton Kaes (Tübingen: Niemeyer, 1978), 38; qtd. in and translated by Hansen, "Early Silent Cinema," 174.

10. Franz Pfemfert, qtd. in Kaes's introduction to *Kino-Debatte*, 10; translation mine. All other translations are mine unless otherwise noted.

11. Herbert Jhering, "UFA und Buster Keaton" (1926), qtd. in ibid., 15.

12. Heide Schlüpmann's essay, which links intellectual attitudes toward the cinema (especially those of Kracauer, Benjamin, and Adorno) with a pervasive patriarchal bias, has been central to my own thinking about theories of cinematic and televisual spectatorship. See her "Kinosucht," *Frauen und Film* 33 (October 1982): 45–52.

13. Siegfried Kracauer, "Das Ornament der Masse," in *Das Ornament der Masse: Essays, 1920–31* (Frankfurt am Main: Suhrkamp, 1963), 50–51.

14. Kracauer, "Kult der Zerstreuung," in *Das Ornament der Masse*, 315; Kracauer, "Das Ornament der Masse," 62; Kracauer, "Die kleinen Ladenmädchen gehen ins Kino," in *Das Ornament der Masse*, 292–293.

15. In saying this, I do not mean to imply that Kracauer, Benjamin, or Brecht settled upon a simple or one-sided interpretation of perception and distraction in the cinema. While the emphasis in their writings seems to me to fall upon an active or intellectual meaning of distraction that, in turn, is combined with a suspicion toward emotional response and identification, all three theorists were alert to the need for identification, recognition, and pleasure in the cinema. (Indeed, as Heide Schlüpmann has argued in "Kinosucht," building upon an earlier argument made by Adorno, Kracauer's own fascination for the cinema was in fact often projected onto the little shop girls he discusses.)

16. Jean-Louis Comolli and Paul Narboni, "Cinema/Ideology/Criticism," *Screen* 12, no. 1 (spring 1971): 26.

17. Stephen Heath, "Narrative Space," *Screen* 17, no. 3 (autumn 1976), 68–112.

18. Stephen Heath, "From Brecht to Film—Theses, Problems," *Screen* 16, no. 4 (winter 1975–76): 39.

19. See the anthology of essays edited by Hal Foster, *The Anti-Aesthetic: Essays on Postmodern Culture* (Port Townsend, Washington: Bay, 1983).

20. Fredric Jameson, "Reflections in Conclusion," in *Aesthetics and Politics*, ed. Ronald Taylor (London: New Left Books, 1977), 209, 211, and "Postmodernism and Consumer Society," in *The Anti-Aesthetic: Essays on Postmodern Culture*, ed. Hal Foster (London: New Left Books, 1977), 112.

21. Jerry Mander, *Four Arguments for the Elimination of Television* (New York: Morrow, 1978), 350–351. As a number of feminist theorists have pointed out, the metaphorics of penetration and rape pervade a number of critical and representational discourses. See, for example, Tania Modleski's remarks regarding Jean Baudrillard's theory of mass communication and David Cronenberg's horror films in her essay "The Terror of Pleasure." See also Teresa de Lauretis's critique of the patriarchal bias in Jacques Derrida and Michel Foucault in her essay "The Violence of Rhetoric: Considerations on Representation and Gender," in *Technologies of Gender: Essays on Theory, Film, and Fiction*, ed. Teresa de Lauretis (Bloomington: Indiana UP, 1987), 31–50.

22. The sociological and psychological studies of television's effects on children are too numerous to list. For a useful overview of these approaches, as well as an extensive bibliography, see Paul M. Hirsch, "The Role of Television and Popular Culture in Contemporary Society," in *Television*, ed. Horace Newcomb, 3d ed. (New York: Oxford UP, 1982), 280–310.

23. Hilde T. Himmelweit, *Television and the Child*, 220, qtd. in Robert S. Alley, "Television Drama," in *Television*, ed. Newcomb, 91.

24. Worthington Miner, "The Terrible Toll of Taboos," in *Television and Radio*, ed. Poyntz Tyler (New York: Wilson, 1961), 171.

25. Paul Robinson, "TV Can't Educate," *The Little, Brown Reader*, ed. Marcia Stubbs and Sylvan Barnett, 3d ed. (Boston: Little, Brown, 1983), 216–219.

26. Ernest van den Haag, "Of Happiness and of Despair We Have No Measure,"

in *Mass Culture: The Popular Arts in America,* ed. Rosenberg and White, 505, 512, 513, 516.

27. Ibid., 533. Van den Haag also writes, and no less revealingly, that while "no pin-up girl can surfeit appetite for a real one . . . the pin-up can spoil the appetites for other images of girls" (525).

28. Dennis Porter, "Soap Time: Thoughts on a Commodity Art Form," in *Television,* ed. Newcomb, 129, 131.

29. Noël Burch, "Narrative/Diegesis—Thresholds, Limits," *Screen* 23, no. 2 (July–August 1982): 33.

30. Cixous, "Castration or Decapitation," 41–55.

31. Jane Feuer, *The Hollywood Musical* (Bloomington: Indiana UP, 1982), 47.

32. See Linda Williams, "Something Else Besides a Mother: *Stella Dallas* and the Maternal Melodrama," *Cinema Journal* 24, no. 1 (fall 1984): 2–27; and Tania Modleski, "Time and Desire in the Woman's Film," *Cinema Journal* 23, no. 3 (spring 1984): 19–30.

33. Tania Modleski, "The Search for Tomorrow in Today's Soap Operas," in *Loving with a Vengeance: Mass Produced Fantasies for Women* (New York: Metheun, 1984), 85–109.

34. Tania Modleski, "The Rhythms of Reception: Daytime Television and Women's Work," in *Regarding Television,* ed. Kaplan, 71.

35. Modleski, "The Search for Tomorrow," 30.

36. Modleski, "The Rhythms of Reception," 69.

37. Ibid.

2. FEMINISM AND FILM HISTORY

The chapter epigraph is from Meaghan Morris, *The Pirate's Fiancée: Feminism, Reading, Postmodernism* (New York: Verso, 1988), 14–15.

1. On the New Historicism, see Brook Thomas, "The New Historicism and the Privileging of Literature," *Annals of Scholarship: Metastudies of the Humanities and Social Sciences* 4, no. 4 (1987): 23–48; David Simpson, "Literary Criticism and the Return to History," *Critical Inquiry* 14 (1988): 721–747; and Gregory Jay, *America the Scrivener: Deconstruction and the Subject of Literary History* (Ithaca: Cornell UP, 1990). On early debates over the relationship between film theory and film history, see Robert C. Allen, "Film History: The Narrow Discourse," *The 1977 Film Studies Annual II* (New York: Redgrave, 1977): 9–16; Charles F. Altman, "Towards a Historiography of American Film," *Cinema Journal* 16, no. 2 (1977): 1–25; Edward Branigan, "Color and Cinema: Problems in the Writing of Film History," *Film Reader* 4 (1979): 16–34; John Ellis, "The Institution of Cinema," *Edinburgh '77 Magazine* 2 (1977): 56–66; Gerald Mast, "Film History and Film Histories," *Quarterly Review of Film Studies* 1 (1976): 297–314; Mark Nash and Steve Neale, "Film History/Production/Memory," *Screen* 18, no. 4 (1977–78): 71–91; Geoffrey Nowell–Smith, "Facts about Films and Facts of Film," *Quarterly Review of Film Studies* 1 (1976): 272–275.

2. See, for example, Robert C. Allen and Douglas Gomery, *Film History: Theory*

and Practice (New York: Knopf, 1985); David Bordwell, Janet Staiger, and Kristin Thompson, *The Classical Hollywood Cinema: Film Style and Mode of Production to 1960* (New York: Columbia UP, 1985).

3. See, for example, David Bordwell, *Making Meaning: Inference and Rhetoric in the Interpretation of Cinema* (Cambridge: Harvard UP, 1989). To be sure, in his final chapter, Bordwell does mention at least one feminist's work on film history. Typically, however, his praise for this work turns entirely on its attention to archival sources and "concrete institutional negotiations among filmmakers, studio executives, and censors," in other words, on its rigorous empirical foundation. While empirical research is, of course, crucial to rethinking film history from a feminist perspective, Bordwell fails to consider the central role played by feminist theory in generating the questions that feminist historians attempt to answer through archival study.

4. Judith Newton, "History as Usual? Feminism and the 'New Historicism,'" *Cultural Critique* 9 (1988): 87–121.

5. Fredric Jameson, *The Political Unconscious: Narrative as a Socially Symbolic Act* (Ithaca: Cornell UP, 1981), 9.

6. The Woolf quote in the epigraph appears in Molly Haskell, *From Reverence to Rape: The Treatment of Women in the Movies* (Harmondsworth: Penguin, 1974), 1.

7. For a compelling analysis of Haskell's *From Reverence to Rape* and Rosen's *Popcorn Venus* as feminist film histories, see Claire Johnston, "Feminist Politics and Film History," *Screen* 16, no. 3 (1975): 115–124.

8. Haskell, *From Reverence to Rape*, xiv.

9. Rosen, *Popcorn Venus*, 9.

10. Jameson, *Political Unconscious*, 38.

11. Haskell, *From Reverence to Rape*, 30.

12. Nancy Miller, "Changing the Subject: Authorship, Writing, and the Reader," in *Feminist Studies/Critical Studies*, ed. Teresa de Lauretis (Bloomington: Indiana UP, 1986), 104.

13. Claire Johnston, "Dorothy Arzner: Critical Strategies," in *The Work of Dorothy Arzner: Towards a Feminist Cinema*, ed. Claire Johnston (London: BFI, 1974), 2.

14. Pam Cook, "Approaching the Work of Dorothy Arzner," in Johnston, *Dorothy Arzner*, 11.

15. Janet Bergstrom, "Rereading the Work of Claire Johnston," 80–88, and Jacquelyn Suter, "Feminine Discourse in *Christopher Strong*," 89–103, both in *Feminism and Film Theory*, ed. Constance Penley (New York: Routledge, 1988).

16. Bergstrom, "Rereading the Work," 84.

17. Constance Penley, "The Lady Doesn't Vanish: Feminism and Film Theory," in *Feminism and Film Theory*, ed. Penley, 2.

18. Suter, "Feminine Discourse," 101, 102.

19. Jean-Louis Baudry, "Ideological Effects of the Basic Cinematographic Apparatus," trans. Alan Williams, *Film Quarterly* 27, no. 2 (1974): 39–47, and "The Apparatus," trans. Jean Andrews and Bertrand Augst, *Camera Obscura* 1 (1979): 104–126; Christian Metz, *The Imaginary Signifier: Psychoanalysis and the Cinema*,

trans. Celia Britton, Annwyl Williams, Ben Brewster, and Alfred Guzzetti (Bloomington: Indiana UP, 1982); Laura Mulvey, "Visual Pleasure and Narrative Cinema," *Screen* 16, no. 3 (1975): 6–18.

20. Jacqueline Rose, "The Cinematic Apparatus: Problems in Current Theory," in *The Cinematic Apparatus,* ed. Teresa de Lauretis and Stephen Heath (New York: St. Martin's, 1980), 172–186.

21. Constance Penley, "Feminism, Film Theory, and the Bachelor Machines," *m/f* 10 (1985): 42.

22. Mary Ann Doane, *The Desire to Desire: The Woman's Film of the 1940s* (Bloomington: Indiana UP, 1987), 4.

23. Charles Eckert, "The Carole Lombard in Macy's Window," *Quarterly Review of Film Studies* 3, no. 1 (1978): 1–22; Jeanne Allen, "The Film Viewer as Consumer," *Quarterly Review of Film Studies* 5, no. 4 (1980): 481–499.

24. Doane refers specifically to Benjamin's most famous essay in English translation, "The Work of Art in the Age of Mechanical Reproduction," in *Illuminations,* trans. Harry Zohn, ed. Hannah Arendt (New York: Schocken, 1969).

25. Doane, *Desire to Desire,* 32.

26. For a sampling of essays on cinema and consumerism, see Michael Renov and Jane Gaines, ed., "Female Representation and Consumer Culture," special issue, *Quarterly Review of Film and Video* 11, no. 1 (1989).

27. Mary Ann Doane, "Feminist Film Theory and the Enterprise of Criticism," typescript.

28. A number of recent feminist studies have addressed precisely this issue. See, for example, Rey Chow, "Silent Is the Ancient Plain: Music, Filmmaking, and the Conception of Reform in China's New Cinema," *Discourse* 12, no. 2 (1990): 82–109; Sandy Flitterman-Lewis, *To Desire Differently: Feminism and the French Cinema* (Urbana: U of Illinois P, 1990); Judith Mayne, *Kino and the Woman Question: Feminism and Soviet Silent Film* (Columbus: Ohio State UP, 1989); and Patrice Petro, *Joyless Streets: Women and Melodramatic Representation in Weimar Germany* (Princeton: Princeton UP, 1989).

29. Judith Mayne, *The Woman at the Keyhole: Feminist and Women's Cinema* (Bloomington: Indiana UP, 1990).

3. GERMAN FILM THEORY AND ANGLO-AMERICAN FILM STUDIES

1. Siegfried Kracauer, *From Caligari to Hitler: A Psychological History of the German Film* (Princeton: Princeton UP, 1947), and *Theory of Film: The Redemption of Physical Reality* (New York: Oxford UP, 1960).

2. Dudley Andrew, *The Major Film Theories: An Introduction* (New York: Oxford UP, 1976), 107, 135. It should be mentioned here that Andrew borrows his characterization of Kracauer from Peter Harcourt. However, throughout his chapter on Kracauer's film theory, Andrew tends to add to Harcourt's description, putting particular emphasis on Kracauer's "incomparable self-confidence and . . . imposing German seriousness."

3. See, for example, Dudley Andrew, "The Neglected Tradition of Phenomenology in Film Theory," in *Movies and Methods*, 2d ed., ed. Bill Nichols (Berkeley and Los Angeles: U of California P, 1985), 625–632.

4. Edward Said, *The World, the Text, and the Critic* (Cambridge: Harvard UP, 1983), 6.

5. Ibid.

6. Erich Auerbach, "Philologie der Weltliteratur," qtd. in ibid.

7. Kracauer, *Theory of Film*, 304.

8. Karsten Witte, "Introduction to Siegfried Kracauer's 'The Mass Ornament,'" *New German Critique* 5 (spring 1975): 59; Heide Schlüpmann, "Phenomenology of Film: On Siegfried Kracauer's Writings of the 1920s," *New German Critique* 40 (winter 1987): 98; Thomas Elsaesser, "Cinema—The Irresponsible Signifier, or 'The Gamble with History': Film Theory or Cinema Theory," *New German Critique* 40 (winter 1987): 85.

9. David Bordwell, "Eisenstein's Epistemological Shift," *Screen* 15, no. 4 (winter 1974–75): 32–46.

10. Peter Wollen, *Signs and Meanings in the Cinema* (Bloomington: Indiana UP, 1969), 56. Following this remark, Wollen adds, "'Realism has always been the refuge of the conservative in the arts, together with a preference for propaganda of a comforting rather than disturbing kind."

11. Louis Althusser, *For Marx*, trans. Ben Brewster (London: New Left Books, 1977).

12. See, for example, Andrew Arato and Paul Breines, *The Young Lukács and the Origins of Western Marxism* (New York: Seabury, 1979).

13. For a historical overview of auteur criticism, see John Caughie, *Theories of Authorship* (London: BFI, 1982).

14. Kracauer, *History*. Phil Rosen and David Rodowick have both stressed Kracauer's disjunctive view of historical time. See Rosen, "History, Textuality, Nation: Kracauer, Burch, and Some Problems in the Study of National Cinema," *Iris* 2, no. 2 (1984): 69–84, and D. N. Rodowick, "The Last Things before the Last: Kracauer and History," *New German Critique* (spring–summer 1987): 109–139.

15. See, for example, Martin Jay, "The Extraterritorial Life of Siegfried Kracauer," *Salmagundi* 31–32 (fall 1975–winter 1976): 49–106.

16. Theodor Adorno, "Der wünderliche Realist: Über Siegfried Kracauer," in *Noten zur Literatur 3* (Frankfurt am Main: Suhrkamp, 1965), 83–108; an English translation of this essay, entitled "The Curious Realist," is included in *New German Critique* 54 (fall 1991) 159–177.

17. Said, *World*, 226.

18. Kracauer, *Theory of Film*, 300, 294.

19. Miriam Hansen has pointed out that Kracauer's early writings also reveal a shift in emphasis, from a concern with metaphysical questions in the early 1920s to a concern with ideology and material practices from 1927 on. See her essay "Decentric Perspectives: Kracauer's Early Writings on Film and Mass Culture," *New German Critique* 54 (fall 1991): 47–76.

20. Adorno, "Letters to Walter Benjamin," *Aesthetics and Politics,* trans. Ronald Taylor (London: New Left Books, 1977), 123.

21. Kracauer, *Theory of Film,* 290.

4. AFTER SHOCK, BETWEEN BOREDOM AND HISTORY

The chapter epigraph is from Fredric Jameson, *Postmodernism, or, The Cultural Logic of Late Capitalism* (Durham: Duke UP, 1991), 71–72.

1. The retrospective viewing of a photographic image is, of course, already on the side of history. As Susan Sontag puts it: "A photograph passes for incontrovertible proof that a given thing happened. The picture may distort; but there is always the presumption that something exists, or did exist, which is like what's in the picture" (*On Photography* [New York: Dell, 1973], 5).

2. On Brassaï's life and work, see Paul Hill and Thomas Cooper, eds., *Dialogue with Photography* (New York: Farrar, 1979). See also the essays and photographs published by Brassaï himself: *The Artists of My Life* (New York: Viking, 1982); *Brassaï* (New York: Pantheon, 1988); *Conversations avec Picasso* (Paris: Gallimard, 1964); *Paris by Night* (New York: Pantheon, 1987); *Paris du nuit* (Paris: Arts et Métiers Graphiques, 1933); *Le Paris secret des années 30* (Paris: Gallimard, 1976).

3. Stephen Meisel, "Flesh and Fantasy," *Rolling Stone,* 13 June 1991, 34–50.

4. After completing a draft of this essay, I came across two books that attempt to chart a history of boredom, particularly in the eighteenth and nineteenth centuries: Reinhard Kuhn's *The Demon of Noontide: Ennui in Western Literature* (Princeton: Princeton UP, 1976) and Wolf Lepenies's *Melancholy and Society,* trans. Jeremy Gains and Dorris Jones (Cambridge: Harvard UP, 1992). But neither Kuhn nor Lepenies distinguish boredom from melancholy or ennui (as I attempt to do here, precisely by emphasizing the visual dimension to perceptual boredom in the twentieth century). And both theorists are uninterested in questions of gender and sexual difference. To be sure, Lepenies's sociological analysis offers a far more expansive and compelling account of boredom than Kuhn's expressly literary approach (which I discuss in chapter 5). And yet even Lepenies reduces the phenomenology of boredom to a particular class condition. Judith N. Shklar alludes to this in her introduction to the English translation of Lepenies's book: "It is not likely that the displaced aristocrat, the excluded bourgeois, and the isolated artist are the only people to be reduced to melancholy by social changes they cannot control in any way. . . . Gender as much as class is a locus of melancholy" (xvi).

5. Quoted in Anders Stephanson, "Regarding Postmodernism—A Conversation with Fredric Jameson," in *Universal Abandon? The Politics of Postmodernism,* ed. Andrew Ross (Minneapolis: U of Minnesota P, 1988), 18. See also Jameson's remarks about the nostalgia film in *Postmodernism,* especially chapter 9, "Nostalgia for the Present."

6. Jameson, *Postmodernism,* 14.

7. Jacqueline Rose, " *The Man Who Mistook His Wife for a Hat* or *A Wife Is Like an Umbrella*—Fantasies of the Modern and Postmodern," in Ross, *Universal Abandon,* 243.

8. On eighteenth-century theories of the sublime, see Lepenies, *Melancholy and Society*; Kuhn, *Demon of Noontide*; and Thomas Weiskel, *The Romantic Sublime: Studies in the Structure and Psychology of Transcendence* (Baltimore: Johns Hopkins UP, 1976). On the relationship between boredom and the sublime, Weiskel writes:

> Clearly, the sublime was an antidote to the boredom that increased so astonishingly throughout the eighteenth century. Addison had celebrated the *Uncommon* along with the *Great* and the *Beautiful* (*Spectator*, no. 412), and Burke began his treatise by laying down a premise that the passions are never engaged by the familiar. Boredom masks uneasiness and intense boredom exhibits the signs of the most basic of modern anxieties, the anxiety of nothingness, or absence. In its more energetic renditions the sublime is a kind of homeopathic therapy, a cure of uneasiness by means of the stronger, more concentrated—but momentary—anxiety involved in astonishment and terror." (18)

9. On the romantic sublime, see Kuhn, *Demon of Noontide*, and Weiskel, *Romantic Sublime*. Giacomo Leopardi explicitly made the connection between boredom and passion when he wrote: "The emptiness of the human heart, the indifference, the absence of any passion is boredom, and yet boredom is passion. . . . Thus it is that the living cannot really ever be without passion. This passion, if the heart at the moment is captured by nothing else, we call boredom. Boredom is proof of the uninterrupted duration of passion. Were it not passion, it would not exist when nothing occupies the soul" (qtd. in Ernest Schachtel, *Metamorphosis: On the Development of Affect, Perception, Attention, and Memory* [New York: Basic Books, 1951], 177n9). Glossing the work of Ernesto Grassi, Schachtel adds that "in the suffocation of boredom man experiences, on the one hand, nothingness and non-being, and—in the unbearable quality of boredom—being" (177).

10. For an interesting discussion of boredom and affect in psychoanalysis and clinical practice, see Schachtel, *Metamorphosis*, and Otto Fenichel, "On the Psychology of Boredom," in *Organization and Pathology of Thought: Selected Sources*, ed. David Rapaport (New York: Columbia UP, 1959), 349–361.

11. The writings of Siegfried Kracauer and Walter Benjamin are especially illuminating in this regard. For an overview of their theories of subjectivity and media, see "Weimar Film Theory," a special issue of *New German Critique* 40 (winter 1987), especially the essays by Miriam Hansen and Heide Schlüpmann. On Kracauer's theories of distraction and boredom, see Kracauer, *Das Ornament der Masse: Essays 1920–31*, ed. Karsten Witte (Frankfurt: Suhrkamp, 1977), especially his essays "Langeweile" ("Boredom") and "Die Wartenden" ("Those Who Wait"). For the English translation of Kracauer's early essays, see Thomas Y. Levin's recent translation, *The Mass Ornament* (Cambridge: Harvard UP, 1995). On the affinities between distraction and shock experience, see Walter Benjamin's "Das Kunstwerk im Zeitalter seiner technischen Reproduzierbarkeit," in *Gesammelte Schriften*, ed. Rolf Tiedemann and Hermann Schweppenhäuser (Frankfurt: Suhrkamp, 1974); first version, 431–469; second version, 471–505. For Benjamin's

(scattered) remarks about boredom, see *Das Passagen-Werk,* ed. Rolf Tiedemann, 2 vols. (Frankfurt: Suhrkamp, 1982).

12. Michèle Huguet, *L'Ennui et ses discours* (Paris: Presses Universitaires de France, 1984), 215. Huguet's definition of ennui is similar to that of Senancour, which was written at the beginning of the nineteenth century: "Ennui is born of the opposition between what we imagine and what we feel, between the poverty of what is and the vastness of what we want; it is born of the diffuseness of desires and the indolence of action; of this state of suspension and incertitude in which a hundred struggling sentiments mutually extinguish themselves; in which we no longer know what to desire, for the simple reason that we have too many desires, nor what to wish because we would wish for everything; in which nothing seems good because we seek the absolute good; . . . in which the heart cannot find satisfaction because the imagination has promised too much; in which we find repellent all good because all good is not radical enough; in which we are tired of life because it is not new" (qtd. in Kuhn, *Demon of Noontide,* 226).

13. Lepenies, *Melancholy and Society.*

14. Weiskel, *Romantic Sublime.*

15. According to *The Oxford English Dictionary,* the verb "to bore" arose after 1750, although its etymology remains unknown. The definitions of *ennui* and *boredom* cited here are taken from *The Random House Dictionary of the English Language,* rev. ed., 1975.

16. Although I speculate here about a modern, visual dimension to boredom suggested by the phrase "unwelcome attentions," I am aware that this phrase equally refers to seventeenth- and eighteenth-century France, specifically to the rules and manner of the salons and the court. The word *attentions,* for example, referred in literary discourses of the time to the attentions of a flirt or suitor, which were more often verbal or written than specifically visual. Given the etiquette of the time, one had to respond in some polite and elaborate manner to these attentions—one had to pay attention—thereby prolonging them, whether wanted or not; hence, a cause of ennui. On seventeenth- and eighteenth-century French society, see Lepenies.

17. Jonathan Crary, "Spectacle, Attention, Counter–Memory," *October* 50 (1989): 102.

18. Jonathan Crary, *Techniques of the Observer: On Vision and Modernity in the Nineteenth Century* (Cambridge: MIT P, 1990), 40.

19. Georg Simmel, "The Metropolis and Mental Life," in *Georg Simmel: On Individuality and Social Forms,* ed. Donald N. Levine (Chicago: U of Chicago P, 1971), 329–330.

20. Kracauer, "The Mass Ornament," trans. Barbara Correll and Jack Zipes, *New German Critique* 5 (1975): 70.

21. Schlüpmann, "Kinosucht," 50.

22. Benjamin, *Das Passagen-Werk,* 962, 162.

23. Kracauer, "Langeweile," 324.

24. Benjamin, *Das Passagen-Werk,* 178; Kracauer, "Die Wartenden," 116.

25. Benjamin, *Das Passagen-Werk*, 164.
26. Gregory Jay, "Postmodernism and *The Waste Land:* Women, Mass Culture, and Others," in *Rereading the New*, ed. Kevin Dettmar (Ann Arbor: U of Michigan P, 1992), 238.
27. Jean-François Lyotard, "The Sublime and the Avant-Garde," trans. Linda Liebmann, *Art Forum* 22 (1984): 40.
28. Maurice Blanchot, "Everyday Speech," trans. Susan Hanson, *Yale French Studies* 73 (1987): 16.
29. Henri Lefebvre, "The Everyday and Everydayness," trans. Christine Levich, with Alice Kaplan and Kristin Ross, *Yale French Studies* 73 (1987): 10.
30. These descriptions of Warhol's films are taken from Stephen Koch, *Stargazer: The Life, World, and Films of Andy Warhol* (New York: Marion Boyars, 1991).
31. Brassaï, qtd. in Hill and Cooper, *Dialogue with Photography*, 40.
32. Madonna, qtd. in Meisel, "Flesh and Fantasy," 44. Madonna may have been reacting to a photo-documentary book published in 1989 entitled *Kiki's Paris: Artists and Lovers, 1900–1930*. This book traces the history—in a voyeuristic, pseudodocumentary style—of artists, models, and prostitutes of the time, and chooses Kiki, "the most well-known woman of Montparnasse," as its emblem and its muse. See Billy Klüver and Julie Martin, *Kiki's Paris* (New York: Abrams, 1989). My reading of the Madonna remake was inspired by Timothy Corrigan's book, *A Cinema without Walls: Movies and Culture after Vietnam* (New Brunswick: Rutgers UP, 1991).
33. Roland Barthes, "Diderot, Brecht, Eisenstein," trans. Stephen Heath, *Screen* 15, no. 2 (1974): 35.

5. HISTORICAL ENNUI, FEMINIST BOREDOM

The chapter epigraph is from Janet Bergstrom and Mary Ann Doane, "The Female Spectator: Contexts and Direction," *Camera Obscura* 20–21 (May–September 1989): 15.

1. Bergstrom and Doane, "Female Spectator," 15.
2. Gianni Vattimo, "*Verwindung:* Nihilism and the Postmodern in Philosophy," *Substance* 53 (1987): 8.
3. Daniel Barbiero, "A Weakness for Heidegger: The German Root of *Il Pensiero Debole*," *New German Critique* 55 (winter 1992): 163.
4. Vattimo, "*Verwindung.*"
5. Juliana Schiesari, *The Gendering of Melancholia: Feminism, Psychoanalysis, and the Symbolics of Loss in Renaissance Literature* (Ithaca: Cornell UP, 1992), 1–2.
6. "On Boredom," special issue, *Documents* 1, no. 1–2 (winter 1993): 91–92.
7. Kuhn, *Demon of Noontide*, 9.
8. Schiesari, *The Gendering of Melancholia*, 16.
9. Andreas Huyssen, "Mass Culture as Woman: Modernism's Other," in *Studies in Entertainment: Critical Approaches to Mass Culture*, ed. Tania Modleski (Bloomington: Indiana UP, 1986), 188.

10. Orrin Klapp, *Overload and Boredom: Essays on the Quality of Life in the Information Society* (New York: Greenwood, 1986), 23.

11. "On Boredom," 92.

12. Benjamin, *Das Passagen-Werk*, 962, 162.

13. Qtd. in Geoff Waite, "On the Politics of Boredom (a Communist Pastiche)," *Documents* 1, nos. 1–2 (winter 1992): 102.

14. Djuna Barnes, *I Could Never Be without a Husband: Interviews by Djuna Barnes*, ed. Alyce Barry (London: Virago, 1985), 253–255.

15. T. S. Eliot, *Selected Essays* (New York: Harcourt Brace, 1950), 379.

16. Jay, "Postmodernism," 238.

17. Hayden White, "The Modernist Event," in *The Persistence of History: Cinema, Television, and the Modern Event*, ed. Vivian Sobchack (New York: Routledge, 1996), 27–35.

6. WORLD-WEARINESS, WEIMAR WOMEN, AND VISUAL CULTURE

1. See my essay "After Shock, between Boredom and History," chapter 4, in this volume.

2. Lawrence Grossberg, "Postmodernity and Affect: All Dressed Up with No Place to Go," *Communication* 10 (1988): 285.

3. Linda Williams, "Corporealized Observers: Visual Pornographies and the 'Carnal Density of Vision,'" in *Fugitive Images: From Photography to Video*, ed. Patrice Petro (Bloomington: Indiana UP, 1995), 8.

4. Lotte Eisner, *The Haunted Screen: Expressionism in the German Film and the Influence of Max Reinhardt*, trans. Roger Greaves (Berkeley and Los Angeles: U of California P, 1969), 194.

5. Kracauer, *From Caligari to Hitler*.

6. Nora Sayre, "The Enduring Art of a Poet of All That Is Fleeting," *New York Times*, October 11, 1998.

7. Peter Sloterdijk, *Critique of Cynical Reason*, trans. Michael Eldred (Minneapolis: U of Minnesota P, 1987).

8. Stephen Brockmann, "Weimar Sexual Cynicism," in *Dancing on the Volcano: Essays on the Culture of the Weimar Republic*, ed. Thomas W. Kniesche and Stephen Brockmann (Columbia, S.C.: Camden House, 1994), 166–167.

9. Ibid., 169. In this essay, Brockmann also interestingly underscores a relationship between twenties America and twenties Berlin, and their respective investments in the status quo:

> The *Neue Sachlichkeit* of the Weimar Republic was seen by its proponents as a return to what Warren G. Harding, in the United States, called "normalcy" after the revolutionary, erotic, idealistic, and utopian hopes and longings of the war and the immediate postwar period. All utopian and idealistic longing was viewed as immature and childish, and the truly realistic course was the renunciation of idealism and the acceptance of the unremarkable, boring, ordinary, quotidian existence of life in an expanding, rationalizing capitalist society. This was supposed to be the end of ideology.

One was disillusioned, cynical, unemotional. One had had enough of grand projects to change the world. As one of the central constituents of utopian thinking and a foundation of prewar ideology, love had to go.

I find these remarks intriguing, although I take issue, however, with Brockmann's attempt to collapse boredom into cynicism, and his neglect of any consideration of women's views on love and disillusionment in this period.

10. See, for instance, Andreas Huyssen's remarks in his "Foreword: The Return of Diogenes as Postmodern Intellectual," in Sloterdijk, *Critique of Cynical Reason,* ix–xxv.

11. Helmut Lethen, *Verhältenslehren der Kalte. Lebensversuche zwischen den Kriegen* (Frankfurt: Suhrkamp, 1994).

12. Maria Tatar, *Lustmord: Sexual Murder in Weimar Germany* (Princeton: Princeton UP, 1995), 14.

13. The best analysis remains Andreas Huyssen, "The Vamp and the Machine: Technology and Sexuality in Fritz Lang's *Metropolis,*" in *New German Critique,* 24–25 (fall–winter 1981–82): 221–237.

14. Kracauer, "*Die Wartenden,*" 116; see also Thomas Y. Levin's English translation, "Those Who Wait," in Kracauer, *The Mass Ornament.*

15. Mary Ann Doane, "The Erotic Barter: *Pandora's Box,*" in *Femmes Fatales: Feminism, Film Theory, Psychoanalysis* (New York: Routledge, 1991), 144, 162.

16. Louise Brooks, "Pabst and Lulu," in Pabst, *Pandora's Box,* 8, qtd. in Doane, "The Erotic Barter," 143.

17. Qtd. in James K. Lyon, *Bertolt Brecht in America* (Princeton: Princeton UP, 1980), 1. See also Wolf von Eckardt and Sander L. Gilman, *Bertolt Brecht's Berlin: A Scrapbook of the Twenties* (Lincoln: Nebraska UP, 1993).

18. Peter Gay, *Weimar Culture: The Outsider as Insider* (New York: Harper and Row, 1970), 20.

19. Joan Rivièré, "Womanliness as a Masquerade," in *Formations of Fantasy,* ed. Victor Burgin, James Donald, and Cora Kaplan (London: Metheun, 1986), 35.

20. On African art and the avant-garde, see Jost Hermand, "Artificial Atavism: German Expressionism and Blacks," in *Blacks and German Culture,* ed. Reinhold Grimm and Jost Hermand (Madison: U of Wisconsin P, 1986), 65–86.

21. On the reception of jazz and jazz culture in Germany of the 1920s, see Nancy Nenno, "Femininity, the Primitive, and Modern Urban Space: Josephine Baker in Berlin," in *Women in the Metropolis,* ed. Katharina von Ankum (Berkeley and Los Angeles: U of California P, 1997), 145–161. See also Cornelius Partsch, "Hannibal ante Portas: Jazz in Weimar," in *Dancing on the Volcano,* ed. Kniesche and Brockmann, 105–116.

22. There is a wealth of new feminist work on Hannah Höch. See, for example, the Walker Art Center Exhibition catalog by Maria Makela, *The Photomontages of Hannah Höch* (Walker Art Center, 1996), and especially the essay by Makela in that volume, which I draw on later. Jula Dech conducted the first groundbreaking work on Höch in her book *Hannah Höch Schnitt mit der Küchenmesser DADA— Spiegel einer Bierbauchkultur* (Frankfurt: Fischer, 1989). For a more recent interpre-

tation, see Maud Lavin, *Cut with the Kitchen Knife: The Weimar Photomontages of Hannah Höch* (New Haven: Yale UP, 1993).

23. Makela, *Photomontages of Hannah Höch*, 85.

24. Gertrud Koch, "Exorcised: Marlene Dietrich and German Nationalism," in *Women and Film: A Sight and Sound Reader*, ed. Pam Cook and Philip Dodd (Philadelphia: Temple UP, 1993), 13.

7. NAZI CINEMA AT THE INTERSECTION OF THE CLASSICAL AND THE POPULAR

1. Eric Rentschler, *The Ministry of Illusion: Nazi Cinema and Its Afterlife* (Cambridge: Harvard UP, 1996); Linda Schulte-Sasse, *Entertaining the Third Reich: Illusions of Wholeness in Nazi Cinema* (Durham: Duke UP, 1996).

2. Sabine Hake, "The Melodramatic Imagination of Detlef Sierck: *Final Chord* and Its Resonances," *Screen* 38: 2 (summer 1997): 129–148; Thomas Elsaesser, "Hollywood Berlin," *Sight and Sound* (November 1997): 14–17.

3. See, for example, Saul Friedlander, ed., *Probing the Limits of Representation: Nazism and the "Final" Solution* (Cambridge: Harvard UP, 1992); Christopher Browning, *Ordinary Men: Reserve Police Battalion 101 and the Final Solution in Poland* (New York: HarperCollins, 1992); and, most recently, Daniel Goldhagen, *Hitler's Willing Executioners: Ordinary Germans and the Holocaust* (New York: Little, Brown, 1996).

4. Schulte-Sasse, *Entertaining the Third Reich*, 5.

5. There have been several different approaches to "classical cinema" in film studies, ranging from ideological analyses in the *Screen* debates of the early 1970s to feminist critiques in the late 1970s to neoformalist approaches in the 1980s. Compare, for example, Comolli and Narboni, "Cinema/Ideology/Criticism"; Bergstrom, "Rereading"; and Bordwell, Staiger, and Thompson, *Classical Hollywood Cinema*. For a useful collection of essays on film classicism from an ideological and feminist point of view, see Philip Rosen, ed., *Narrative/Apparatus/Ideology* (New York: Columbia UP, 1986).

6. Thomas Elsaesser, "Film History and Visual Pleasure: Weimar Cinema," in *Cinema Histories, Cinema Practices*, ed. Patricia Mellencamp and Philip Rosen (Frederick, Md.: University Publications of America, 1984), 72.

7. There are some good reasons for this, of course. As Richard Maltby and Ruth Vasey explain: "'The America of the movies presented itself less as a geographical territory than as an imaginative one, and it was also a territory that deliberately made itself available for assimilation in a variety of cultural contexts. Hollywood's geographical location has always been elusive, whether in Los Angeles or Berlin; the America of American movies was as imaginary to the residents of Des Moines or Atlanta as it was to the citizens of Brussels or Budapest" ("The International Language Problem: European Reactions to Hollywood's Conversion to Sound," in *Hollywood in Europe: Experiences of a Cultural Hegemony*, ed. David W. Ellwood and Rob Kroes [Amsterdam: Vrije UP, 1994], 69). Rather than explore this phe-

nomenon, however, film scholars often repeat Hollywood's own universalizing tendencies by assuming Hollywood cinema as the model for all filmmaking, as I explain further on.

8. Linda Williams makes this point in the introduction to the anthology she edits entitled *Viewing Positions: Ways of Seeing Film* (New Brunswick: Rutgers UP, 1995): "Gunning's timely description of the difference between early cinema's spectatorial relations and those of classical narrative has recently begun to vie with Laura Mulvey's classic formulation of the spectatorial relations of classical cinema as one of the most frequently cited concepts in the field" (10). Williams takes a position at a considerable distance from Mulvey's (a position that Williams did much to amplify and refine in the 1970s and 1980s), arguing that Gunning's work attests to "the hunger for a new paradigm of spectatorial relations" (20n14). While the "hunger" is no doubt real, I am struck by Williams's tendency throughout this introduction to collapse feminist film theory into something she calls "gaze theory" (the theory of a "singular, unitary spectator"). "Gaze theory" sounds to my ear like "Frisco" (for San Francisco)—a shorthand used by people unfamiliar or new to the area.

9. For feminist critiques of Gunning's work along these lines, see Mayne, *Woman at the Keyhole,* and Connie Balides, "Scenarios of Exposure in the Practice of Everyday Life: Women in the Cinema of Attractions," *Screen* 34, no. 1 (spring 1993): 19–37.

10. Tom Gunning, "The Cinema of Attraction: Early Film, Its Spectator, and the Avant-Garde," *Wide Angle* 8, nos. 3–4: 64. Gunning elaborates on this argument in his essay "An Aesthetic of Astonishment: Early Film and the (In)Credulous Spectator," *Art & Text* 34 (1989): 31–45.

11. See, for example, Rick Altman, ed., *Genre: The Musical* (London: Routledge and Kegan Paul, 1981), and Feuer, *Hollywood Musical.*

12. See, for example, Richard Dyer and Ginette Vincendeau, *Popular European Cinemas* (London: Routledge, 1992), 1.

13. Nataša Ďurovičová, "Some Thoughts at an Intersection of the Popular and the National," *Velvet Light Trap* 34 (fall 1994), 4. I am indebted to this essay and the author for many insights into recent debates on popular cinema in the U.S. and in Europe. The title of this essay is also indebted to Ďurovičová's title and to her formulation of conceptual tensions and precarious categories in film studies.

14. Heide Schlüpmann, "Early German Cinema: Melodrama and Social Drama," 206–219, and Thomas Elsaesser, "Author, Actor, Showman: Reinhold Schünzel and *Hallo Caesar!* 72–86.

15. Nataša Ďurovičová, "Translating America: The Hollywood Multilinguals, 1929–1933," in *Sound Theory/Sound Practice,* ed. Rick Altman (New York: Routledge, 1992), 150.

16. Thomas J. Saunders, *Hollywood in Berlin: American Cinema and Weimar Germany* (Berkeley and Los Angeles: U of California P, 1994), 247.

17. See, for example, Elsaesser, "Film History" and "Lulu and the Meter Man: Louise Brooks, Pabst, and *Pandora's Box,*" *Screen* 24, nos. 4–5 (July–October 1983): 4–36.

18. Elsaesser, "Hollywood Berlin."

19. See, for example, Joseph Garncarz, "Hollywood in Germany: The Role of American Film in Germany, 1925–1990," in *Hollywood in Europe*, ed. Ellwood and Kroes, 94–117. Garncarz argues that during the period 1925–71, "German-made films were more popular than American films within the domestic market [and] German film audiences selected American films for viewing according to the standards developed within the native German film industry." According to Garncarz, it was only after the 1970s that "American films established themselves as German audiences' preferred films [and] German commercial films started to become increasingly like American films, beginning a trend which has continued until the present" (95).

20. Klaus Kreimeier, *Die Ufa-Story: Geschichte eines Filmkonzerns* (Munich: Hanser, 1992).

21. Katie Trumpener has initiated research in this area. My remarks here are indebted to her paper "Obsessive Monologues, Modernist Songs: Towards the Reunification of the Postwar German Cinemas," delivered at the University of Iowa, Institute for Cinema and Culture, November 1997. This paper will appear in a forthcoming book coauthored by Trumpener and Sabine Hake and published by Routledge Press, entitled *German National Cinema*.

22. Karsten Witte, "Visual Pleasure Inhibited: Aspects of the German Revue Film," *New German Critique* 24–25 (fall–winter 1981–82): 238–263.

23. Rentschler, *Ministry of Illusion*, 14.

24. Susan Sontag, "Fascinating Fascism," 93, qtd. in ibid., 39–40.

25. Renstchler, *Ministry of Illusion*, 16.

26. Richard Dyer, "Entertainment and Utopia," in *Genre*, ed. Altman, 175–189.

27. Witte, "Visual Pleasure Inhibited," 244.

8. The Hottentot and the Blonde Venus

1. Rivièré, "Womanliness as a Masquerade," 35.

2. For a broader consideration of this issue, see Petro, *Joyless Streets*, especially chapter 3.

3. See, for example, chapter 6 in this volume, where I discuss the complex and interesting work of Hannah Höch, especially her photomontage *Liebe im Busch* (1925), which references the Rhineland controversy and which resonates with both Riviere's essay and a film like *Blonde Venus*. In this regard, see Makela, *Photomontages of Hannah Höch*.

4. See, for example, the collection of essays included in *Blacks and German Culture*, ed. Reinhold Grimm and Jost Hermand (Madison: U of Wisconsin P, 1986).

5. Jean Walton, "Nightmare of the Uncoordinated White-Folk: Race, Psychoanalysis, and *Borderline*," *Discourse* 19, no. 1 (winter 1997): 88–109. In this essay, Walton argues that race substitutes for and subsumes gender in the masquerade (the white woman substitutes the black male body for her own): "The true 'father figures' in this imagined scenario set in the 'Southern States of America' would

not be the attacking 'negro' but rather the white male authorities representing 'justice'. To propitiate the (white) fathers, the white woman fantasizes that she can substitute the black male body for her own. This suggests that the 'masquerade' involves a degree of identification and desire across imagined racially defined differences—indeed, a trafficking in the eroticized black male body." My own analysis of *Blonde Venus* suggests that a more complex operation of identification and displacement may be at play, extending beyond an eroticized black male body to include a black female body as well. This analysis is indebted to Tara McPherson's work on southern femininity in her dissertation, "Reconstructing Dixie: Place, Race, and Femininity in the Deep South," which is forthcoming in book form from Duke University Press.

6. See, for example, the collection of essays included in *America and the Germans: An Assessment of a Three-Hundred-Year History*, ed. Frank Trommler and Joseph McVeigh (Philadelphia: U of Pennsylvania P, 1985).

7. Nancy Nenno provides an excellent account of Baker's career in Europe in her essay "Femininity."

8. Lynn Haney, *Naked at the Feast: A Biography of Josephine Baker* (New York: Dodd, Mead, 1981); the quotations from various critics that I cite further on in the text are derived from this biography (which does not footnote its sources), 64–67.

9. Nenno, "Femininity," 155.

10. On this issue, see, for example, Saunders, *Hollywood in Berlin*.

11. Mulvey, "Visual Pleasure"; E. Ann Kaplan, *Women and Film: Both Sides of the Camera* (New York: Methuen, 1983), 49–60; Lea Jacobs, *The Wages of Sin: Censorship and the Fallen Woman Film, 1928–1942* (Madison: U of Wisconsin P, 1991); Andrea Weiss, "'A Queer Feeling When I Look at You': Hollywood Stars and Lesbian Spectatorship in the 1930s," in *Multiple Voices in Feminist Film Criticism*, ed. Diane Carson, Linda Dittmar, and Janice R. Welsch (Minneapolis: U of Minnesota P, 1994), 330–342; Janet Staiger, "The Romances of the Blonde Venus: Movie Censors Versus Movie Fans," *Canadian Journal of Film Studies* 6, no. 2 (autumn 1997): 5–20.

12. For an excellent discussion of New York culture at this time, see Marybeth Hamilton, *When I'm Bad, I'm Better: Mae West, Sex, and American Entertainment* (Berkeley and Los Angeles: U of California P, 1997).

13. Jacobs, *Wages of Sin*, 89.

14. Mary Ann Doane, "Dark Continents: Epistemologies of Racial and Sexual Difference in Psychoanalysis and the Cinema," in *Femme Fatales*, 211–212.

15. Lynne Frame, "Gretchen, Girl, Garçonne? Weimar Science and Popular Culture in Search of the Ideal New Woman," in *Women in the Metropolis*, ed. von Ankum, 14.

16. Rony, *The Third Eye* (Durham: Duke UP, 1996), 199.

17. Josephine Baker and Jo Bouillon, *Josephine*, trans. Mariana Fitzpatrick (St. Martin's/Marek, 1985), 84.

18. Rony, *The Third Eye*, 203.

9. Film Feminism and Nostalgia for the Seventies

1. Jeff MacGregor, "Copying Copies: The Sad Slide from Stardom to Celebrity," *New York Times,* March 19, 2000.

2. Morris, *Pirate's Fiancée.*

3. My question was inspired by the theories of history advanced by Siegfried Kracauer, especially in his final work, *History.*

4. B. Ruby Rich, *Chick Flicks: Theories and Memories of the Feminist Film Movement* (Durham: Duke UP, 1998), 6.

5. Janet Bergstrom, "American Feminism and French Film Theory," *Iris* 10 (April 1990): 185.

6. Bergstrom and Doane, "The Female Spectator," 15.

7. Bergstrom, "American Feminism," 189.

8. Ibid.

9. Williams, introduction to *Viewing Positions,* 11. In this introduction, Williams cites Mulvey's "Visual Pleasure" and Gunning's "Cinema of Attraction, as well as the elaboration of his earlier argument in the later "An Aesthetic of Astonishment."

10. I have written more extensively about this in chapter 5 in this volume.

11. I have elaborated this argument, in the context of recent debates on Weimar and Nazi cinema, in chapter 7 in this volume.

12. Rich, *Chick Flicks,* 117.

WORKS CITED

Adorno, Theodor. "Der wunderliche Realist. Über Siegfried Kracauer." *Noten zur Literatur 3*, 83–108. Frankfurt am Main: Suhrkamp, 1965; reprinted in translation as "The Curious Realist: On Siegfried Kracauer," in *New German Critique* 54 (fall 1991): 159–177.

———. "Letters to Walter Benjamin." *Aesthetics and Politics*. Trans. Ronald Taylor. London: New Left Books, 1977.

———. *Notes to Literature*. Vols. 1, 2. Ed. Rolf Tiedemann, trans. Shierry Weber Nicholson. New York: Columbia UP, 1991, 1992.

Allen, Jeanne. "The Film Viewer as Consumer." *Quarterly Review of Film Studies* 5, no. 4 (1980): 481–499.

Allen, Robert C. "Film History: The Narrow Discourse." *The 1977 Film Studies Annual II*, 9–16. New York: Redgrave, 1977.

Allen, Robert C., and Douglas Gomery. *Film History: Theory and Practice*. New York: Knopf, 1985.

Alley, Robert S. "Television Drama." *Television: The Critical View*, ed. Horace Newcomb, 89–121. 3d ed. New York: Oxford UP, 1982.

Althusser, Louis. *For Marx*. Trans. Ben Brewster. London: New Left Books, 1977.

Altman, Charles F. "Towards a Historiography of American Film." *Cinema Journal* 16, no. 2 (1977): 1–25.

Altman, Rick, ed. *Genre: The Musical*. London: Routledge and Kegan Paul, 1981.

———. "Television/Sound" in *Studies in Entertainment: Critical Approaches to Mass Culture*, ed. Tania Modleski, 39–54. Bloomington: Indiana UP, 1986. Originally "The Sound Track in Television," presented at the 1984 SCS Conference, 28–31 March 1984, Madison, Wisconsin.

Andrew, Dudley. *The Major Film Theories: An Introduction*. New York: Oxford UP, 1976.

———. "The Neglected Tradition of Phenomenology in Film Theory." *Movies and Methods*, ed. Bill Nichols. 2d ed. Berkeley and Los Angeles: U of California P, 1985.

———. "The 'Three Ages' of Cinema Studies and the Age to Come." *Publications of the Modern Language Association* 115, no. 3 (May 2000): 341–351.

Arato, Andrew, and Paul Breines. *The Young Lukács and the Origins of Western Marxism*. New York: Seabury, 1979.

Baker, Josephine, and Jo Bouillon. *Josephine*. Trans. Mariana Fitzpatrick. New York: Harper and Row, 1977.

Balides, Connie. "Scenarios of Exposure in the Practice of Everyday Life: Women in the Cinema of Attractions." *Screen* 34, no. 1 (spring 1993): 19–37.

Barbiero, Daniel. "A Weakness for Heidegger: The German Root of *Il Pensiero Debole*." *New German Critique* 55 (winter 1992): 159–172.

Barnes, Djuna. *I Could Never Be without a Husband: Interviews by Djuna Barnes*. Ed. Alyce Barry. London: Virago, 1985.

Barthes, Roland. *Camera Lucida: Reflections on Photography*. Trans. Richard Howard. New York: Hill, 1981.

———. "Diderot, Brecht, Eisenstein." Trans. Stephen Heath. *Screen* 15, no. 2 (1974): 33–39.

Baudry, Jean–Louis. "The Apparatus." Trans. Jean Andrews and Bertrand Augst. *Camera Obscura* 1 (1979): 104–126.

———. "Ideological Effects of the Basic Cinematographic Apparatus." Trans. Alan Williams. *Film Quarterly* 27, no. 2 (1974): 39–47.

Benjamin, Walter. *The Arcades Project*. Trans. Howard Eiland and Kevin Mc-Laughlin. Cambridge: Harvard UP, 1999.

———. "Das Kunstwerk im Zeitalter senier technischen Reproduzierbarkeit." *Gesammelte Schriften*, ed. Rolf Tiedemann and Hermann Schweppenhäuser. First version, 431–166. Second version, 471–505. Frankfurt am Main: Suhrkamp, 1974.

———. *Das Passagen-Werk*. Ed. Rolf Tiedemann. 2 vols. Frankfurt am Main: Suhrkamp, 1982.

———. *Selected Writings, 1913–1926*. Trans. Marcus Paul Bullock and Michael William Jennings. Cambridge: Harvard UP, 1996.

———. *Selected Writings, 1927–1934*. Trans. Marcus Paul Bullock, Michael William Jennings, Howard Eiland, and Gary Smith. Cambridge: Harvard UP, 1999.

———. "A Short History of Photography." Trans. Stanley Mitchell. *Screen* 13, no. 1 (1973): 5–26. Originally published in three parts in the *Literarische Welt* (1931).

———. "The Work of Art in the Age of Mechanical Reproduction." *Illuminations*, ed. Hannah Arendt, trans. Harry Zohn, 217–251. New York: Schocken, 1969.

Bergstrom, Janet. "American Feminism and French Film Theory." *Iris* 10 (April 1990): 183–197.

———. "Rereading the Work of Claire Johnston." *Feminism and Film Theory*, ed. Constance Penley, 80–88. New York: Routledge, 1988.

Bergstrom, Janet, and Mary Ann Doane. "The Female Spectator: Contexts and Directions." *Camera Obscura*, no. 20–21 (May–September 1989): 5–27 (special issue on "The Spectarix").

Blanchot, Maurice. "Everyday Speech." Trans. Susan Hanson. *Yale French Studies* 73 (1987): 12–20.

Bordwell, David. "Eisenstein's Epistemological Shift." *Screen* 15, no. 4 (winter 1974–75): 32–46.

————. *Making Meaning: Inference and Rhetoric in the Interpretation of Cinema*. Cambridge: Harvard UP, 1989.

Bordwell, David, Janet Staiger, and Kristin Thompson. *The Classical Hollywood Cinema: Film Style and Mode of Production to 1960*. New York: Columbia UP, 1985.

Branigan, Edward. "Color and Cinema: Problems in the Writing of Film History." *Film Reader* 4 (1979): 16–34.

Brassaï. *The Artists of My Life*. New York: Viking, 1982.

————. *Brassaï*. New York: Pantheon, 1988.

————. *Conversations avec Picasso*. Paris: Gallimard, 1964.

————. *Graffiti*. Paris: Temps, 1961.

————. *Henry Miller grandeur nature*. Paris: Gallimard, 1975.

————. *Paris by Night*. New York: Pantheon, 1987.

————. *Paris de nuit*. Paris: Arts et Métiers Graphiques, 1933.

————. *Le Paris secret des annés 30*. Paris: Gallimard, 1976.

Brockmann, Stephen. "Weimar Sexual Cynicism." *Dancing on the Volcano: Essays on the Culture of the Weimar Republic*, ed. Thomas W. Kniesche and Stephen Brockmann, 166–167. Columbia, S.C.: Camden House, 1994.

Browning, Christopher. *Ordinary Men: Reserve Police Battalion 101 and the Final Solution in Poland*. New York: HarperCollins, 1992.

Buck–Morris, Susan. *The Dialectics of Seeing: Walter Benjamin and the Arcades Project*. Cambridge: MIT P, 1989.

Burch, Noël. "Narrative/Diegesis–Thresholds, Limits." *Screen* 23, no. 2 (July–August 1982): 16–33.

Burgin, Victor. *Thinking Photography*. London: Macmillan, 1982.

Butler, Alison. "Feminist Theory and Women's Films at the Turn of the Century," *Screen* 41, no. 1 (spring 2000): 73–78.

Caughie, John. *Theories of Authorship*. London: BFI, 1982.

Chow, Rey. "Silent Is the Ancient Plain: Music, Filmmaking, and the Conception of Reform in China's New Cinema." *Discourse* 12, no. 2 (1990): 82–109.

Cixous, Hélène. "Castration or Decapitation." Trans. Annette Kuhn. *Signs: Journal of Women in Culture and Society* 3, no. 1 (autumn 1981): 44.

Comolli, Jean–Louis, and Paul Narboni. "Cinema/Ideology/Criticism." Reprinted in translation in *Screen* 12, no. 1 (spring 1971): 27–36, and in *Movies and Methods*, ed. Bill Nichols, 23–30. Berkeley: U of California P, 1976.

Cook, Pam. "Approaching the Work of Dorothy Arzner." *The Work of Dorothy Arzner: Towards a Feminist Cinema*, ed. Claire Johnston. London: BFI, 1974.

Corrigan, Timothy. *A Cinema without Walls: Movies and Culture after Vietnam*. New Brunswick: Rutgers UP, 1991.

Crary, Jonathan. "Spectacle, Attention, Counter–Memory." *October* 50 (1989): 97–107.

————. *Suspensions of Perception: Attention, Spectacle, and Modern Culture*. Cambridge: MIT P, 2000.

————. *Techniques of the Observer: On Vision and Modernity in the Nineteenth Century*. Cambridge: MIT P, 1990.

Dech, Jula. *Hannah Höch Schnitt mit der Küchenmesser DADA—Spiegel einer Bierbauchkultur.* Frankfurt am Main: Fischer, 1989.

de Lauretis, Teresa. *Alice Doesn't: Feminism, Semiotics, Cinema.* Bloomington: Indiana UP, 1984.

———. "The Violence of Rhetoric: Considerations on Representation and Gender." *Technologies of Gender: Essays on Theory, Film, and Fiction,* ed. Teresa de Lauretis, 31–50. Bloomington: Indiana UP, 1987.

Doane, Mary Ann. *Femme Fatales: Feminism, Film Theory, Psychoanalysis.* New York: Routledge, 1991.

———. *The Desire to Desire: The Woman's Film of the 1940s.* Bloomington: Indiana UP, 1987.

———, "Feminist Film Theory and the Enterprise of Criticism." Typescript. Author files.

———. "The 'Woman's Film': Possession and Address." *Re–Vision: Essays in Feminist Film Criticism,* ed. Mary Ann Doane, Patricia Mellencamp, and Linda Williams. AFI Monograph Series 3. Frederick, Md.: University Publications of America, 1983.

Döblin, Alfred. "Das Theater der kleinen Leute." *Kino–Debatte: Literatur und Film, 1909–1929,* ed. Anton Kaes, 38. Tübingen: Niemeyer, 1979.

Ďurovičová, Nataša. "Some Thoughts at an Intersection of the Popular and the National." *Velvet Light Trap* 34 (fall 1994): 3–9.

———. "Translating America: The Hollywood Multilinguals, 1929–1933." *Sound Theory/Sound Practice,* ed. Rick Altman, 138–153. New York: Routledge, 1992.

Dyer, Richard. "Entertainment and Utopia." *Genre: The Musical,* ed. Rick Altman, 175–189. London: Routledge and Kegan Paul, 1981.

Dyer, Richard, and Ginette Vincendeau. *Popular European Cinemas.* London: Routledge, 1992.

Eckert, Charles. "The Carole Lombard in Macy's Window." *Quarterly Review of Film Studies* 3, no. 1 (1978): 1–22.

Eisner, Lotte. *The Haunted Screen: Expressionism in the German Film and the Influence of Max Reinhardt.* Trans. Roger Greaves. Berkeley and Los Angeles: U of California P, 1969.

Eliot, T. S. *Selected Essays.* New York: Harcourt Brace, 1950.

Ellis, John. "The Institution of Cinema." *Edinburgh '77 Magazine* 2 (1977): 56–66.

Elsaesser, Thomas. "Author, Actor, Showman: Reinhold Schünzel and *Hallo Caesar!*" *Popular European Cinemas,* ed. Richard Dyer and Ginette Vincendeau, 72–86. London: Routledge, 1992.

———. "Cinema—The Irresponsible Signifier, or 'The Gamble with History': Film Theory or Cinema Theory." *New German Critique* 40 (winter 1987): 65–89.

———. "Film History and Visual Pleasure: Weimar Cinema." *Cinema Histories, Cinema Practices,* ed. Patricia Mellencamp and Philip Rosen, 47–84. Frederick, Md.: University Publications of America, 1984.

———. "Hollywood Berlin." *Sight and Sound* (November 1997): 14–17.

————. "Lulu and the Meter Man: Louise Brooks, Pabst, and *Pandora's Box.*" *Screen* 24, nos. 4–5 (July–October 1983): 4–36.

Fenichel, Otto. "On the Psychology of Boredom." *Organization and Pathology of Thought: Selected Sources,* ed. David Rapaport, 349–361. New York: Columbia UP, 1959.

Feuer, Jane. *The Hollywood Musical.* Bloomington: Indiana UP, 1982.

Fielder, Leslie. "The Middle against Both Ends." *Mass Culture: The Popular Arts in America,* ed. Bernard Rosenberg and David Manning White, 537–547. New York: Free Press, 1957.

Flitterman-Lewis, Sandy. *To Desire Differently: Feminism and the French Cinema.* Urbana: U of Illinois P, 1990.

Foster, Hal, ed. *The Anti–Aesthetic: Essays on Postmodern Culture.* Port Townsend, Wash.: Bay, 1983.

Frame, Lynne. "Gretchen, Girl, Garçonne? Weimar Science and Popular Culture in Search of the Ideal New Woman." *Women in the Metropolis: Gender and Modernity in Weimar Culture,* ed. Katharina von Ankum, 12–40. Berkeley and Los Angeles: U of California P, 1997.

Friedlander, Saul, ed. *Probing the Limits of Representation: Nazism and the "Final" Solution.* Cambridge: Harvard UP, 1992.

Garncarz, Joseph. "Hollywood in Germany: The Role of American Film in Germany, 1925–1990." *Hollywood in Europe: Experiences of a Cultural Hegemony,* ed. David W. Ellwood and Rob Kroes, 94–117. Amsterdam: Vrije UP, 1994.

Gay, Peter. *Weimar Culture: The Outsider as Insider.* New York: Harper and Row, 1970.

Giedion, Siegfried. *Mechanization Takes Command: A Contribution to Anonymous History.* New York: Oxford UP, 1948.

Goldhagen, Daniel. *Hitler's Willing Executioners: Ordinary Germans and the Holocaust.* New York: Little, Brown, 1996.

Grimm, Reinhold, and Jost Hermand, eds. *Blacks and German Culture.* Madison: U of Wisconsin P, 1986.

Grossberg, Lawrence. "Postmodernity and Affect: All Dressed Up with No Place to Go." *Communication* 10 (1988): 271–293.

Gunning, Tom. "An Aesthetic of Astonishment: Early Film and the (In)credulous Spectator." *Art & Text* 34 (1989): 31–45.

————. "The Cinema of Attractions: Early Film, Its Spectator, and the Avant-Garde." *Wide Angle* 8, nos. 3–4 (1986): 63–70.

Hake, Sabine. "The Melodramatic Imagination of Detlef Sierck: *Final Chord* and Its Resonances." *Screen* 38, no. 2 (summer 1997): 129–148.

Hamilton, Marybeth. *When I'm Bad, I'm Better: Mae West, Sex, and American Entertainment.* Berkeley and Los Angeles: U of California P, 1997.

Haney, Lynn. *Naked at the Feast: A Biography of Josephine Baker.* New York: Dodd, Mead, 1981.

Hansen, Miriam. "Benjamin, Cinema, and Experience: 'The Blue Flower in the Land of Technology.'" *New German Critique* 40 (1987): 179–224.

―――. "Decentric Perspectives: Kracauer's Early Writings on Film and Mass Culture." *New German Critique* 54 (fall 1991): 47–76.

―――. "Early Silent Cinema: Whose Public Sphere?" *New German Critique* 29 (spring–summer 1983): 147–183.

Haskell, Molly. *From Reverence to Rape: The Treatment of Women in the Movies.* Harmondsworth: Penguin, 1974.

Heath, Stephen. "From Brecht to Film—Theses, Problems." *Screen* 16, no. 4 (winter 1975–76): 34–45.

―――. "Narrative Space." *Screen* 17, no. 3 (autumn 1976): 68–112. (Reprinted in Heath, *Questions of Cinema* [Bloomington: Indiana UP, 1981].)

Hermand, Jost. "Artificial Atavism: German Expressionism and Blacks." *Blacks and German Culture,* ed. Reinhold Grimm and Jost Hermand, 65–86. Madison: U of Wisconsin P, 1986.

Hill, Paul, and Thomas Cooper, eds. *Dialogue with Photography.* New York: Farrar, 1979.

Hirsch, Paul M. "The Role of Television and Popular Culture in Contemporary Society." In *Television: The Critical View,* ed. Horace Newcomb, 280–310. 3d ed. New York: Oxford UP, 1982.

Houston, Beverle. "Viewing Television: The Metapsychology of Endless Consumption." *Quarterly Review of Film Studies* 9, no. 3 (summer 1984): 183–195.

Huguet, Michèle. *L'Ennui et ses discours.* Paris: Presses Universitaires de France, 1984.

Huyssen, Andreas. Foreword to *Critique of Cynical Reason,* by Peter Sloterdijk, ix–xxv. Trans. Michael Eldred. Minneapolis: U of Minnesota P, 1987.

―――. "Mass Culture as Woman: Modernism's Other." *Studies in Entertainment: Critical Approaches to Mass Culture,* ed. Tania Modleski, 188–207. Bloomington: Indiana UP, 1986.

―――. "The Vamp and the Machine: Technology and Sexuality in Fritz Lang's *Metropolis.*" *New German Critique* 24–25 (fall–winter 1981–82): 221–237.

Jacobs, Lea. *The Wages of Sin: Censorship and the Fallen Woman Film, 1928–1942.* Madison: U of Wisconsin P, 1991.

Jameson, Fredric. *The Political Unconscious: Narrative as a Socially Symbolic Act.* Ithaca: Cornell UP, 1981.

―――. *Postmodernism, or, The Cultural Logic of Late Capitalism.* Durham: Duke UP, 1991.

―――. "Reflections in Conclusion." *Aesthetics and Politics,* ed. Ronald Taylor, 196–213. London: New Left Books, 1977.

Jay, Gregory S. *America the Scrivener: Deconstruction and the Subject of Literary History.* Ithaca: Cornell UP, 1990.

―――. "Postmodernism and *The Waste Land:* Women, Mass Culture, and Others." *Rereading the New,* ed. Kevin Dettmar, 221–246. Ann Arbor: U of Michigan P, 1992.

Jay, Martin. "The Extraterritorial Life of Siegfried Kracauer." *Salmagundi* 31–32 (fall 1975–winter 1976): 49–106.

Johnston, Claire. "Dorothy Arzner: Critical Strategies." *The Work of Dorothy Arzner: Towards a Feminist Cinema,* ed. Claire Johnston. London: BFI, 1974.

———. "Feminist Politics and Film History." *Screen* 16, no. 3 (1975): 115–124.

Kaplan, E. Ann, ed. *Feminism and Film.* New York: Oxford UP, 2000.

———. *Regarding Television.* American Film Institute Monograph Series, vol. 115. Frederick, Md.: University Publications of America, 1984.

———. *Women and Film: Both Sides of the Camera.* New York: Methuen, 1983.

Klapp, Orrin. *Overload and Boredom: Essays on the Quality of Life in the Information Society.* New York: Greenwood, 1986.

Klüver, Billy, and Julie Martin. *Kiki's Paris: Artists and Lovers, 1900–1930.* New York: Abrams, 1989.

Koch, Gertrud. "Exorcised: Marlene Dietrich and German Nationalism." *Women and Film: A Sight and Sound Reader,* ed. Pam Cook and Philip Dodd, 10–15. Philadelphia: Temple UP, 1993.

———. *Siegfried Kracauer: An Introduction.* Trans. Jeremy Gaines. Princeton: Princeton UP, 2000.

Koch, Stephen. *Stargazer: The Life, World, and Films of Andy Warhol.* New York: Marion Boyars, 1991.

Kracauer, Siegfried. "Cult of Distraction." Trans. Thomas Y. Levin. *New German Critique* 40 (1987): 91–96.

———. "Das Ornament der Masse." *Das Ornament der Masse: Essays 1920–31.* Ed. Karsten Witte. Frankfurt am Main: Suhrkamp, 1977.

———. *From Caligari to Hitler: A Psychological History of the German Film.* Princeton: Princeton UP, 1947.

———. *History: The Last Things Before the Last.* New York: Oxford UP, 1969.

———. "The Mass Ornament." Trans. Barbara Correll and Jack Zipes. *New German Critique* 5 (1975): 67–76.

———. *The Mass Ornament: Weimar Essays.* Trans. Thomas Y. Levin. Cambridge: Harvard UP, 1995.

———. *Theory of Film: The Redemption of Physical Reality.* New York: Oxford UP, 1960.

Kreimeier, Klaus. *Die Ufa-Story: Geschichte eines Filmkonzerns.* Munich: Hanser, 1992.

Kuhn, Reinhard. *The Demon of Noontide: Ennui in Western Literature.* Princeton: Princeton UP, 1976.

Lavin, Maud. *Cut with the Kitchen Knife: The Weimar Photomontages of Hannah Höch.* New Haven: Yale UP, 1993.

Lefebvre, Henri. "The Everyday and Everydayness." Trans. Christine Levich, with Alice Kaplan and Kristin Ross. *Yale French Studies* 73 (1987): 7–11.

Lepenies, Wolf. *Melancholy and Society.* Trans. Jeremy Gaines and Dorris Jones. Cambridge: Harvard UP, 1992. Originally published as *Melancholie und Gesellschaft.* Frankfurt am Main: Suhrkamp, 1969.

Lethen, Helmut. *Verhältenslehren der Kälte. Lebensversuche zwischen den Kriegen.* Frankfurt am Main: Suhrkamp, 1994.

Lyon, James K. *Bertolt Brecht in America*. Princeton: Princeton UP, 1980.

Lyotard, Jean-François. "The Sublime and the Avant–Garde." Trans. Lisa Liebmann. *Art Forum* 22 (1984): 36–43.

Makela, Maria. *The Photomontages of Hannah Höch*. Exhibition catalogue. Minneapolis: Walker Art Center, 1996.

Maltby, Richard, and Ruth Vasey. "The International Language Problem: European Reactions to Hollywood's Conversion to Sound." *Hollywood in Europe: Experiences of a Cultural Hegemony*, ed. David W. Ellwood and Rob Kroes, 68–93. Amsterdam: Vrije UP, 1994.

Mander, Jerry. *Four Arguments for the Elimination of Television*. New York: Morrow, 1978.

Mast, Gerald. "Film History and Film Histories." *Quarterly Review of Film Studies* 1 (1976): 297–314.

Mayne, Judith. *Kino and the Woman Question: Feminism and Soviet Silent Film*. Columbus: Ohio State UP, 1989.

———. *The Woman at the Keyhole: Feminist and Women's Cinema*. Bloomington: Indiana UP, 1990.

McPherson, Tara. *Reconstructing Dixie: Race, Place, and Femininity in the Deep South*. Durham: Duke UP, forthcoming.

Meisel, Steven. "Flesh and Fantasy." *Rolling Stone*, 13 June 1991, 34–50.

Mellencamp, Patricia. *A Fine Romance . . . Five Ages of Film Feminism*. Philadelphia: Temple UP, 1995.

Metz, Christian. *The Imaginary Signifier: Psychoanalysis and the Cinema*. Trans. Celia Britton, Annwyl Williams, Ben Brewster, and Alfred Guzzetti. Bloomington: Indiana UP, 1982.

Miller, Nancy. "Changing the Subject: Authorship, Writing, and the Reader." *Feminist Studies/Critical Studies*, ed. Teresa de Lauretis, 102–120. Bloomington: Indiana UP, 1986.

Miner, Worthington. "The Terrible Toll of Taboos." *Television and Radio*, ed. Poyntz Tyler. New York: Wilson, 1961.

Modleski, Tania. *Old Wives' Tales: Feminist Re-Visions of Film and Other Fictions*. New York: New York UP, 1998.

———. "The Rhythms of Reception: Daytime Television and Women's Work." *Regarding Television*, ed. Ann E. Kaplan, 67–75. American Film Institute Monograph Series, vol. 115. Frederick, Md.: University Publications of America, 1984.

———. "The Search for Tomorrow in Today's Soap Operas." *Loving with a Vengeance: Mass Produced Fantasies for Women*, 85–109. New York: Metheun, 1984.

———. "The Terror of Pleasure: The Contemporary Horror Film and Postmodern Theory." *Studies in Entertainment: Critical Approaches to Mass Culture*, ed. Tania Modleski, 155–166. Bloomington: Indiana UP, 1986.

———. "Time and Desire in the Women's Film." *Cinema Journal* 23, no. 3 (spring 1984): 19–30.

Morris, Meaghan. *The Pirate's Fiancée: Feminism, Reading, Postmodernism*. New York: Verso, 1988.

Mulvey, Laura. "Hollywood Cinema and Feminist Theory: A Strange but Persistent Relationship." *Iris* 26 (1998): 23–32.

———. "Visual Pleasure and Narrative Cinema." *Screen* 16, no. 3 (1975): 6–18.

Nash, Mark, and Steve Neale. "Film History/Production/Memory." *Screen* 18, no. 4 (1977–78): 71–91.

Nenno, Nancy. "Femininity, the Primitive, and Modern Urban Space: Josephine Baker in Berlin." *Women in the Metropolis*, ed. Katharina von Ankum, 145–161. Berkeley and Los Angeles: U of California P, 1997.

Newton, Judith. "History as Usual? Feminism and the 'New Historicism.'" *Cultural Critique* 9 (1988): 87–121.

Nowell–Smith, Geoffrey. "Facts about Films and Facts of Film." *Quarterly Review of Film Studies* 1 (1976): 272–275.

"On Boredom." Special issue, *Documents* 1, nos. 1–2 (winter 1993).

Partsch, Cornelius. "Hannibal ante Portas: Jazz in Weimar." *Dancing on the Volcano: Essays on the Culture of the Weimar Republic*, ed. Thomas W. Kniesche and Stephen Brockmann, 105–116. Columbia, S.C.: Camden House, 1994.

Penley, Constance. "Feminism, Film Theory, and the Bachelor Machines." *m/f* 10 (1985).

———. "The Lady Doesn't Vanish: Feminism and Film Theory." *Feminism and Film Theory*, ed. Constance Penley, 1–24. New York: Routledge, 1988.

Petro, Patrice. *Fugitive Images: From Photography to Video.* Bloomington: Indiana UP, 1995.

———. *Joyless Streets: Women and Melodramatic Representation in Weimar Germany.* Princeton: Princeton UP, 1989.

———. "Modernity and Mass Culture in Weimar: Contours of a Discourse on Sexuality in Early Theories of Perception and Representation." *New German Critique* 40 (1987): 115–146.

Porter, Dennis. "Soap Time: Thoughts on a Commodity Art Form." *Television: The Critical View*, ed. Horace Newcomb, 129–131. 3d ed. New York: Oxford UP, 1982.

Renov, Michael, and Jane Gaines, eds. "Female Representation and Consumer Culture." Special issue, *Quarterly Review of Film and Video* 11, no. 1 (1989).

Rentschler, Eric. *The Ministry of Illusion: Nazi Cinema and its Afterlife.* Cambridge: Harvard UP, 1996.

Rich, B. Ruby. *Chick Flicks: Theories and Memories of the Feminist Film Movement.* Durham: Duke UP, 1998.

Rivière, Joan. "Womanliness as a Masquerade." *Formations of Fantasy*, ed. Victor Burgin, James Donald, and Cora Kaplan, 35–44. London: Metheun, 1986.

Robinson, Paul. "TV Can't Educate." *The Little Brown Reader*, ed. Marcia Stubbs and Sylvan Barnett, 216–219. 3d ed. Boston: Little, Brown, 1983. Originally published in *New Republic* (12 August 1978).

Rodowick, D. N. "The Last Things Before the Last: Kracauer and History." *New German Critique* 41 (spring–summer 1987): 109–139.

Rony, Fatimah Tobing. *The Third Eye: Race, Cinema, and the Ethnographic Spectacle.* Durham: Duke UP, 1996.

Rose, Jacqueline. "The Cinematic Apparatus: Problems in Current Theory." *The Cinematic Apparatus,* ed. Teresa de Lauretis and Stephen Heath, 172–186. New York: St. Martin's, 1980.

———. "The Man Who Mistook His Wife for a Hat, or A Wife Is Like an Umbrella: Fantasies of the Modern and Postmodern." *Universal Abandon? The Politics of Postmodernism,* ed. Andrew Ross, 237–250. Minneapolis: U of Minnesota P, 1988.

Rosen, Marjorie. *Popcorn Venus: Women, Movies, and the American Dream.* New York: Avon, 1973.

Rosen, Philip. "History, Textuality, Nation: Kracauer, Burch, and Some Problems in the Study of National Cinema." *Iris* 2, no. 2 (1984): 69–84.

———, ed. *Narrative/Apparatus/Ideology.* New York: Columbia UP, 1986.

Ross, Andrew, ed. *Universal Abandon? The Politics of Postmodernism.* Minneapolis: U of Minnesota P, 1988.

Said, Edward. *The World, the Text, and the Critic.* Cambridge: Harvard UP, 1983.

Sartre, Jean-Paul. "The Journey and the Return." *Essays on Language and Literature.* Port Washington, N.Y.: Kennikat, 1964.

Saunders, Thomas J. *Hollywood in Berlin: American Cinema and Weimar Germany.* Berkeley and Los Angeles: U of California P, 1994.

Schachtel, Earnest G. *Metamorphosis: On the Development of Affect, Perception, Attention, and Memory.* New York: Basic, 1951.

Schiesari, Juliana. *The Gendering of Melancholia: Feminism, Psychoanalysis, and the Symbolics of Loss in Renaissance Literature.* Ithaca, N.Y.: Cornell UP, 1992.

Schlüpmann, Heide. "Early German Cinema: Melodrama and Social Drama." *Popular European Cinemas,* ed. Richard Dyer and Ginette Vincendeau, 206–219. London: Routledge, 1992.

———. "Kinosucht." *Frauen und Film* 33 (1982): 45–52.

———. "Phenomenology of Film: On Siegfried Kracauer's Writings of the 1920s." *New German Critique* 40 (winter 1987): 97–114.

Schulte-Sasse, Linda. *Entertaining the Third Reich: Illusions of Wholeness in Nazi Cinema.* Durham: Duke UP, 1996.

Sekula, Allan. "On the Invention of Photographic Meaning." *Thinking Photography,* ed. Victor Burgin, 84–109. London: Macmillan, 1982.

Simmel, Georg. "The Metropolis and Mental Life." *Georg Simmel: On Individuality and Social Forms.* Ed. Donald N. Levine. Chicago: U of Chicago P, 1971. Reprinted from *Social Sciences III: Selections and Selected Readings.* Trans. Edward A. Shils. U of Chicago P, 1948. Originally published as "Die Grosstadt und das Geistesleben." *Die Grosstadt: Jahrbuch der Gehe–Stiftung* (1903).

Simpson, David. "Literary Criticism and the Return to History." *Critical Inquiry* 14 (1988): 721–747.

Sklar, Robert. *Movie-Made America.* New York: Random House, 1975.

Sloterdijk, Peter. *Critique of Cynical Reason.* Trans. Michael Eldred. Minneapolos: U of Minnesota P, 1987.

Sontag, Susan. *On Photography.* New York: Dell, 1973.

Staiger, Janet. "The Romances of the Blonde Venus: Movie Censors Versus Movie Fans." *Canadian Journal of Film Studies* 6, no. 2 (autumn 1997): 5–20.

Stam, Robert. *Film Theory: An Introduction.* New York: Blackwell, 1999.

Stam, Robert, and Toby Miller. *A Companion to Film Theory.* New York: Blackwell, 1999.

———, eds. *Film and Theory: An Anthology.* New York: Blackwell, 2000.

Stephanson, Anders. "Regarding Postmodernism: A Conversation with Fredric Jameson." *Universal Abandon? The Politics of Postmodernism,* ed. Andrew Ross, 3–30. Minneapolis: U of Minnesota P, 1988.

Suter, Jacquelyn. "Feminine Discourse in *Christopher Strong.*" *Feminism and Film Theory,* ed. Constance Penley, 89–103. New York: Routledge, 1988.

Tatar, Maria. *Lustmord: Sexual Murder in Weimar Germany.* Princeton: Princeton UP, 1995.

Thomas, Brook. "The New Historicism and the Privileging of Literature." *Annals of Scholarship: Metastudies of the Humanities and Social Sciences* 4, no. 4 (1987): 23–48.

Trommler, Frank, and Joseph McVeigh, eds. *America and the Germans: An Assessment of a Three-Hundred-Year History.* Philadelphia: U of Pennsylvania P, 1985.

Trumpener, Katie. "Obsessive Monologues, Modernist Songs: Towards the Reunification of the Postwar German Cinemas." *German National Cinema,* ed. Katie Trumpener and Sabine Hake. London: Routledge, forthcoming.

van den Haag, Ernest. "Of Happiness and of Despair We Have No Measure." *Mass Culture: The Popular Arts in America,* ed. Bernard Rosenberg and David Manning White, 504–535. Glencoe, Ill.: Free Press, 1957.

Vattimo, Gianni. "*Verwindung:* Nihilism and the Postmodern in Philosophy." *Substance* 53 (1987).

von Eckardt, Wolf, and Sander L. Gilman. *Bertolt Brecht's Berlin: A Scrapbook of the Twenties.* Lincoln: Nebraska UP, 1993.

Waite, Geoff. "On the Politics of Boredom (a Communist Pastiche)." *Documents* 1, no. 1–2 (winter 1992).

Walton, Jean. "Nightmare of the Uncoordinated White-Folk: Race, Psychoanalysis, and *Borderline.*" *Discourse* 19, no. 1 (winter 1997): 88–109.

"Weimar Film Theory." Special issue, *New German Critique* 40 (winter 1987).

Weiskel, Thomas. *The Romantic Sublime: Studies in the Structure and Psychology of Transcendence.* Baltimore: Johns Hopkins UP, 1976.

Weiss, Andrea. "'A Queer Feeling When I Look at You': Hollywood Stars and Lesbian Spectatorship in the 1930s." *Multiple Voices in Feminist Film Criticism,* ed. Diane Carson, Linda Dittmar, and Janice R. Welsch, 330–342. Minneapolis: U of Minnesota P, 1994.

White, Hayden. "The Modernist Event." *The Persistence of History: Cinema, Television, and the Modern Event,* ed. Vivian Sobchack, 27–35. New York: Routledge, 1996.

Williams, Linda. "Corporealized Observers: Visual Pornographies and the 'Carnal Density of Vision'." *Fugitive Images: From Photography to Video*, ed. Patrice Petro, 3–41. Bloomington: Indiana UP, 1995.

————. "Something Else Besides a Mother: *Stella Dallas* and the Maternal Melodrama." *Cinema Journal* 24, no. 1 (fall 1984): 2–27.

————, ed. *Viewing Positions: Ways of Seeing Film*. New Brunswick: Rutgers UP, 1995.

Witte, Karsten. "Introduction to Siegfried Kracauer's 'The Mass Ornament'." *New German Critique* 5 (spring 1975): 59–66.

————. "Visual Pleasure Inhibited: Aspects of the German Revue Film." *New German Critique* 24–25 (fall–winter 1981–82): 238–263.

Wollen, Peter. *Signs and Meanings in the Cinema*. Bloomington: Indiana UP, 1969.

Young, Donald. "Social Standards and the Motion Picture." *Annals of the American Academy of Political and Social Sciences* 128 (November 1926): 147.

INDEX

ABOUT THE AUTHOR

Patrice Petro is a professor of English and Film Studies at the University of Wisconsin–Milwaukee, where she is also the director of the Center for International Education. She is the author of *Joyless Streets: Women and Melodramatic Representation in Weimar Germany* (1989) and editor of *Fugitive Images: From Photography to Video* (1995).